MW00622421

A FEAST OF
FOLKLORE

Epicurus and His Influence on History
Strange Ways to Die in History: The Heroic, Tragic and Funny

A FEAST OF FOLKLORE

*The Bizarre Stories
Behind British Food*

BEN GAZUR

unbound

First published in 2024

Unbound
c/o TC Group, 6th Floor King's House, 9–10 Haymarket, London SW1Y 4BP
www.unbound.com

Text design by Jouve (UK), Milton Keynes

A CIP record for this book is available from the British Library

ISBN 978-1-80018-316-2 (hardback)
ISBN 978-1-80018-317-9 (ebook)

Printed in Great Britain by Clays Ltd, Elcograf S.p.A.

1 3 5 7 9 8 6 4 2

With thanks to the patrons of this book:

Tom Brereton
Candice Carty-Williams
Lottie Joy Cragg
Michael Cragg
Leslie DeBauche
Bhanu Dhir
Amy Feltman
Julie Gazur
Tony Gazur
Julie Giles
Keith Gregory
Duncan & Holly
Hammond

Jan Hunter
Edith Laird
Daire Mhurain
Mark Pahlow
Alistair Renwick
Sam Sharp
Matthew William
Beresford Spencer
Claude Tarazi
Liz Thompson
Susan Wicks
Cara Wilson
Eryn Young

Dedicated to my nans, Nanny Gazur and
Nanny-in-the-Country, and all the nans
who told us the old stories.

Contents

Introduction

The other day I spilled some salt while cooking. Almost unconsciously I took a pinch and threw it over my left shoulder. Doubtless many of us would have done the same and not given it too much thought. Folklore can have a power that is hard to understand until we examine it.

Where did the idea that salt should be thrown over the shoulder if spilled come from? It was pondering such questions that led to me writing this book. It turns out that there is not a singular answer. Some point to salt being given to visitors as a symbol of the host–guest relationship which was formed by dining together. To spill this was a sign that trouble would come between the two and so a little was sacrificed to ward off this omen.

Others suggest that spilling salt offered hospitality to evil spirits or even the Devil himself. Since evil always approached from the left, *sinister* side then tossing salt over the left shoulder was a means of driving these spirits away.

Explanations like this are often given but are seldom satisfactory. Such is the way with folklore. Written sources are sometimes hideously late and we cannot interrogate the originators of these beliefs. There are those who consider all folk beliefs, rituals and tales to hold some sort of truth which can be gleaned because they are universal. I am not so sure. There must have been a first person to take a pinch of salt and throw it over their shoulder. What were they thinking? In most cases it is impossible to know. Our ignorance of history does not necessarily mean that we can project anything we want onto it; the meanings we give to a ritual may be utterly unrelated to its original connotations. A child seeing a parent unthinkingly tossing salt over their shoulder may carry on the ritual without ever asking why they do it and so the secret is lost. I think that we examine folklore not because it is true but because it tells us something about ourselves. But you should always take anyone's opinion on folklore with the idiomatic pinch of salt.

There is no definition of folklore that would please a Platonist. There are always exceptions and special cases. For the purposes of this book, folklore encompasses any of the traditions that have built up across the centuries. In particular *A Feast of Folklore* will examine some of the weirder traditions and beliefs about food which make Britain such a fruitful place to study folklore.

Food is the universal ingredient in all our lives. Man may not live by bread alone but no one can go without food. Magic and rituals often use what is closest to hand, and food was always available in people's homes to be incorporated into some aspect of folklore. Even dining together gave opportunities for superstition. Thirteen at a table was unlucky because it mirrored the number of those at the Last Supper. Folklore is such a bountiful area of history to study because it records, if distantly, something that was shared by people who were often never otherwise noticed by grand historians of the past. We will see people trying to ward off illnesses with only what they had in their larder. Can we imagine the desperation of a parent whose child was struggling to breathe and there was no help any doctor could give? What wouldn't we try to help them? We will see the importance placed by common people on weddings, christenings and death through the foods special to each event.

With writing about folklore there is a dilemma. If folklore is not written down it is easily lost or not remembered. Yet once folklore is written down it becomes fixed and dead, like a butterfly with a pin through its body. As with the example of salt, there is rarely one singular version of any bit of folklore or folk tale. The one that gets written down is the one that survives and all the other variants are lost or smothered. Remember when you read anything in this book that there were a hundred alternatives that must have existed as each individual interacted with the stories they were told.

There is a fascination with folklore that will never truly die. Traditions can be lost to the mists of time as people forget the value of them, but new ones are born every day. I well remember being told in the playground not to eat crisps that were green because they were fatally toxic. When I was ill my nan would serve me eggy bread and Lucozade, original flavour, because they were the best thing for the body. These are surely bits of folklore of a modern vintage.

Long may folklore continue to be generated. It adds a little bit of spice both to our meals and to our lives.

Vegetable Lore

The amount of vegetables that we are told should make up a good proportion of our daily fare is loaded with folklore. Even the idea that we should eat five portions of fruit and veg per day is apocryphal: it was simply the maximum that scientists thought they could effectively convince British people to consume. From old remedies that were based on 'correspondences' – a walnut looks like a brain so is good for brain disorders – to folk tales about giant turnips, vegetables are ubiquitous in folklore.

Vegetables were so important to our ancestors' diets that ensuring a good crop became a vital matter of survival. Every community relied on growing their own food. Procuring a bountiful harvest was a matter of life and death, and folklore provided a way of passing on important cultivation tips. If you are thinking of establishing an allotment you might want to follow this advice from Devon: any crop planted on Good Friday will 'come up goody'.[1]

The most popular piece of allotment folklore about sowing vegetables is one involving exposure of the buttocks. To test whether it is time to plant your crops you should pull down your trousers and sit on the ground. If the soil is warm enough to sit on comfortably with your naked bum, it is time for the seeds to go in.

ONIONS AND GARLIC

Knowing your onions is a proverbial way of saying you know something well. Even for gardeners it can indeed be tricky to tell the bulbs of different alliums apart. Folk have always known that onions have a place in the medicine cabinet.

One of the most persistent powers attached to onions is that they act as magnets for bacteria and viruses. By hanging an onion in the home all the infectious bugs from the outside world could be sucked up and thus stop the family falling ill. One family from Orkney would keep an onion cut in half in the pantry and the children were given strict instructions never to touch it – it had all the germs in the house in it.[1] It may be that this stems from the miasma theory of infection and the pungent aroma of onions was driving out the sickening stenches that were thought to cause illness.

This woodcut of an onion from 1547 would probably not help much in getting to know your onions.

When smallpox struck Sheffield in 1927 many houses hung an onion outside in hopes of stopping it from infecting the home. In other places the onion was hung in the house as a warning of illness. When an infectious person had entered the home the onion would turn black from absorbing their illness.

The *Daily Chronicle* reported the health-preserving properties of onions as a fact in 1915.

The virtues of the onion were never more plainly demonstrated than during the great cholera epidemic in London in 1849. Saffron Hill was practically free of it, although the surrounding neighbourhood suffered severely. The Board of Health investigated, and discovered that it was due to the fact that all the cholera-proof houses were occupied by the Italian organ-grinders who consumed huge quantities of onions, which were hanging in strings from the ceilings of their rooms. When this was made known Londoners just reeked of onions! In many rural districts this superstition is still scrupulously observed. The onions are left blackened in appearance when they are considered to have become impregnated with the impurities of the air, and are then either consigned to the dustbin or burnt, and fresh bunches substituted.[2]

There were other rituals for carrying off disease in an onion. One victim of scarlet fever was observed taking the outer layers of an onion from the house and burying them in a place where no one would dig them up. By doing this it was thought the illness had been safely disposed of.

Sometimes the onion was best placed on, or in, the body to help the healing process. Those with a toothache in Lincolnshire were advised to roast an onion and then drape the outer layers on the big toe.[3] The cure for earache seems to make more sense as this involved taking a small onion and warming it in the fire before inserting it into the affected ear. Ulster lore tells us that the best cure for chilblains is to rub them with a cut onion, though I cannot believe this would improve the whiff of the patient's feet.[4]

Onions have also found their place in several forms of magic and rite. The Pitt Rivers Museum in Oxford has an onion in its collection that is pierced with multiple pins.[5] This charmed object was discovered in a pub in Rockwell Green in Somerset in 1872 by Edward Burnett Tyler when a strong wind dislodged it from the chimney where it had been hanging. Attached to the desiccated vegetable was a label bearing the name John Milton.

It seems that Milton had annoyed the publican at some point and so he had been hanged in vegetable form. By drying the onion out and stabbing it, the landlord was probably hoping that some sympathetic harm could be caused to the human Milton, in a similar way to how voodoo dolls are supposed to work. Interestingly, the onion, and others like it, was hidden from sight and only drew attention when knocked from the fireplace. It was not the implicit threat of a tortured onion that was supposed to harm Milton, as the victim never saw it, but the very act of producing the item which worked the charm.

Onions had uses other than inflicting harm on your enemies. For a simple weather forecast simply check your vegetable cupboard.

> Onion's skin very thin
> Mild winter's coming in;
> Onion's skin thick and tough,
> Coming winter cold and rough.[6]

Garlic is held to be a miracle cure by many today. Allicin, the sulphur-containing compound which gives garlic its pungency, has been claimed to cure everything from the common cold to heart disease. There are those who claim that a garlic clove used as a suppository in the anus or vagina can 'cleanse the body', whatever that may mean. There is a long history to garlic being used in medicine.

The seventeenth-century botanist Nicholas Culpeper discussed the virtues of garlic, as well as the 'offensiveness of the breath of him that hath eaten Garlick'.[7] He also informs us that: 'It provokes urine, and women's courses, helps the biting of mad dogs and other venomous creatures, kills worms in children, cuts and voids tough phlegm, purges the head, helps the lethargy, is a good preservative against, and a remedy for any plague, sore, or foul ulcers; takes away spots and blemishes in the skin, eases pains in the ears, ripens and breaks imposthumes, or other swellings.'

The medical uses of garlic are still touted to this day. A study of traditional cures in Ulster found that garlic leaves should be chewed to help an asthmatic, its seeds steeped in whisky were good for those with measles and that when bulbs were inserted into socks it could ease whooping cough.[8]

LEEKS

Leeks are the heraldic symbol of the Welsh. In Shakespeare's *Henry V* Fluellen is spotted wearing his leek even though St David's Day is past. When Pistol mocks him for this, saying that the smell of leeks makes him 'qualmish', Fluellen forces the leek on him for his insults.

> I say, I will make him eat some part of my leek, or
>   I will peat his pate four days. Bite, I pray you; it
>   is good for your green wound and your ploody coxcomb.[1]

How this slightly strange association came to be is the subject of a martial tale. In the sixth century, the Welsh were being menaced by the Anglo-Saxons. St David told the Welsh to place a leek on their helmets before a battle, which would certainly have helped distinguish friend from foe during the confusion of battle – few people use leeks as personal attire unless instructed.[2]

The Welsh triumphed and St David became the patron saint of Wales, and the leeks remained a proud symbol of the country.

Others claim that the link between the Welsh and leeks dates from the seventh century, when King Cadwaladr gave leeks to his soldiers to identify themselves. Still others claim that Welsh archers at the Battle of Crécy in 1346 fought in a field of leeks, and so plucked them as a symbol of their victory.

Culpeper offered up a medical cure that he charmingly calls 'Pilulæ Fœtidæ Or Stinking Pills'.[3] It involves several herbs and spices mixed with various plant materials and odiferous other ingredients. Leek juice forms the syrup that binds it all together. These pills 'purge gross and raw flegm, and diseases thereof arising; gouts of all sorts, pains in the back-bone, and other joints: it is good against leprosies, and other such like infirmities of the skin'. Culpeper adds, perhaps unnecessarily, 'I fancy not the receipt much'.

POTATOES

The well-known story of potatoes being introduced to Europe by Sir Walter Raleigh is unfortunately just a myth, for potatoes were already well known to Europeans by his time. There probably never was a scene of an enraptured Queen Elizabeth I gushing over a bulbous tuber. However, after their arrival, potatoes soon became a staple of the table and of medicinal food folklore, particularly among the poor. There was no one so destitute they could not afford a spud to ease their maladies.

The Victorians had a fondness for keeping potatoes in their pockets. Anecdotes abound of potato cures and the Pitt Rivers Museum has a beautifully preserved potato that was carried around as a cure for rheumatism.[1] According to some, for this cure to be efficacious the potato had to be pilfered from a grocer; it absolutely could not be paid for. The potatoes were sometimes worn around the neck in special pouches. By having them near to the skin it was thought that they could absorb rheumatism; as the potato withered with time so the condition would dwindle. How long this might take is not recorded. One believer in the potency of potatoes was known to have carried one around with him for eight years. There are reports of people still placing a potato in their beds as a way of curing cramps and fevers.[2]

Potatoes have a curious property when they are cut. On exposure to air they rapidly darken. This oxidation can make potatoes appear greyish or black and has led to some of the odd beliefs that can still be found online. A myth with no easily discernible source has it that in the past slices of potato were placed on the feet of people suffering from flu. As the slices turned black it was thought the illness was being sucked from the afflicted. Now TikTok influencers swear that a potato in the sock will pull everything from viruses to unspecified toxins out of the body.[3] Their evidence? That the potato turns black, something that, as we know, will happen anyway.

Other cures involving potatoes include washing a child with rickets in water that has had spuds steeped in it and warts being charmed away by rubbing them with pieces of raw potato.[4] Some claim that the potato must be cut in half and only one half rubbed on the wart. The two pieces are then joined back together and either planted or thrown over the shoulder.[5] Throwing things over your shoulder, and putting them behind you forever, is a common motif in folklore. The wart would disappear from the body and appear on the potato as it began to grow.

To get the best crop of potatoes you were supposed to plant them on Good Friday. Being subterranean crops they were always at risk of being stolen by the Devil so planting on a holy day helped keep his influence to a reasonable minimum.

BEANS

According to legend, during the tumultuous reign of King Stephen in the twelfth century, the village of Woolpit in Suffolk was visited by two exceedingly strange children who loved beans.[1] The villagers stumbled across them living wild in the woods. These children had green skin, could speak no English and would not eat any human food. It was only when they saw some green beans that the pair could be convinced to consume anything at all.

The green children were taken in by Richard de Calne and were slowly tempted to include food in their diet other than beans. Gradually normal colour returned to their bodies. Once taught to speak English the children revealed they came from a land where the sun never fully rose above the horizon, casting

Not everyone considered beans to be wholesome. The ancient philosopher Pythagoras banned his followers from eating them as he believed the beans might contain human souls. Human beans, perhaps?

everything into a perpetual twilight. Everyone in their land was green, too. In a Narnian turn of events, after straying into a cave the children had found themselves in a new world where the villagers discovered them.

If all this sounds like a fairy tale, there are hints in the historical record of something like the discovery of children occurring at Woolpit around this time. Two separate chroniclers writing in the decades afterwards, William of Newburgh and Ralph of Coggeshall, claim to have had reports of these prodigious children.[2] In times of anarchy many such strange stories tend to spring up.

Beans may be a spur to the creation of children – with more usual skin colours, one hopes. It was said that beans, particularly the smell of bean plants blooming, caused lust. One person in Oxfordshire commented, 'There ent no lustier scent than a beanfield in bloom'.[3] In Suffolk when the beans were flowering it was said 'It wouldn't be long before the missus was calving'. Nicholas Culpeper agreed with this as he assigned beans to the influence of Venus. French beans were said to 'engender sperm', but then they *are* French.[4]

Should a baby result from the lusty aroma of beans, you can also use the bean field to cure them of whooping cough. Carry the child through the field and the aroma will drive the sickness from them.

Some areas of Britain are apparently more fond of beans than others. 'If you shake a Leicestershire man by the collar you can hear the beans rattle inside him.'[5] The same county also advises that sleeping in a bean field will either give you awful dreams or send you mad. In Hertfordshire the saying 'bean for a pea' was used to refer to someone who was very stingy, as in 'she would not so much as give you a bean for a pea!'

If you want to get a bumper crop of beans, you may wish to remember some Devonshire advice: always plant four times as many beans as you want to germinate.

One for the mouse,
One for the crow,
One for the rot,
One to grow.

Be careful when you plant your beans. If you sow them on St Thomas's Day you might get a nasty surprise. If any of the beans come up white with mould it is a sure omen that a death is coming to the household.

Beans were most susceptible to the good luck of planting crops on Good Friday. In *A Book of Exmoor* by F. J. Snell we hear the account of one country vicar who was new to his parish but thought he had established a good rapport with his flock. On Good Friday he was startled to find his pews empty save for a few older ladies. He immediately concluded that the congregation's absence was down to something he had done. After the sermon he tentatively questioned one of the ladies present. With great gentleness, as if speaking to a simpleton, she informed the nervous vicar that everyone spent Good Friday planting their beans in hopes that they would germinate by the Monday, like Jesus returning from the tomb.

Beans can be good for the skin. If you suffer from warts you should take the soft inside of a broad bean pod and rub it against the protrusion. This will transfer the wart to the plant. Then either toss the pod over your shoulder or carefully bury it somewhere private.[6] As the pod rots, so will the wart. And water made from boiling bean blossoms clears the face of blemishes.

PEAS

Peas feature in one of Britain's true culinary delights – mushy peas. This staple of chip shops, often a lurid green, has an older traditional form. Carlin peas are a brownish or blackish variety of peas that were once very popular in parts of Britain, so much so that the fifth Sunday of Lent was known as 'Carlin Sunday' or 'Pea Sunday'.[1]

One Scottish song, however, does not make the eating of carlin, or carling, peas sound much fun.

> There'll be all the lads and lassies
> Set down in the midst of the ha',
> With sybows, and ryfarts, and carlings
> That are bath sodden and raw.[2]

It makes sense that peas should become associated with Lent. As one of the few foods you were permitted to eat during this time they took on an almost holy aspect. Some even thought that it was bad luck to eat peas outside of Lent – you might choke on them if you tried to do so.

The greyish carling peas could be soaked overnight and fried in butter, often served simply seasoned with vinegar, salt and pepper. This hearty dish was sometimes eaten at special festivities held on the tops of hills. Whoever was lucky enough to get the last pea was told that they would be the next to marry. Alternatively, a bean hidden among the carling peas could predict the positive marriage prospects of the person to whom it was served.

Few people shell their own peas today, but, if you do, you should count the number of peas in each pod. To find just a single pea lurking inside is a sign of good luck. The same is true for nine nestled together, though some say that one must be removed and tossed over the shoulder if you wish to ward off bad luck.[3]

Peas were once the answer for people who could not wake up in time for work. If you could not afford an alarm clock there was an entire industry of employment for people known as 'knocker uppers'.[4] They would walk around the neighbourhood and use long sticks to tap at the windows of their clients to wake them up. For some, however, a different method was used.

Mary Smith was one of the last knocker uppers in twentieth-century London and she would patrol the streets armed with her pocket watch, a blow pipe and a bag of dried peas. At the appointed hour she would unleash a barrage of peas against your window before moving on to her next house. For this she charged the princely sum of sixpence per week. So if you happen to live with a slugabed, next time you cannot rouse them from their slumbers just pelt them with peas.

CABBAGES AND SPROUTS

Cabbages have a bad reputation. The smell of boiling cabbage is one that haunts many a childhood memory. Nicholas Culpeper gave another reason to fear cabbage on the menu: 'Cabbages are extremely windy, whether you take them as meat or as medicine, as windy meat as can be eaten, unless you eat bag-pipes or bellows.'[1] The Welsh were also not always fans of the humble cabbage, saying, somewhat cryptically, 'If thou desirest to die, eat cabbage in August'.[2]

Cabbages do have their uses, however. Even today breastfeeding women may be told to ease the pain by placing a cabbage leaf in their bra. Indeed, scientific research has found strong evidence that cabbage leaves on the chest do reduce pain and the hardness of engorged breasts.[3] Fevers could be alleviated by having hot cabbage leaves draped over the feet, it was thought, though to my knowledge no scientific analysis of this cure has ever been conducted.

On Jersey there is a variety of cabbage which grows with long stalks. These can be dried and turned into walking sticks. They were once very popular and were often bought by visitors to the island, with 30,000 being exported annually.[4] The trade in cabbage stalk canes has dwindled in recent years but a few can still be found.

Those looking to predict the nature of their future spouse need look no further than the nearest cabbage field – so long as they don't mind a little criminal damage. It was once traditional for young ladies to sneak onto a farm and steal a cabbage, roots and all.[5] They would then examine the soil that came up with the cabbage. A lot of earth clinging to the roots meant a prosperous match would be made while a clean cabbage presaged an inadequate husband.

Other variations of this rite involved the girls being blind-folded as they picked a cabbage. Should she choose a withered and dry cabbage from the field it was a sign she would wed an old man. A fine green and luscious vegetable predicted that a hand-some young man was in her future. A small cabbage meant she would be widowed at a young age. A rotten cabbage, as in so many things, meant nothing good.

Brussels sprouts are a much maligned vegetable but few would really accuse them of being infested with devils no matter how much they dislike the taste. Yet that is what folklore says, though pinning down sources for this belief is difficult. Why do we cut crosses into the base of Brussels sprouts before boiling them? Most will say it is to help them cook but according to lore the holy cross is to let out the demons. Chefs will tell you that while a cross may let the devils out it also makes for mushy and flavour-less sprouts.

CARROTS

It is not often that folklore can be pinpointed to a specific time in history but with a popular tradition about carrots we are on fairly safe ground. Ask anyone to name a benefit of eating carrots and many will say they help you to see in the dark. There may have been ideas about the importance of these vitamin A-rich vegetables to eyesight before the Second World War but it was certainly amplified by the conflict.[1]

A majority of German air raids over Britain took place at night and yet the RAF was able to shoot down many of the enemy planes. This was in part due to the development of Airborne Interception radar (AI) that gave British pilots the ability to find the foe in darkness, but the government of the day did not want this technological marvel to become common knowledge. How then to explain the British night-time prowess? The government let it be known that their aces were eating lots of carrots and so had excellent night vision. Propaganda posters reinforced this notion and many still believe it to this day.

There is one folklore cure involving carrots that, though not British, is just too good not to include here. Dr Walter J. Hoffman published *Folk Medicine of the Pennsylvania Germans* in 1899 and described a rather peculiar remedy for jaundice. 'Hollow out a carrot, fill it with the patient's urine and hang it, by means of a string, in the fireplace. As the urine is evaporated and the carrot becomes shrivelled, the disease will leave the patient.'[2]

TURNIPS, SWEDES AND MANGELWURZELS

Turnips and swedes have a poor culinary reputation. In 2023, at the height of a fruit and vegetable shortage, the then environment minister Thérèse Coffey suggested in the House of Commons that people might celebrate some of Britain's native produce, such as the turnip.[1] Roundly mocked for her attitude of 'let them eat turnip', it was pointed out that, though turnips can indeed be delicious, they are a poor substitute for tomatoes in a sauce.

The disdain for turnips is not a particularly modern one. Rustics were mocked as 'turnip eaters'. During the First World War, when the Germans were suffering from starvation they had to live, or otherwise, through the *Steckrübenwinter* – the Turnip Winter – named for the only food available to them. When the

Emperor Vespasian displeased the people of Hadrumetum they pelted him with turnips for his perceived stinginess.[2]

But turnips do have their uses, particularly in folklore. To cure whooping cough you can make a soothing syrup from them.[3] Simply slice your turnip several times and place sugar between the layers before restacking them. As the sugar dissolves, a syrup will drain from the vegetable. Collect this and give it to the sick person. Others preferred to make the syrup by roasting the turnip in a bag with sugar.

In another example of larceny being required in order for folklore to work, young maids after a husband were encouraged to filch a turnip from a field.[4] The girl would then peel the turnip in a single unbroken strand. This peel had to be buried in the garden while the rest of the turnip was hung behind a door. The first man to enter through the door was destined to be her spouse.

Turnips also have a frankly terrifying use in the celebration of Halloween. Before the pumpkin became common in Britain, children would carve jack-o'-lanterns with monstrous faces. These hollowed-out turnips, or occasionally mangelwurzels (a type of beet with large swollen roots used to feed livestock), then had small candles placed in them.[5] The smell of singed turnip is not one that is soon forgotten . . .

Punkie Night is an event in Somerset held on the last Thursday of October which sees punkies, or lanterns, made from swedes and mangelwurzels in profusion. According to legend it began when a group of men, possibly the worse for wear after a day of drinking, were late returning home from a fair. Their wives decided to set out in the dark in search of their absent husbands and used lanterns carved from vegetables. If these lanterns had the grimacing faces that most punkies have, they probably hoped to get across their displeasure at having to roam about in the dark.

Punkie Night developed into a carnival of door-to-door begging similar to modern-day trick-or-treating. Children would process around the neighbourhood and knock on doors demanding

candles or a small sum of money. On opening the door the householder would be faced with a sea of hovering and horrific lanterns
as the children chanted a threatening rhyme insisting on a candle
(a light) if the homeowner did not want to be punked (a fright).

This model of a punkie carved from a root vegetable gives some idea of the
nightmares they might have inspired.

PARSLEY

Parsley seems to have one of the worst reputations of all herbs
found in British gardens. The problems start when you try to
plant it. According to folklore it will not germinate unless you
swear profusely and volubly while sowing the seeds. This may be
because the herb is strongly associated with the Devil.

It was said that you needed to plant parsley three times – twice
for the Devil and once for yourself – if you were to have any
hope of a good crop. It is true that parsley seeds take more time
than most to germinate. It can take up to a month for the

shoots to show so gardeners have no idea if they are successfully growing or not. What is the parsley doing for all that time? Some said it takes so long because the seeds have to travel to Hell and back seven times before they grow upwards.[1]

Some folk were so superstitious about parsley that they would not so much as handle the seeds. If they truly wanted them to grow they had to place the seeds on an open Bible and blow them onto the ground. Planting them on Good Friday, the holiest day of the year, was another option to try and ward off the Devil's influence.[2]

Once you had managed to get the seeds to grow you couldn't even take the parsley with you if you moved house. Transplanting parsley was said to cause bad luck or even a death in the home. One lady from Oxfordshire, a Mrs Calcutt, remembered how her grandmother transplanted some and her husband died within the year.[3] But the successful growing of parsley might get the neighbours talking. A garden with parsley growing in profusion was a sign that it was the woman who was in charge of the house. In Monmouthshire they had a little rhyme about it.

> Where the mistress is the master,
> The parsley grows the faster.[4]

This bit of sexist folk wisdom is also applied to homes where rosemary is grown.

Fruit Lore

The prologue to 'The Reeve's Tale' from Chaucer's *Canterbury Tales* may not make sense to anyone who has not had the pleasure of eating a medlar.[1] Few enough have. In Chaucer's tale an ageing man compares himself to a medlar, a fruit that is not considered ripe until it is rotten. Instead of naming the medlar, Chaucer vividly conjures up its appearance by calling it an 'open-ers' – an open arse.

The medlar is a fruit that rarely makes it to market and even those who do come across fresh medlars may not think you can eat them, partly for reasons that Chaucer makes clear. Small and similar to the crab apple, the medlar has a little brown opening on top that fits Chaucer's anatomical description.

If you pick a medlar from the tree and try to bite into it, you are in for a nasty surprise. In its fresh state the fruit is tooth-gratingly hard, astringent and full of large stones.

How, then, did medlars get the reputation of being one of England's greatest fruits? The secret is to blet them.

Blet is not a word in most people's culinary vocabulary.[2] From the French verb *blettir*, meaning to become overripe, it essentially means you have to let medlars rot before you eat them. Rotten food is generally off-putting but with medlars it is necessary if you don't want to vomit them up. Once the medlar is picked it is left to soften by decay and as it does so the inedible fruit transforms itself into something with a luscious texture and a taste similar to apple sauce.

The medlar's popularity may have withered but the British love

The distinctly anal appearance of the medlar fruit, as well as the difficulty of eating it, has led to a diminished popularity in recent centuries.

affair with fruit has always been strong. King John was rumoured to have died from eating a surfeit of peaches, though it may have been poison or dysentery that really did him in.[3] Given our uncertain summers, the joy that was found in brilliant red strawberries nestling in hay beds or russet honey-sweet apples hanging from bending branches is only too understandable. Fruit can be enjoyed all year long today but with seasonality came something special. Our ancestors found there was more to savour in fruit than the fresh sensation of their juices on the tongue. Each harvest brought with it the chance to relive the folklore they associated with fruit.

APPLES

'The sweetest apples are always at the top of the tree.'

This country saying must have sent many scrumpers scrambling up trees in orchards in search of the ultimate illicit fruit.

Apples were for centuries the fruit that most people would have eaten most often. From sharp, acerbic cooking apples to rosy red ones that crunch and release floods of juice, there was an apple for every palate. The number of apple varieties proliferated as farmers and hobbyists cross-bred them in pursuit of the ultimate apple. Britain is home to 2,500 cultivars out of around 7,000 developed worldwide.[1]

What better gift to give a loved one than an apple as sweet as they are? One of the traditional ways to share love was to share an apple. Eat half yourself and give the other half to the one you love and passion will grow between you as fruitful as a tree from an apple pip. It was once thought that apples should be given as Valentine's Day gifts. Given the Christian association of the apple with the Garden of Eden it was also perhaps suggestive of wanting to sin with the one you desired. Though perhaps not the best way to woo a partner – look what happened to Adam and Eve.

Some places created entire festivals around the humble apple and its prognosticatory power in the matters of love. In Cornwall, 31 October is not simply Halloween, it also marks the day of Allantide – or St Allan's Day.[2] Today some question the historical existence of the local bishop who became St Allan but it has not quenched the desire for his apples. If you happened into Cornwall on Allantide in earlier centuries you would have been bombarded with fruiterers willing to sell you large, shiny red apples. The larger the apple the greater the magic attached. Eating these apples gave good luck, and gifting them was even better. For young girls, and probably not a few boys, the apples went under their pillows at night as they were said to give them dreams of their future lovers. With an apple under your pillow you have to wonder what the quality of your night's sleep was like.

Sometimes a game would be played with the Allan apples that consisted of two pieces of wood nailed together in a cruciform shape and suspended from the ceiling. At the end of each piece of wood a lit candle was placed, four in all. Then four apples were

Halloween apple bobbing could range from the familiar water bobbing, to dodging globules of hot wax from candles perilously near your face.

tied to the construction. The 'fun' was in seeing who could pull an apple free with their teeth without getting splashed with hot wax. Well, they had to pass the long October night somehow.

A New Year's Day tradition in some parts of Wales saw children going door-to-door with an apple into which they had stuck sprigs of rosemary and other bits of foliage. Three sticks were embedded in the bottom of the apple. When the children knocked on a door they would sing a little song in hope of receiving small gifts and give the cheery reminder that before the next year arrived many of them would be dead.[3] This tradition was known as Calennig, as was the apple tripod itself. Arthur Machen recorded his experience of Calennig in the nineteenth century:

When I was a boy, which is a good many years ago, there was a very queer celebration on New Year's Day in the little Monmouthshire town where I was born, Caerleon-on-Usk. The town children – village children would be nearer the mark since the population of the place amounted to a thousand souls or thereabouts – got the big-gest and bravest and gayest apple they could find in the loft, deep in the dry bracken. They put bits of gold leaf upon it. They stuck raisins into it. They inserted into the apple little sprigs of box, and then they delicately slit the ends of hazel nuts, and so worked that the nuts appeared to grow from the ends of the box leaves, to be the disproportionate fruit of these small trees. At last, three bits of stick were fixed into the base of the apple, tripod-wise; and so it was borne round from house to house; and the children got cakes and sweets, and – those were wild days, remember – small cups of ale. And nobody knew what it was all about.[4]

Sometimes when gangs of young children came to the door it was to beg you to give them apples – if you didn't have some-thing better to offer. This tradition usually took place around 23 November, but in Armscote, Warwickshire, apples were begged so that villagers could make apple fritters for Shrove Tuesday. Because 23 November is St Clement's Day, the children were called Clementers and, because it was also near St Catherine's Day, the begging was called Catterning.

In Worcestershire, as boys went around on St Clement's Day to beg for apples, they would sing:

> Catteny, Clemeny, year by year,
> Some of your apples and some of your beer;
> Some for Peter, some for Paul,
> Some for God who made us all.
> Clemeny was a good old man,
> For his sake give us some,
> Some of the best, and some of the worst,
> And pray God give you a good night's rest.
> Plum, plum, cherry, cherry,
> All good things to make us merry.
> Up the ladder and down the pan,

Give us a red apple and we'll be gone.
Missis and master, sit by the fire,
While we poor children are trudging in the mire,
All for the apples that grow on the tree.
So missis and master, come listen to me.[5]

Others wanted something a little more uplifting along with their apple:

Give us good ale to make us merry,
Apples to roast and nuts to crack,
And a barrel of cider on the tap.
Up the ladder and down the can,
Give us a red apple and we'll be gone.[6]

St Swithin's Day, 15 July, is more famous for predicting the weather than for predicting the apple harvest but for apple farmers it was an important day. The old saying goes:

St Swithun's day if thou dost rain
For forty days it will remain
St Swithun's day if thou be fair
For forty days 'twill rain nae mare.

You might therefore think that apple farmers would hate to see it rain on that day but in fact a downpour on St Swithin's was an answer to their prayers. Rain on 15 July was considered a blessing from St Swithin and was seen as him christening the apples.[7] Rain was a sign of divine protection for the harvest and meant that early ripening varieties were sure to come in soon. In Warwickshire it was said: 'You won't have the jam made till the apples are christened . . . We never eat or cut apples until St Swithin has christened them.'[8]

Of course the best way to ensure a good fall of apples was to

Wassail them – feeding the apple trees with cider, firing guns at them and toasting them with many a drink, a song, and a cake placed in the branches.

The behaviour of the apple trees was important beyond the crop itself. Any action that seemed to go against nature was seen as a portent. The apple trees blossoming out of season was a sign that other untimely events would take place.

> A bloom upon the apple-tree when the apples are ripe,
> Is a sure termination to somebody's life.[9]

Once you had your apples, the next question was what to do with them. If you're anything like me you want a warming and hearty apple pie. At Marldon in Devon a fair is held in honour of a gigantic apple pie, and an unlucky apple seller called George Hill.[10] Since 1888 the fair has been held fairly irregularly, sometimes with a gap of several decades.

George Hill was known for having a faithful donkey that he would ride between St Marychurch and Marldon. Each day he would load the panniers onto his donkey with apples and sell them in St Marychurch, sometimes bringing to town a vast apple pie 'the size of a kitchen table'. This was drawn on a decorated cart and pulled by two donkeys bedecked in flowers and ribbons. Anyone who wanted a slice of pie was welcome to have one, if they paid for it.

After selling his apples or pie he would head home with his bags stuffed full of clothes and linen to wash. A hard day of trading often prompted George to fall into a deep slumber as he rode back, but luckily for him his donkey could be relied on to guide him home.

One day thieves took advantage of George's somnolent nature and filched his entire load of clothes and sheets. The shock is said to have broken his spirit and led to George's death soon after. In his honour a fair was arranged to celebrate the apples he brought to the town.

Over the years the fair has changed. Participants recall how large pies served at the fair in the past used to be baked in several sections before being pieced together on the cart, so large were they. Today an Apple Pie Princess is chosen and crowned. While in the past she was pulled on a cart by donkeys, much like the original apple pie, today she is more likely to ride in a cart drawn by local teenagers. Apple pies of enormous size can still be had, though, for those with a gigantic hunger.

Crab apples generally have a bad reputation. In fact, partly because I didn't listen properly, and I love scatological humour, I thought they were called 'crap apples'. They are fairly crappy as apples go unless you enjoy biting into something unpleasantly sharp and woody in texture. Yet it is from the crab apple, rather than crustaceans, that we can trace the name of the Egremont Crab Fair. Held in Cumbria in September, when the crab apple is in season, the fair can be traced back to 1267.[11]

The fair includes a 'Parade of the Apple Cart', which may date from a time when Baron de Multon came to town with a cart of crab apples and tossed them to the people to celebrate the end of a harvest. Luckily for all involved, the apples used today are sweet eating apples and everyone goes home happy. In place of a cart a man in a van distributes the apples. In the past cakes were sometimes tossed to the crowd, but, alas for fans of pie fights, this no longer occurs.

Tossing apples is not always a wholly jolly affair. When a new bailiff was elected in Kidderminster a period of lawlessness known as the Kellums was tolerated. Each Michaelmas the newly elected official led a parade through the town but instead of being cheered he would be struck by cabbage stalks and apples thrown by the locals. One correspondent to the *Gentleman's Magazine* in 1790 observed the anarchy and how on every level of social respectability people took the chance to attack a public official. It was not just a handful of apples tossed either, he noted: 'I have known forty pots of apples expended at one house.'[12] Before you start saving up your apples to express your dissatisfaction with your elected representatives, you should know that the Kellums was abolished at the very end of the eighteenth century.

In Oxfordshire in the village of Northmoor, Eastertime saw a great apple toss. After church everyone would throw masses of apples at each other across the churchyard. When one newly appointed vicar left the church, unaware of what was happening, he was struck several times. Whether this caused a new Fall of Man is unknown.

Sometimes the priest was the deliberate target. St Cynehelm's Day in the ancient village of Kenelstowe was celebrated with a rite called 'Crabbing the Parson',[13] whereby the unfortunate cleric would be pelted with crab apples by his parishioners. One account of such an event described how the parson would try to walk as quickly as possible between buildings to avoid the barrage. Unfortunately he could not dodge them all, with 'not a few telling with fearful emphasis on his burly person, amid the intense merriment of the rustic assailants'. The tradition is said to have begun when a clergyman stole some apple dumplings and hid them up his sleeve. When one slipped out of the sleeve and hit a parishioner on the head during service the parishioner fired back with a crab apple.

If you want a more productive use for your crab apples, a Shropshire remedy calls for the juice, known as crab-varjis, to be applied to a sprain on the grounds that it will 'swage the swellin'. A mouldy eating apple is said to cure a stye if you press the fruit to it. To cure a wart an apple should be cut in half and one piece rubbed on the protuberance. The warty half of the apple should then be given to a pig while you eat the other.

Apples, of course, have long been considered medicinal: we all know the saying 'an apple a day keeps the doctor away'. Certainly it is one of the five-a-day that doctors recommend. The people of Devonshire say: 'Ait a happle avore gwain to bed, an' you'll make the doctor beg his bread.'[14] Other versions of the folklore suggest an onion a day. Oxfordshire lore has the best of both worlds: eat an apple in the morning and an onion at night.

While the Golden Apple of Discord bearing the words 'To the fairest' sparked the Trojan War in Greek mythology, there were apparently apples of peace. On Guernsey, if a group of men were fighting it was said that they could be calmed if an apple marked with the letters H A O N was thrown among them.[15] What those letters represent and how they could pacify obstreperous men is just another piece of folklore that remains baffling.

PEARS

The most famous pear tree in British culture may well be the one in which a partridge perches in the Twelve Days of Christmas. While that tree was a gift, others have treated their pear trees rather more rudely. When a man in Yorkshire thought himself cursed with the evil eye it was not that he was under its baleful influence but, rather, that the mere act of him looking at others was hurting them.[1] His remedy was to open his door in the morning and stare at a pear tree. Since the evil eye was most potent in the morning, by directing his glance at the pear tree it bore the brunt of his inadvertent curses. Naturally the tree died as a result of this, but at least the man felt his neighbours had been spared.

Others might have looked forward to seeing a little pear foliage. One English custom saw men creep out of their homes at night to decorate the cottages of their neighbours with boughs from pear trees, and each of which was imbued with a meaning. If you awoke to find a pear branch at your door it indicated that someone in your household was fair of face. Much better than briar, meaning liar, or holly for those given to folly.

Hot Baked Wardens have nothing to do with baking your church warden in a pie. These goodies make a brief appearance in Shakespeare's *The Winter's Tale* when the Clown declares, 'I must have saffron to colour the warden pies'. But what was a warden and how do you bake one?

Warden is simply an Old English word for pear – though it is often applied to cooking varieties that might need a culinary lift to make them tasty. Precisely when pears first arrived in Britain is unknown but some Anglo-Saxon charters record pear trees as boundary markers, as in a grant from 937 in Topsham in Devon describing how a stream 'ran to the pear tree and then along a dyke'.[2] When the Abbess of Shaftesbury planted pear trees along her lands in the tenth century she did not know she was also planting churches. Seven pear tree churches were built next to these trees, though only one survives today.

We know of Hot Wardens, or Hot Warden Pies, being sold in Bedford in the thirteenth century by boys who would cry their wares to passers-by, especially around St Jude's Day. But how can you make some for yourself? Luckily Thomas Dawson's *The Good Huswifes Jewell*, published in 1585, has a recipe for the pie.

> You must bake your Wardens first in a Pie [dish], and then take all the wardens and cut them in foure quarters, and coare them, and put them into a Tarte pinched, with your Suger, and season them with Suger, Synamon and Ginger, and set them in the Ouen, and put no couer on them, but you must cutte a couer and laye in the Tart when it is baked, and butter the Tarte and the couer too, and endore it with suger.[3]

Alternatively you can take the wardens, peel and quarter them, boil them to soften, then poach in red wine with spices, and bake in a puff pastry case.

Those who find pears a hard fruit to swallow might want to try the delights of perry, an alcoholic drink made from fermented pears. It has a fearsome reputation for getting drinkers very drunk – and it is an old reputation. In John Gerard's *The Herball, Or Generall Historie of Plantes*, published in 1597, Gerard describes how 'Wine made of the juice of pears called in English Perry, is soluble, purgeth those that are not accustomed to drinke thereof; notwithstanding it is as wholesome a drink being taken in small quantity as wine; it comforteth and warmeth the stomach, and causeth good digestion'.[4] Be careful not to purgeth after too much perry.

ORANGES AND LEMONS

Oranges and lemons,
Say the bells of St Clement's.

So begins the well-known nursery rhyme that often ends with innocent young children being decapitated. Such is the law of the playground. But behind the rhyme lies the special nature of citrus fruit. A relatively rare import in times gone by, an orange or lemon would have been quite the treat – even when the only varieties known were the bitter citron and marmalade oranges. Certainly something to sing about.

Apart from in schools up and down the country, you can hear the rhyme sung in the church of St Clement Danes in London every year in March. When the bells of the church were repaired and rehung in 1920 the vicar, William Pennington-Bickford, decided to hold a special service.[1] The Oranges and Lemons service saw children from a local school being given the fruit by London's Danish community and the bells rang out the well-known tune.

Some people claim that St Clement Danes became associated with oranges and lemons because in former years the church's land backed onto the River Thames and fruit boats passing along the river had to pay a toll as they went. Or perhaps the boats simply unloaded their citrus fruits near the church.[2] While St Clement Danes does have the bells to support its claim, St

Clement's Eastcheap also regards itself as the St Clement's of the rhyme.

No Christmas for me was complete without being given an orange. No matter what exciting thing waited for me wrapped up downstairs, it was the orange, which invariably worked its way into the toe of my stocking, that most amused me. Why were my parents so obsessed with putting an orange there? There was already a perfectly good bowl of oranges on the table. It was just one of those inscrutable things adults did. Of course, I now know they were simply carrying on a tradition, something their parents had done, and theirs before them. Traditions are the living history of folklore.

The origin of the tradition is debated. Some see the oranges as a reference to the balls of gold St Nicholas – yes, that one – threw through a window to help three poverty-stricken girls. Others trace it to the Great Depression in the United States. In times of hardship even an orange can bring joy.

If your children prefer not to be given an orange but would rather earn it, they can try their hand at 'A Lug and a Bite' – a game played in Lancashire.[3] The game begins with a child throwing the orange to their playmates. A mad scramble for it ensues and the first to reach it bites down hard. It will take some willpower to hold on as their competitors begin lugging down as hard as they can on the fruit-bearer's ears. Once the pain has reached a sufficient pitch the orange is dropped and the scrum begins again.

Marginally less painful was the tradition of orange rolling, or orange pelting, that took place in Dunstable.[4] There on Good Friday residents would clamber up the steep slopes near Pascombe Pit to take part. Hundreds gathered to catch the oranges tossed or rolled from the top. Pathé films from the 1930s show the scrums that could form around the tumbling fruit. Some people wore garish clothes or top hats to attract the attention of the pelters. A top hat made for a top target. Not only were oranges a tasty treat, they were a valuable commodity – the canny person who had been pelted could collect the oranges and sell them on.

Though the origins of this tradition are lost in the fog of the eighteenth century, the demise of orange pelting can be exactly pinpointed to rationing during the Second World War. With oranges and other imports in short supply, orange pelting was cancelled and, despite sporadic attempts to bring it back, the oranges no longer roll at Pascombe Pit. Which is a shame given the description that appeared in the *Dunstable Gazette* on a particularly windy day on which the orange pelting took place in 1900.

> A few courageous young people endeavoured to climb the Downs. Many of them belonged to the fair sex, and, as the wearing of bloomers has by no means yet become general, the wind played havoc with their skirts, and the result may be much more decorously imagined than described. No staid and sober journalist such as the writer of this article would ever dream of looking in that direction while the wind played such mad pranks with these ladyes faire; nevertheless it may easily be imagined that a wonderfully pretty display of multi-coloured petticoats was seen, while here and there a gleam of white, while the fair ones were executing most marvellous evolutions in frantic – but generally futile – endeavours to retain a serene and stately comportment.[5]

One of the concerns about resurrecting orange pelting is fear of injuries to children if they fall in the pursuit of the oranges. But oranges were sometimes a source of good health. It is well known today (though disputed by some historians) that the past stank. Open sewers, butchers in towns and a lack of hygiene made the smellscape of the past somewhat more noisome than the one we enjoy today (if you ignore car fumes). In the past smell was not just a matter of happiness, though – it could be deadly serious. The miasma theory of infection suggested that bad smells could actually cause bad health. To avoid breathing in the poisonous aromas of the city the wealthy turned to pomanders.

Pomanders used expensive and fragrant ingredients to drive the sickening fumes away. Often highly decorated and made from gold and silver, they could only belong to the uppermost members of society. Cardinal Wolsey is said to have introduced the poor man's pomander, or Comfort Apple, and it came in the form of an orange.[6]

One account describes him 'holding in his hand a very fair orange, whereof the meat or substance within was taken out, and filled up again with the part of a sponge, wherein was vinegar, and other confections against the pestilent airs; the which he most commonly smelt unto, passing among the press, or else when he was pestered with many suitors'.[7] He could, of course, have pelted his smelly suitors with the orange to drive them away.

CHERRIES

Cherry trees which bear fruit edible for humans are not native to Britain but were brought here by Romans, who first encountered them in the Near East. It was once said that you could trace the ancient roads the Romans used by looking for the cherry trees that grew beside them – presumably from cherry stones spat out by marching soldiers.[1]

The wild cherry trees that used to grow in Britain produced such astringent fruit that they were fit only for birds. Their vivid red skins must have proved a helpful warning to those foolhardy or hungry enough to try them.

Over the centuries during which eating cherries grew in Britain, however, they were incorporated into many aspects of folk life. Building on a tale in the apocryphal gospel of pseudo-Matthew involving an infant Jesus and a date palm, 'The Cherry-Tree Carol' seems to date from the fifteenth century. It tells the story of how

Joseph, apparently still bitter and distrustful of his pregnant wife
Mary, refuses to bring her some of the cherries she craves. When he
tells her to get the man who impregnated her to fetch the cherries,
the unborn Jesus causes the trees to bow down.

> Joseph was an old man,
> and an old man was he,
> When he wedded Mary,
> in the land of Galilee.
> Joseph and Mary walked
> through an orchard good,
> Where was cherries and berries,
> so red as any blood.
> Joseph and Mary walked
> through an orchard green,
> Where was berries and cherries,
> as thick as might be seen.
> O then bespoke Mary,
> so meek and so mild:
> 'Pluck me one cherry, Joseph,
> for I am with child.'
> O then bespoke Joseph,
> with words most unkind:
> 'Let him pluck thee a cherry
> that brought thee with child.'
> O then bespoke the babe,
> within his mother's womb:
> 'Bow down then the tallest tree,
> for my mother to have some.'
> Then bowed down the highest tree
> unto his mother's hand;
> Then she cried, 'See, Joseph,
> I have cherries at command.'
> O then bespake Joseph:
> 'I have done Mary wrong;

But cheer up, my dearest,
and be not cast down.'
Then Mary plucked a cherry,
as red as the blood,
Then Mary went home
with her heavy load.
Then Mary took her babe,
and sat him on her knee,
Saying, 'My dear son, tell me
what this world will be.'
'O I shall be as dead, mother,
as the stones in the wall;
O the stones in the streets, mother,
shall mourn for me all.
Upon Easter-day, mother,
my uprising shall be;
O the sun and the moon, mother,
shall both rise with me.'[2]

Many places in Britain once celebrated the end of the cherry harvest by baking a pie. Today one of the few places to hold a cherry pie festival is the Plough Inn in Cadsden.[3] While it was traditionally held on the first Sunday in August, unfortunately global warming is now playing havoc with folk traditions as well as the climate. Local farms which might once have been able to provide cherries now end their cherry season in the middle of July. Seasonality may lead to adjustments in many other celebrations as we come to terms with the earth we have created.

If you do get some cherries, whether from a farm or a supermarket, one of the most popular uses for them has been to predict the future. Take some cherries, or other stoned fruit, and arrange them around the outside of a plate. To know when you will marry count them off as you chant 'This year, next year, sometime, never'.[4] Whichever one you end on will be your future.

Cuckoos, with their murderous and parasitical life cycle, might seem like poor creatures to turn to for a glimpse of your tomorrows. The first cuckoo has always marked a turning point in the year, but cuckoos can also be used to predict how many more years you have to live.[5] This is related to cherries because it was once thought that cuckoos could only call out once they had filled their greedy bellies three times over with cherries.

Once they had done this, if you saw one in a tree then it was the perfect time to call out to them yourself:

> Cuckoo, cherry tree,
> Come down, tell me,
> How many years afore I dee?[6]

The number of times you heard the cuckoo afterwards indicated just how many more years you could look forward to. If you were a wise person with a lot of patience and willing to wait for a cuckoo to keep calling, maybe you were the sort of person who would live a long time.

PLUMS

Nothing beats the glut of plums when they start falling from the trees. The soft, sweet flesh of a good plum is a joy. Given the shortness of their season, people have found many ways of cooking them up into delicious dainties. Some, like Plum Shuttles (a fruited bun: Shuttles is pronounced Shittles), were given as Valentine's Day gifts, while others were just hearty puddings. One plum pudding rhyme is admirably tolerant of the different ways in which people enjoyed their pudding.

> Plum pudding hot, plum pudding cold,
> Plum pudding in the pot, nine days old;

Some like it hot, some like it cold,
Some like it in the pot nine days old.[1]

Medical advice suggests, however, that pudding left in a pot for nine days is probably not good for the health.

Plum charming takes something of a similar form to Wassailing. In 2013 in Pershore, Worcestershire, a local solicitor named Paul Johnson could be found in plum orchards, dressed in purple robes and a tricorn hat, serenading the trees with a clarinet. His aim was to 'wake up' the trees so that they would get on with the business of producing the plums that are part of Pershore's history.[2] It is said that plums became vital to the area in the 1830s after the landlord of a pub discovered a new variety of plum known as the Pershore Yellow Egg.

Those hoping for a good crop of plums should be warned that they are likely to get a season of bad health, for it was thought that when plums were plentiful cholera was sure to follow. There were other ways in which plums were bad for the health. In 1905, the *Folklore Journal* recorded the belief of a factory girl that over-ripe plums could be positively fatal. 'There was a young girl in our street ate a whole pound of plums, I think it was, and there was maggots in them. And they grew inside her. They took her to the hospital, but they couldn't do nothing for her: they had to get consent to smother her!'[3]

BERRIES

The bramble has long provided sustenance for the needy or the greedy. Most years they produce a huge number of lush blackberries. Known variously throughout the country as black-blegs, bumblekites, gatterberries and skaldberries, they would have been much sought after as a free and plentiful addition to otherwise dreary diets. But they were not available all year round.

When should you stop picking blackberries? That is the central question that has troubled British folklore for at least three centuries. The most common date given is Old Michaelmas, 10 or 11 October.

St Michael is said to have cast the Devil bodily out of heaven after the old rascal's failed rebellion. Falling for days, he is said to have finally landed face first in a bramble patch. Anyone who has taken a similar tumble knows how painful the clinging thorns of the blackberry bush can be. No doubt nursing some nasty scratches, the Devil is said to have risen up and cursed the blackberry – making it unsafe to eat blackberries after St Michael's Day.[1]

One writer in 1727 remarked that 'after Michaelmas the D—l casts his club over them' on this day.[2] This suggests he merely made the fruit unpalatable and soft. Others believe that the Devil made a more intimate intervention in the blackberry harvest. Some places in Britain hold that the Devil spat on the blackberries, while others prefer to steer children away from them on the grounds that the Devil either urinated or defecated on them at Michaelmas. There were more sanitary rumours as well, that the Devil simply trotted up and down the hedgerows on Michaelmas to squash fruit with his trotters.

What happened to those who did eat a blackberry after Michaelmas? Charlotte Latham, writing in the 1860s, was told by a friend of the horror that greeted her request for blackberries a single day after Michaelmas. She was told in no uncertain terms of the risk she was taking. 'If any person were to eat one on the eleventh, they or someone belonging to them would die or fall into great trouble before the year was out. No, nothing should persuade me to let any child of mine go blackberrying on the 11th of October.'[3] There are reports of some country folk so scared of the Devil that they would never touch a blackberry at any time of the year.

The Cornish treated blackberries after Michaelmas as a game

of Russian roulette. They held that Lucifer touched a single blackberry on that date and it became fatally poisonous. As they could not tell which fruit he had touched, to eat any one of them was to take your life in your hands.

The bramble was not entirely cursed, however. Should a child come down with whooping cough the cure administered in Devon involved passing them under an arch of bramble and saying:

> In bramble, out cough,
> Here I leave the whooping cough.[4]

In Cornish tradition the first blackberry of the season was held to be an infallible cure for warts. Those on the Isle of Man would have to forgo this treatment because on no account should the first blackberry of the year be picked – it had to be left for fairy folk. If not, all the blackberries would be full of grubs. Having once picked wild blackberries and left them in a tub overnight, nothing prepared me for the crawling mass of larvae that I found wiggling inside the next day. Since then, I have been happy to leave all the blackberries for the little folk to eat.

The strawberry has long been considered to be at the pinnacle of British produce. In the seventeenth century a Dr Butler was recorded as saying: 'Doubtless God could have made a better berry, but doubtless God never did.' The plump, large strawberries we enjoy today are, of course, not the work of God but the product of human interference. It took me some time to make the connection between the fragrant but tiny wild strawberries found on banks and verges with those that stained my lips pink when I was taken to a pick-your-own farm. We had our own family folklore about eating too many during these trips as my father convinced me that they weighed you on the way in and out to check you hadn't eaten any. It was their method of making sure more ended up in the punnet than down my gullet. Children, who are often the most beguiled by the flavour of the strawberry, could suffer from their influence even before birth. A mother eating too many strawberries risked her child being born with a scarlet birthmark on their body.[5]

In Oxfordshire, just before the Second World War, a tradition existed whereby men in straw hats were seen as potential bringers of good fortune. After first touching their elbows, children who saw such a man would recite:

> Strawberry man, Strawberry man,
> Bring me good luck,
> Today or tomorrow,
> To pick something up.[6]

A pebble or small object then had to be thrown over the left shoulder if the charm was to work.

Nobody is quite sure why gooseberries are called gooseberries. Looking to the French does not help matters as they call gooseberries 'mackerel berries'. In some places in England they were known as goose-gogs or goozegogs.

Children were often told that they were not given birth to by their mother but, rather, found under a gooseberry bush. Some have suggested that 'gooseberry bush' was slang for pubic hair. That would certainly explain why children come from such a bush.

On the Isle of Wight a sprite known as the Gooseberry-wife guarded the unripe fruit of the gooseberry bush. She lurked there in the shape of a large, furry caterpillar and was used by generations of parents to keep their children away from overly green gooseberries – an upset tummy was the least of their concerns.[7]

'If ye goos out in the gearden, the gooseberry-wife'll be sure to ketch ye.'

Eating unripe gooseberries was also said to be the cause of head lice.[8] Best all round to wait until they are ready to be picked.

The village of Hartlebury in Worcestershire seems to have had gooseberry bushes with the ability to prognosticate. Should a gooseberry bush in your garden die and shrivel up while laden with fruit it was a sure sign that there would soon be a death in the family.[9]

A fascinating study of traditional cures from Ulster published in 2009 found that many people thought that prodding a stye with a thorn was a sure cure for the swelling – but it had to be the thorn from a gooseberry bush.[10] Some of the rites for this cure were quite complex. The thorn had first to be passed through a wedding ring, or wielded by the seventh son of a seventh son. Alternatively, twelve separate thorns had to be used to stab the stye, with each being cast first over the left and then over the right shoulder until they were all gone. It should be said that jabbing possibly dirty thorns into the skin is probably not a great way of curing a bacterial infection.

I don't want to go on and on about gooseberries: when someone tells a long and pointless tale they are said to be beating the Devil around the gooseberry bush. I wouldn't want to appear a gooseberry fool.

RAISINS

Most British people in the past would only have known grapes in their dried form – the raisin. These sweet brown nuggets were popular in all manner of foods from sweet pastries to dishes we might think of as savoury today. They also played a role in medicine. You might still find people who claim that 'drunken raisins' help those with arthritis.[1] All you need to do is soak some raisins in gin and consume them when the pain is bad. However, while gin may help you deal with the agony of arthritis, doctors do not recommended it.

You might want to try drunken raisins if you happen to be going poaching. I was once told by someone who enjoyed a bit of pheasant without paying for it that his preferred method of

Nothing says 'festive event' like small children snatching flaming raisins
from a bowl of flammable liquid.

catching them was to soak raisins in vodka. These were then left
out overnight and were apparently irresistible to pheasants and
would get them blackout drunk. In the morning all he had to
do was pick up the pheasants where they lay and shove them in
his bag.

That method of hunting may be illegal – you'll have to ask a
lawyer – but there is a game that was enjoyed by generations of
children which, if played today, would definitely see a parent
charged with reckless child endangerment. Snap-dragon was
once a feature of many a Christmas festivity.

To play snap-dragon all you need are raisins, brandy, a fire and
a complete lack of concern for personal safety. The raisins were
soaked in the brandy and set alight. The gathered guests would
then take up spoonfuls of the flaming mixture and place it in
their mouths. The 'fun' comes from the appearance this gives the

players of breathing fire like a dragon or demon. Needless to say this caused numerous burns to many of those taking part but it did not stop snap-dragon being a widespread activity for several centuries. It appears as flap-dragon in several Shakespeare plays, Michael Faraday discussed the physics of the game, and Lewis Carroll in one of his *Alice* books described the snap-dragon-fly whose 'body is made of plum pudding, its wings of holly-leaves, and its head is a raisin burning in brandy'.[2]

NUTS

> Here we come gathering nuts in May,
> Nuts in May, nuts in May,
> Here we come gathering nuts in May,
> On a cold and frosty morning.[1]

If children were sent out to gather nuts before they were ripe they would have had to be careful not to attract the attention of mischievous spirits. Nut groves are said to be protected by a spirit variously known as Churn Milk Peg or Melsh Dick.[2] Where hazelnuts grow she will sit smoking her pipe to make sure that no nuts are taken before they are ready. Should a child be so foolish as to try and take one she will pinch them hard and chase them off.

Sunday was an ill time for gathering nuts. One person in the 1870s recalled his grandmother knowing of an exceedingly wicked man who broke the sabbath to go nutting.[3] The malefactor was horrified to find that no matter how many nuts he picked from the tree they reappeared back on the tree in greater numbers. Why an infinite number of nuts should be scary rather than a goldmine is not recorded.

In Sussex the Devil was said to have offered his help to those who went out collecting nuts on a Sunday. The nuts picked on the Sabbath brought terrible bad luck. This may explain the Sussex idiom 'As black as the de'il's nutting-bag'.

Another dangerous time for gathering nuts was Devil's Nutting Day on 21 September. The strangely conical hill called Alcock's Arbour near Alcester, Warwickshire, was said to have come into being when the Devil was out collecting nuts on that day.[4] Having stripped hundreds of trees, the Devil's hands were full when the Virgin startled him, causing him to drop them. As they fell to the ground the hill was created but ever after it was unlucky to pick nuts on that date. A saying warned people not to risk it:

> The devil as common people say,
> Doth go nutting on Holy-rood day
> And sure such leachery in some doth lurk,
> Going a nutting do the devil's work.[5]

Nuts with their hard shells were once used as tiny works of art and carving, but they also featured in amulets. In the National Museum of Wales there is an amulet from east London carried by a First World War soldier that consists of a hazelnut hung in gold.[6] Other nuts required modification to become magical.

You can cure whooping cough by opening a nut and replacing the kernel with a living spider. One wise woman from Syresham, Northamptonshire, in the nineteenth century was well known for providing this cure. Others favoured a woodlouse rather than a spider. A reminiscence of nineteenth-century doctor John Sebastian Helmcken from London suggests that the magic worked by some sympathy between the insect and the cough.[7] As the trapped animal rotted, the cough would wither away too. According to his memoirs the spider in the nut should be worn around the neck in a satin bag.

As a child Helmcken was given just such a nut but at first refused to wear it and his mother pooh-poohed the idea of this charm working. Eventually he was persuaded to wear it with a bag of sweets and, finding that the spider did not bite him, let the nut rest on his neck. His whooping cough disappeared and, when the nut was opened, the spider was found to have been reduced to its insubstantial shell. The 'crone' who had suggested this cure was triumphant. 'Didn't I tell you so? Now don't laugh at me any more!'

Nuts need not only be shared with others; they can be enjoyed on one's own. One All Hallows' Eve in Wales it was the custom to toss nuts on the fire to predict your health for the year ahead. If they flared into a bright flame then the thrower would enjoy good health and live to repeat the act the following year.

Not all nuts need to be cast into the flames to be of use, however. When two nuts grow in a single shell they are called St John's Nuts. You can use these nuts as powerful charms against witches and others who would seek to cast evil charms over you. In some places, though, it was not simply enough to have the nuts about your person – you had to load them into a gun. Perthshire folklore said that witches could not be harmed by a lead bullet so St John's Nuts had to be fired at them instead.[8] As ever it was bad luck to bite the bullet – no one should eat St John's Nuts as it was said they bring terrible misfortune. The canny people of Northamptonshire felt it was only bad luck to consume both the kernels in a double nut so got the best of both worlds by eating one and casting the other over their shoulder. Shropshire lore says that such double nuts kept in the pocket are a good cure for toothache.

Some nut folklore is simply nutty. In Kingston upon Thames, those who went to church near Michaelmas would not go with any expectation of hearing a sermon but, rather, to disrupt it. Each person took a load of nuts with them to munch on cheerfully throughout the service. Known as Crack-Nut Sunday, the service could be incredibly noisy. One observer in the nineteenth century remarked: 'The cracking noise was often so powerful, that the minister was obliged to suspend his reading, or discourse, until greater quietness was obtained.'[9] No one knows how this annual act of ecclesiastical disobedience came about – perhaps something to do with a local election – but it was firmly cracked down on by the twentieth century.

One curious saying collected in Oxford has it that 'a good nut year is a good baby year'.[10] Nutting, it seems, is imperative for the procreative act. A year when many children were born was called a 'nutty year'. Nutting has long been proverbially good for getting pregnant. What young men and women got up to while out looking for nuts was not always food-related.

Going nutting gave young people an opportunity to spend some time alone in the woods away from the prying eyes of chaperones.

Meat and Animal Lore

The language of meat in English is fascinating and reveals class structures going back nearly 1,000 years. When we sit down for a meal we do not eat cow, we eat beef. Nor do we feast on pig, we have some pork. Many meats have not shared their names with the animals they come from since the Norman Conquest of 1066. The elite classes that came to England spoke French while most of the population continued to speak forms of Old English. Most of the upper classes would only see farm animals when they were served up cooked at their dining table. A sheep was a *mouton* to them, so we eat mutton today. The poorer people who actually raised the animals continued to call them scēap and so we still see sheep grazing in fields. Similar verbal repercussions can be seen in the French *porc* and *boeuf* that grace our plates.

Some traditions involving meat are very specific as to the species of animal and even the cut which must be used while others take a more universal approach. One cure for whooping cough involved tying a bit of raw meat around the patient's neck.[1] The doctor who witnessed this assumed it to be related to the hanging of a worm around a child's neck. As the worm dried and shrivelled it was thought the illness would leave the body. He noted that the meat must have been placed on its string some days earlier as it had begun to go off and smell.

Perhaps the most popular myth about British food is that the word sirloin is derived from an English king being so pleased

with a piece of beef at a feast that he knighted it on the spot, dub-
bing it 'Sir Loin'. This fanciful tale can be traced back to at least
the seventeenth century though the king who did the knighting
changes in the telling across time. Early sources tend to cite the
gourmand Henry VIII while Jonathan Swift gives credit for this
bon mot to James I. In Samuel Johnson's *Dictionary of the English
Language* no specific king is mentioned but the popular legend
reappears.

Alas, the truth is that sirloin is merely a cut of meat whose
name comes from the French word meaning 'over the loin'.

While many of our treasured tales of meat and animal folklore
disappear like the steam rising from a roast chicken, there are
definite examples of meat being used in folk magic, rituals, rites
and medicine.

BEEF

Those who lived in the North of England were very clear about
what constituted a good New Year:

> I wish you a merry Christmas,
> And a happy New Year,
> A pantry full of roast beef,
> And a barrel full of beer.[1]

No New Year could possibly be prosperous unless meat was on
the menu. Beef has always been an expensive foodstuff, often
only served on special occasions, so eating beef really was a cause
for celebration. Opening your house to guests and treating them
to beef, cake and drink must have made one feel like a generous
noble. Welcoming others to rich fare at New Year in the North of
England was known, somewhat improbably, as 'fadging' or
'eating fadge'.[2]

In Scotland the eating of the first meat of the year was a special moment because it presaged another year of life. A saying explains how fresh meat overcomes the curses of those predicting scarcity:

> A death-shroud on the grey, bitter grey, old woman,
> Who said she would not taste the fresh meat,
> I will taste the fresh meat,
> And will be alive for it next year.[3]

By eating the produce and bounty that the coming year promised you were joining your vitality to that of the world around you and ensuring another year of life.

The relative absence of beef on the common person's table has made it somewhat scarce in folk rituals and charms. In Cornwall one folklorist did discover an old woman who kept an infallible amulet for good luck in her pocket at all times – the dried tip of an ox's tongue.[4] It was also said that when tongue was served the tip should be sliced off and kept in a purse. This ensured that whoever had the tongue would never lack for money.[5]

Sir James Young Simpson, a famous nineteenth-century doctor, related how his father could remember a brutal ritual taking place involving a cow. When Simpson's grandfather found the cattle on his farm were suffering from a murrain, or infectious illness, he decided that there was an evil spirit that needed to be placated. With the aid of the farm hands one of the cows was buried alive.[6]

In Dorset a bullock's heart was considered a good source of protection against fairies. Hanging one in your chimney was thought to keep the mischievous spirits from entering the house and creating havoc. In the Pitt Rivers Museum there is a cow's heart that has been pierced with thorns and nails and dried in a chimney.[7] Such charms may have been an offensive sort of magic where the pain inflicted on the heart was supposed to be inflicted on some desired target, human or supernatural.

PORK

Pork was more plentiful for many people than beef. A whole pig might be beyond most purses but a bit of dried bacon could be found in even the humblest kitchens. Because pigs were more common there were more opportunities for traditions and superstitions to form. One bit of pork lore says that you should never eat pork in a month without the letter R in it. Pork does indeed spoil quickly in the heat and the warmer months in Britain do lack an R. Pigs were handy creatures as livestock as they could be let loose to eat whatever they could forage and then later slaughtered to provide food for the table. This has not always been a success. History relates how pigs have been used to clean up human waste. This helps to get rid of faeces but has the unfortunate side effect of spreading parasites, a route of infection my lecturer in epidemiology referred to as from 'turd to table'. They also occasionally

In 1457 a sow was placed on trial in Lavigny, France, for the murder and consumption of a child. Her piglets were spared because of their tender age.

had the unfortunate habit of finding swaddled babies left on the ground and devouring them. Homicidal pigs were sometimes put on trial and sentenced for their crimes. Still, seeing pigs roaming in the street was once commonplace.

St Anthony of Egypt was the patron saint of swineherds and his name was also invoked against a painful skin condition often called St Anthony's Fire. One of the most frequently used charms against such illnesses involved pig lard. This double association with the saint and pigs gave rise to the tantony pig, the smallest piglet of a litter.

Every part of the pig could find a use. Black pudding is mostly made from pig blood, pig fat, some type of cereal and a variety of herbs and spices. Pennyroyal was so firmly associated with black pudding that it was known as pudding-yerb in Yorkshire. Black puddings are somewhat controversial today because some people find the eating of congealed blood makes them feel queasy. In the seventeenth century it was at the heart of a religious debate. In 1652 the future Bishop of Lincoln, Thomas Barlow, wrote a pamphlet titled *The triall of a black-pudding. Or, The unlawfulness of eating blood proved by Scriptures, before the law, under the law, and after the law. By a well wisher to ancient truth*.[1]

Those who enjoy a black pudding might like to visit Ramsbottom on the second Sunday of September. There they will be able to partake in the World Black Pudding Throwing Championship.[2] Locals claim that the sport has been taking place since the Wars of the Roses but its current incarnation only dates from the 1980s. Competitors take turns hurling black puddings at Yorkshire puddings on a raised platform. Whoever knocks the most down is declared world champion.

Before you prepare your pork you should pay attention to the time of the month. If a pig is killed when the moon is waning, the meat will wither away before you get a chance to eat it. In Yorkshire it was also thought that if a woman was menstruating when she salted and preserved bacon it would quickly go off.[3] Nor was every part of the pig safe to eat. Eating the marrow of a pig bone was, according to Norfolk folklore, a one-way ticket to the madhouse.[4]

Pigs could be handy in getting a good marriage to help in the production of babies in the first place. At Northrepps in Norfolk, a song was sung by children suggesting that if a girl's father owned a pig she was a promising prospect for marriage.

Good morrow, Valentine!
How do it hail!
When Father's pig die,
You shall ha' its tail.

Good morrow, Valentine!
How thundering Hot!
When Father's pig die,
You shall ha' its jot.[5]

In this case the tripe of the pig was known as its jot. From the song this seems to have been something desirable. Once you got married, however, you might not be pleased with the results. One joke at the expense of porcine and crude husbands recorded how 'Her'l never want for bacon as her's allus got a hog in the house'.[6]

Sometimes, just sometimes, a marriage can lead to long-lasting love and affection. Some would think that such a state of affairs was its own reward but there is a ceremony where a happy couple can earn a prize for having a harmonious marriage.

The Dunmow Flitch is a side of bacon that is awarded to any couple who can truthfully claim that they have been married for at least a year and a day without ever once regretting their marriage – so long as they pass the Flitch Trials.[7] The Flitch Trial involves the swearing of an oath and production of witnesses that can confirm a couple's matrimonial harmony. A popular, though probably mythical, account of the origins of this tradition dates it to the twelfth century in the village of Little Dunmow in Essex. Reginald Fitzwalter and his lady wife disguised themselves as poor folk and visited the prior of the local abbey. There they declared they had been married for a year and a day and sought the prior's blessing on their union. As well as holy words the prior gave them a side of bacon. Fitzwalter then revealed his true identity and bestowed lands on the abbey on the condition that the profits were used to distribute bacon to those who could make a similar claim about their marriage.

The Dunmow Flitch became a byword for a happy union. Chaucer's fourteenth-century Wife of Bath, herself a victim of unhappy marriages, referred to it in her tale in *The Canterbury Tales*.

> The bacon was nat fet for hem, I trowe,
> That som men han in Essex at Dunmowe.

The earliest officially recognised winner of the flitch is one Richard Wright of Norwich in 1445. Oddly his wife, who was also integral to his bringing home the bacon, is not mentioned. Some uncharitable historians have commented that the bacon

This engraving of the Dunmow Flitch of 1751 shows a successful couple being carried aloft with their prize bacon being paraded in front of them.

was given to unusually kind husbands during this period who rarely beat their wives. The Flitch Trials fell into abeyance for some years but were revived in the Victorian age. Today the bacon is given away at Dunmow every four years.

There have been accusations that some awards of bacon were not entirely fair. It was reported in the early nineteenth century that one couple who had successfully claimed the prize had certain natural (if unfortunate) advantages in their marriage: the husband was deaf and the wife blind.[8]

Once you had your bacon there were ways of using it that did not include frying it up. If you had a wart that you wanted to be rid of you were advised to steal a piece of bacon from a butcher and rub it on the wart. The meat was then buried and, as the purloined pork rotted in the ground, the wart would wither.[9]

This might sound like the rankest sort of superstition but Francis Bacon believed in it. Bacon's philosophical works did much to codify the scientific method that has brought about so many advances. He described how Lady Paulet, wife of the English ambassador to Paris, showed him the charm.

The taking away of warts by rubbing them with somewhat that afterwards is put to waste and consume, is a common experiment: and I do apprehend it the rather because of mine own experience. I had from my childhood a wart upon one of my fingers; afterwards when I was about sixteen years old, being then at Paris, there grew upon both my hands a number of warts, at the least a hundred, in a month's space. The English ambassador's lady, who was a woman far from superstition, told me one day she would help me away with my warts: whereupon she got a piece of lard with the skin on, and rubbed the warts all over with the fat side; and amongst the rest that wart which I had had from childhood; then she nailed the piece of lard, with the fat towards the sun, upon a post of her chamber window, which was to the south. The success was that within five weeks' space all the warts went quite away, and that wart which I had so long endured for company.[10]

Should you just need a bit of good luck then procure yourself the nose of a pig. One writer from Cornwall recorded witnessing a crowd watching a girl trying to toss the nose of a pig over the roof of her house.[11] Apparently if you could do this, with your back to the house, and the nose fell into the back garden, it was good luck. Be careful, though: should the nose not make it, bad luck would follow, not least because you would now have a rotting pig's nose stuck on your roof.

For a pork-based celebration you can visit the Church of the Holy Cross in Avening, Gloucestershire. On the Sunday nearest 14 September, every other year, Pig Face Day is held.[12] Despite its name, this has nothing to do with the libellous suggestion that former prime minister David Cameron may have been intimate with a porcine partner. There are two stories about how this strangely named feast may have been created.

The bringing in of a boar's head was once the centrepiece of many a grand meal.

In one version it came about simply because a large boar was terrorising the community. When it was finally caught and killed, the boar was strung up and displayed for all to see. Then it was cooked and fed to the village, with cuts of meat from the face being thought particularly lucky.

The other version involves a tale of royal revenge. Matilda of Flanders once sought the hand of a nobleman called Brittic who owned the lands at Avening. After he had rejected her multiple times, her love turned to hatred. She did eventually make a good match when she married William of Normandy, otherwise known as William the Conqueror. Using her influence as queen, she had Brittic stripped of his lands and thrown into prison, where he died. Guilt about her part in his demise is said to be why Matilda ordered the construction of a church in Avening. To reward the builders she presented a roast boar to the workmen and Pig Face Day became an annual event.

If you ask someone who isn't from Britain whether they would like to eat toad in the hole they would probably wonder once again whether British cooks were a few sandwiches short of a picnic. In fact, toad in the hole is a much loved dish. Today we know it as pork sausage baked in crisp batter and usually served with lashings of savoury gravy. But how did the dish get its name?

The etymology I was taught, probably incorrectly, is that it comes from the Fortean phenomenon of entombed animals. From the mid-eighteenth century there are recurrent stories of ancient animals emerging from stones that had just been quarried from the earth. Writers from Benjamin Franklin to Charles Dickens noted examples of these mysterious, trapped animals. When the rocks were split open out flopped frogs and toads.[13] Some were described as fitting perfectly within the hollows left behind in the stone, as if the rock had formed around them.

A more humorous tale recounts a golfer making an excellent shot and sinking his ball from a great distance. When the players approached the green a toad which had been lurking in the hole crawled out and carried the ball with it. The culinary toad in the hole was then created in mock celebration of this event.

In reality the name toad in the hole can be dated back to at least 1787 in Francis Grose's *A Provincial Glossary*, in which it is noted that in Norfolk the dish is known by the equally excellent name pudding-pye-doll.[14] Dishes made from putting meat in batter and baking it can be found in earlier texts but the first mention of an 'in-the-hole' recipe is Hannah Glasse's of 1747 for 'pigeons in a hole', where pigeons take the place of the more familiar sausages.

LAMB AND MUTTON

The town of Kirtlington in Oxfordshire has a long association with lambs and festivities. In 1679 Thomas Blount recorded how on the Monday after Whitsun all the maidens would meet and have their thumbs tied behind their backs.[1] In this unlikely fashion they then chased after a lamb and whoever managed to take hold of it with her teeth was crowned the 'Lady of the Lamb'. The lamb was then killed and its skin held aloft on a long pole and carried in procession with the winning lady. The next day the lady and her friends would feast on the lamb.

Later versions of this tradition at the location refer to the festival as Lamb Ale. In the nineteenth century young ladies no longer hunted the lamb with their teeth; rather, the Lady of the Lamb was elected by the lord of the day. The firstborn lamb of the season was bedecked in ribbons and carried on the shoulders of a man and paraded through the town. This lamb was then supposed to be killed to make pies that were given out to all present. Most prized of all was the Head Pie, made with the lamb's head, wool and all, inside. This pie had to be purchased, though why anyone would want it is not recorded.

The village of Holne in Devon had a standing stone that was

the site of sacrifice into the early modern era. On May Day the young men of the village would chase down a male lamb and drag it to the stone. There it was tied down, its throat was cut and it was roasted whole, without anything being removed from it. At noon a struggle would begin to win the meat. It was thought that eating a bit of the lamb would bring luck for the coming year so the men set to with fists and knives to carve off a morsel. It is said that some men would gallantly carry some of the meat to their beloved, who did not enter the fray.[2]

This was not a case of rustic barbarity, however; young would-be gentlemen could be just as brutal. At Eton College the scholars were treated to a ram hunt every year.[3] This consisted of the well-dressed boys chasing the ram down as it ran through the streets. One year the ram managed to escape to the river and swim into Windsor, just across the water. When the Eton boys pursued it into the marketplace and exposed their revelries to the locals, it caused a minor scandal. Thereafter the rams were hamstrung to prevent them making an escape and bludgeoned to death within the confines of the school. In 1747 the hunt was abolished and pasties made from the meat of an already slaughtered ram were distributed instead.

Sheep bones and sheep flesh appear many times in charms, spells and cures across the British Isles. In the Highlands of Scotland the shoulder blade of a black sheep that had been removed without being touched with iron was considered to be powerful.[4] When cleaned without the use of knives it could be held up by a person over their left shoulder while another tried to glimpse visions through the thinnest part of the bone. Everything from births to burials could be gleaned in this way.

This practice was known as *Slinneineachd*, and many types of animal scapula could be used, though the shoulder blade of a bear was thought to be particularly effective.[5] Because even the smallest blemish on the bone would render it useless, they were usually prepared by boiling the meat from them. The natural

shapes and marks of the bone were read by those who had the
ability to interpret them.

One reader of the bones was a man called Mac a' Chreachaire,
who lived on the island of Barra.[6] Whenever there was a feast at
the castle belonging to clan MacNeil he would be called on to
examine the bones and read the future for his hosts. Mac a'
Chreachaire was asked to divine the fate of the clan's castle one
evening and refused to reveal what he saw. Under duress he announced that, when certain unlikely things happened, the castle
would be 'a cairn for thrushes'. Of course, as in all such tales, these
things came to be and the castle was indeed left in ruins.

In Yorkshire a girl was recorded as having used a blade from a
shoulder of mutton to snare her desired lover. She took the bone
and stabbed a knife through the thinnest part and, with the knife
still embedded, buried it in the garden. This inflicted such pain
on her intended beau that he soon came round and paid court to
her. The girl was so shocked by the efficacy of her magic and
ashamed to have employed it against the man that she promised
never to try it again.

An 1860 chapbook called *The Universal Fortune Teller* reveals
that this spell might have been used more than once. It advises
that those who seek 'to know if their present sweet-heart will
marry you' should turn to the bone. With the shoulder blade of
a lamb in one hand and a borrowed knife in the other, the maiden
should stab the bone once a night for nine days before going to
bed. As they stabbed it they should recite the words:

> 'Tis not this bone I mean to stick,
> But my lover's heart I mean to prick;
> Wishing him neither rest nor sleep
> Till he comes to me to speak.[7]

Should your sheep have been 'overlooked' by an ill wisher who
has cursed your flock then you could use your sheep, or part of

them, to fight back. In the Horniman Museum in London there is a dried sheep's heart that has been pierced with nails and pins.[8] The handwritten label states that it was collected in Exmouth in 1912. The reasoning behind impaling a heart seems to have been that you could turn the magic back on the person who had cast it. Stabbing the heart and then burning or roasting it would inflict the same pain on the one who cursed the sheep.

If you suffered from cramps you might resort to the use of a cramp-bone. This was the kneecap of a sheep that was worn next to the skin as a way of warding off the pain. The cure for rheumatism was more dramatic – and traumatic for the poor animal.

The patient was to be taken to a live black sheep. While living, the creature was flayed. The warm skin was then draped over the rheumatic person and the animal strength of the sheep would heal the human. The folklorist who recorded this rite stated that his source had only heard of this being done once, in the early nineteenth century.[9]

Food folklore never stands still and even the oldest dishes can accrue new meanings. Haggis, despite being the national dish of Scotland, was first mentioned in an English manuscript in the 1430s. From the earliest written records the description of a haggis has been somewhat off-putting. An early recipe reminds cooks that 'bowel noght þou shalle forsake'.[10] That haggis contains the heart, lungs and liver of a sheep, mixed with oats, herbs and spices all boiled in its own stomach, is a fact everyone knows, but fewer know how delicious it truly is.

The Scots like to have a little fun with the reputation of haggis. Modern folklore tells of the 'wild haggis' that roams the Highlands. These creatures are sometimes described as having longer legs on one side of their body than the other to cope with the steep slopes they live on. This has led to two different species evolving with one having longer left limbs and the other longer right limbs. Because of their physiological differences each species has to run in different ways up mountains or they will lose their balance and plunge to their deaths. Of course, the two species cannot interbreed and the male would have to turn around to mount the female and would tumble down the hill if it tried.

Stuffed examples of the wild haggis can be found in several Scottish museums.[11] In size and shape they resemble the regular haggis, have the heads of rodents and often a luxurious head of hair. Be careful should you decide to try and snare a haggis for yourself. The poet James J. Montague wrote in 1924:

> My heart's in the Highlands, twa strings on my bow
> To hunt the fierce haggis, man's awfu'est foe.
> And weel may my bairn ha' a tear in his ee.
> For I shallna come back if the haggis hunts me.[12]

FOWLS

Millions of families will be familiar with the squabbles between children after Christmas dinner as to who gets to pull the wishbone of the turkey or chicken. Whoever pulls the wishbone, or furcula, and gets the larger piece, is supposed to be granted their wish. Few will know that this practice may well have sexual connotations.

The antiquary John Aubrey, writing in the seventeenth century, describes how the wishbone, then called the merrythought, was placed on the nose like a pair of spectacles. The wearer then shook it loose, the wishbone was pulled and the pieces placed in one person's hand like straws. Whoever drew the longer bone got their wish. But it is Aubrey's explanation of how the merrythought derived its name that gives one pause: ''tis called the merrythought, because when the fowle is opened, dissected, or carv'd, it resembles the pudenda of a woman.'[1]

Whether this is true or not, I leave it to the imagination of the reader. As Freud would no doubt say, sometimes a wishbone is

Wishbones have been symbols of both fertility and fortune for centuries.

just a wishbone. Others prefer to say that the merrythought simply refers to the 'merry thought' that one wanted to come true.

On New Year's Eve a girl could guarantee a husband by hanging a wishbone over the door of her house and the first man to pass under it would become her husband. If Aubrey's explanation of the wishbone is true, it may have been a symbolic hanging of the lady's more intimate charms that were enticing a future spouse.

When a hen crowed it was always seen as a terrible sign. Sometimes it was thought that a crowing hen was actually a witch in disguise. In the Hebrides it was said that a crowing hen was as bad as a whistling woman.[2] To cure the hen a part of its tail was cut off, or, more drastically, the hen's head. It is not recorded what the cure for an annoying human whistler is. The Welsh concurred with this assessment of female whistlers and hens:

A whistling woman and a crowing hen
Are only fit for the devil and his den.[3]

Gender nonconformity in roosters was punished, too. When a rooster laid an egg in 1474 in Basel it was placed on trial and convicted. The rooster was burned as if it were a heretic.

If chickens were not being consigned to the flames, other threats awaited them. In Wales hens that failed to produce eggs before Shrove Tuesday were considered useless, dragged out of the hen house, then thrashed to death by the household.[4]

Chickens could be used in the detection of witches. If someone thought they might have been bewitched they could steal a black hen and remove its heart.[5] This was then stabbed with many pins and placed in the fire. This would draw the spirit of the witch to the door of the house at midnight – if any of the neighbours were known to have passed a sleepless night then they were clearly the witch.

Warnings from chickens have turned up from time to time in British history. In the unrest of the Wars of the Roses we are told that a monstrous chicken emerged from the sea in 1457. The *Chronicles* of Raphael Holinshed record how: 'In the moneth of Nouember, in the Ile of Portland not farre from the towne of Weimouth, was séene a cocke comming out of the sea, hauing a great crest vpon his head, and a great red beard, and legs of halfe a yard long: he stood on the water & crowed foure times, and euerie time turned him about, and beckened with his head, toward the north, the south, and the west, and was of colour like a fesant, & when he had crowed thrée times, he vanished awaie.'[6]

Geese have traditionally had a better reputation than chickens in folklore. The loud honking of the sacred geese of Juno was supposed to have saved Rome when invaders attempted to sneak into the Capitol. Other familiar tales that mention geese include the proverbial goose that laid the golden egg – though that story ends less happily for that bird since it was dissected to find the source of the gold.

In Adlestrop, Gloucestershire, there is a field in which ancient megaliths can be seen. These are said to have been formed when a woman walking her geese to market was asked by a witch if she could buy one. On being refused, as revenge the witch turned them all to stone. A variation of this story relates how the owner of the geese used to illicitly take her flock to graze on common land and was punished when her geese were all turned to stone.[7]

The idea of walking geese anywhere might strike us as strange but in the days before refrigeration livestock would be driven to market as it was easier than trying to preserve their flesh. When droves of turkeys were walked long distances they wore leather booties to protect their feet. This was less common for geese as geese are famously intractable. The phrase 'to shoe a goose' was an idiom meaning someone was attempting a foolish task. In Beverley Minster, Yorkshire, there is an early wood carving of a blacksmith attempting to hammer a horseshoe onto a goose, a doubly foolish endeavour.

To eat a goose is considered lucky– for the diner at least, less so for the bird. At Michaelmas goose was the most prized of meals; to go without one then was a sign that the rest of your year would not be prosperous. One legend had it that this association with good fortune came about because Queen Elizabeth I was feasting on goose when brought news of the destruction of the Spanish Armada in 1588. Though the association may date from this time, we can trace the eating of goose for Michaelmas to at least the fifteenth century. In Yorkshire goose pies were made to celebrate St Stephen's Day, 26 December, and given to neighbours, though one was always kept in the house and only eaten on Candlemas, 2 February.

Perhaps the most surprising tale told of geese was that they sprung from barnacles.[8] The goose barnacle, which has colours similar to those of the barnacle goose and a long stalk like a goose's neck, was thought by some, such as the twelfth-century Gerald of Wales, to be the embryonic form of the bird. The fact that the geese were spontaneously generated by rotting wood in water meant that they were not born of flesh and so, according to some Irish bishops, it was perfectly fine to eat goose during Lent. Images of geese growing by hanging from trees were common in medieval bestiaries, though the myth that geese came from trees or barnacles did not end in the medieval period.

In 1807 a spectacle was advertised in London whereby paying visitors could view geese in their aquatic form.

> Wonderful curiosity called the Goose Tree, Barnacle Tree, or Tree bearing geese, taken up at sea on the 12th January, 1807, by Captain Bytheway, and was more than twenty men could raise out of the water – may be seen at the Exhibition Rooms, Spring Gardens, from ten o'clock in the morning till ten at night, every day. The Barnacles which form the present exhibition possess a neck upwards of two feet in length, resembling the windpipe of a chicken; each shell contains five pieces, and notwithstanding the many thousands which hang to eight inches of the tree, part of the fowl may be seen from each shell. Sir Robert Moxay, in the Wonders of Nature and Art, speaking of this singularly curious production, says, that in every shell he opened he found a perfect sea-fowl, with a bill like that of a goose, feet like those of water-fowl, and the feathers all plainly formed.[9]

Similar tales were sometimes told about ducks forming from shellfish, but this was probably less widely believed as duck eggs were common. If you wanted a duck of your own you simply had to head down to your local pond. At Wantage in Oxfordshire, duck chasing was an organised affair. For at least 200 years live ducks were released into the pond and men and boys leaped into the water to grab hold of them. Those who wrestled a duck into submission got to keep it.

Photographs exist of this event from the mid-twentieth century showing how crowded the competition for ducks could be. In 1956 there were twelve ducks and so twelve races were run. Not everyone was happy with this event, however, the RSPCA receiving several complaints that year with allegations of cruelty. Organisers had no time for such grumbles. 'Our races are not terrible like stag or fox hunting. The difference seems to be that our races are the poor man's entertainment while stag and fox hunting are rich men's sports.'[10] Alas, such class commentary did not save the races, which were ended in 1960.

A more celebrated duck hunt has survived, and coincidentally takes place in one of the most privileged seats of learning in Britain.[11] Once every hundred years All Souls College, Oxford, undertakes the Hunting of the Mallard. According to tradition this ceremony began when a marvellously large duck flew out of a drain that was broken into as the foundations of the college were being sunk in 1437.

Every hundred years, 1901 and 2001, for instance, sees a gathering of members of the college. A duck, once real but now a wooden model, is stuck on a high pole to be carried in procession. Accompanying them is an individual who has been elected 'Lord Mallard' for the occasion and is carried on a chair around the quadrangle. In 1901 the future Archbishop of Canterbury Cosmo Lang was the Lord Mallard and he recalled being carried around for two hours after midnight as the traditional Mallard Song was sung.[12]

Sung twice a year without the full hunt being performed, the Mallard Song has some quite interesting lyrics. They praise the size and prowess of the mallard and compare it favourably to the geese that saved Rome and the swan form Jupiter adopted before ravishing Leda. One verse underlines the 'swapping' – meaning prodigious – size of the mallard seen at the foundation of the college.

> He was swapping all from bill to eye,
> He was swapping all from wing to thigh;
> His swapping tool of generation
> Out swapped all ye wingged Nation.

The Victorians were not keen to loudly hymn the large penis, or 'tool of generation', and so that verse was suppressed for several years. The corkscrew shape of a duck's penis is a remarkable sight and worthy of a song. Though as one lecturer told me, ducks are 'surprisingly rapey', so perhaps best if you never do see one in all its 'swapping' glory.

At the conclusion of the Mallard Hunt overseen by Cosmo Lang, the duck was removed from its pole and pitched into a bonfire. Lang recalled how 'some of the junior fellows could not be restrained from eating portions of its charred flesh'. In 1632, the Archbishop of Canterbury George Abbot was not impressed by the irrepressible exuberance of All Souls hunters. 'Civil men,' he wrote, 'should never so far forget themselves under pretence of a foolish mallard, as to do things barbarously unbecoming.'

Swans are not commonly considered for eating, but for centuries they graced the tables of the very wealthiest. The collective noun for swans, a herd, dates from the time when they were considered livestock like many other farm animals. Generally only the young of the swan, the cygnets, were eaten. In the eighteenth century the writer John Rutty explained that swans were 'most succulent, but hard of digestion, except when very young'.[13]

Today, as is well known, all swans in England belong to the Crown. In fact, this is only partially true. The monarch has rights over all unmarked swans that swim in open water across the country. From time to time the Crown has allowed favoured organisations or courtiers to claim swans of their own by marking them. This is done by cutting characteristic notches into the birds' bills. A register of such marks was kept so that owners of swans could be recognised.

Today, apart from the Crown, only two London guilds – the Vintners' Company and the Dyers' Company – still exercise their right to mark swans. Each year the Swan Upping ceremony sees officials from the guilds rowing up the Thames to capture and mark their swans. When a swan or cygnet is spotted, those in the boats shout 'All up!' The ownership of cygnets is derived from whichever company (sometimes neither does) owns the parent swans. Marker rings are now attached to the swans and cygnets instead of their beaks being cut.[14]

The Vinters' Company used to hold an annual Swan Feast where their birds were eaten with much ceremony. The cooked cygnets would be carried in to the tune of 'Greensleeves'. While the feast remains, the swans are no longer on the menu.

RABBITS AND HARES

Rabbits are not native to Britain. For a long time it was thought that they were introduced by the Normans in the eleventh century but a rabbit tibia discovered at a Roman villa reveals that they were probably here 1,000 years earlier.[1] As is well known, you only need a couple of lusty rabbits to be overrun by hundreds of their descendants.

Since their introduction rabbits have been made the centre of some unusual ceremonies.

In the Bedfordshire village of Biddenham, on 22 August residents would gather to parade a white rabbit that had been festooned with red ribbons through the streets as they sung a hymn to St Agatha. Whenever an unmarried maid met the white rabbit she would point at it with two fingers of her left hand and say:

> Gustin, Gustin, lacks a bier!
> Maidens, maidens, bury him here.[2]

Why they said this is unknown, and whether it was in order to improve their chances of marriage or for some other reason is also lost. The ritual had died out by the end of the nineteenth century. Similarly, nobody knows why people say 'Rabbits!' or 'White rabbits!' for luck when they wake up on the first day of a new month .

One of the most unusual rabbit tales in English folklore comes from 1726, and was widely reported and investigated at the time. A young lady from Godalming, Surrey, named Mary Toft began to give birth to rabbits.[3] As *Mist's Weekly Journal* reported on 19 November that year:

From Guildford comes a strange but well-attested Piece of News. That a poor Woman who lives at Godalmin, near that Town, was about a Month past delivered by Mr John Howard, an Eminent Surgeon and Man-Midwife, of a creature resembling a Rabbit but whose Heart and Lungs grew without its Belly, about 14 Days since she was delivered by the same Person, of a perfect Rabbit: and in a few Days after of 4 more; and on Friday, Saturday, Sunday, the 4th, 5th, and 6th instant, of one in each day: in all nine, they died all in bringing into the World. The woman hath made Oath, that two Months ago, being working in a Field with other Women, they put up a Rabbit, who running from them, they pursued it, but to no Purpose: This created in her such a Longing to it, that she (being with Child) was taken ill and miscarried, and from that Time she hath not been able to avoid thinking of Rabbits. People after all, differ much in their Opinion about this Matter, some looking upon them as great Curiosities, fit to be presented to the Royal Society, etc. others are angry at the Account, and say, that if it be a Fact, a Veil should be drawn over it, as an Imperfection in human Nature.[4]

Though the idea of a pregnant woman being so taken with a desire to eat rabbits that she gives birth to a litter is ridiculous, it was widely believed at the time, and by some even today, that the emotional state of an expectant mother could cause physical changes to a developing child. Birthmarks were sometimes called 'mother spots', and were thought to be caused by a mother's experiences while pregnant.

Toft began producing bloody masses and lumps of flesh during the last months of her pregnancy and when she went into labour more body parts were produced. A neighbour called in one John Howard, a 'man midwife', to see what was going on. When he examined Toft he found nothing wrong with her and no more parts of animals. When Toft went into labour on another occasion he found that she gave birth to a rabbit's leg, three cat's legs and the backbone of an eel. The presence of the cat's legs was thought to be due to a cat that habitually slept on Mary's bed. More rabbit parts followed.

The case came to the attention of Nathaniel St André, a surgeon and anatomist attached to the court of King George I. When he examined Mary Toft he helped to deliver her next rabbit baby. He later wrote:

> She was lodged over against Mr. Howard's House, we found her dress'd in her Stays, sitting on the Bed-side with several Women near her. I immediately examined her, and not finding the Parts prepared for her Labour, I waited for the coming on of fresh Pains, which hapned in three or four minutes, at which time I deliver'd her of the entire Trunk, strip'd of its Skin, of a Rabbet of about four Months growth, in which the Heart and Lungs were contained with the Diaphragm entire. I instantly cut off a piece of them, and tried them in Water; they seemed but just specifically lighter than it, and Mr. Molyneux pressing them to the Bottom they rose again very slowly; the Heart was very large, and its Foramen Ovale entirely open; the Lungs were remarkably small, and of a much darker Colour than commonly the Lungs are of such Rabbets, who have breathed for some time. No Person but my self touch'd her, from the first time that I had examined her, to the time of her being deliver'd by me: Her Pains were pretty smart, and lasted for some Minutes; they went off the Moment she was deliver'd, and

she seem'd chearful and easy; walked by herself from the Bed-side to the Fire, and sat on a Chair, where I examined her; and found, that in the Course of the Fallopian Tubes, there were some Inequalities, but more sensibly on the right side of her Belly; which made me conjecture that the Rabbets were bred in those Tubes, and only came into the Uterus, when they gave her those Agitations, which, according to the account of Mr. Howard and of several other Persons, were sensibly felt many Hours before their Exclusion.

As there was no Blood nor Water that issued from the Vagina, after I had delivered her, I again examined that Part, and found it not in the least inflamed or lacerated ... she again fell into Labour-Pains, though more sudden and short than the former; at which time I again deliver'd her of the Head of the Rabbet, with the Furr on, part of one of the Ears being torn off, also without any Blood or Moisture.[5]

Another doctor, Cyriacus Ahlers, who was present at a birth, found no signs of Toft being pregnant and thought he saw her squeezing her thighs together to prevent something falling out of her private parts. When another obstetrician examined Toft he found that she had delivered what looked to him like a hog's bladder; it even smelled of urine.

Firmly convinced of the genuine nature of her condition, St André arranged to have her taken to London to show off his prodigious discovery. The courtier John Harvey described in a letter the sensation she created: 'Every creature in town, both men and women, have been to see and feel her: the perpetual emotions, noises and rumblings in her Belly are something prodigious; all the eminent physicians, surgeons and man-midwives in London are there Day and Night to watch her next production.' Toft became a celebrity, with the artist William Hogarth producing a satirical cartoon called 'Cunicularii [The Rabbit Men], or the Wise Men of Godliman in Consultation'. This shows Toft struggling in labour, a doctor up to his elbow inside the poor woman, and a litter of

Hogarth's print of the Mary Toft affair shows a rabbit being smuggled
into the birthing chamber.

little bunnies on the floor. St André began work on a pamphlet
recording the history of the case.

His 'A short narrative of an extraordinary delivery of rabbets
[sic] perform'd by Mr. John Howard surgeon at Guilford' came
out in December 1726. It included several sworn affidavits by
people who had witnessed the events and, with the doctor's use
of scientific language and examinations, appeared to put any
doubts to rest. At least for a few days.

Others who had investigated the affair found that people close to
Mary Toft were buying an unusual number of rabbits. Under pres-
sure and interrogation Mary confessed to her part in the hoax. After
suffering a miscarriage she was convinced that by 'giving birth' to
rabbits she would make enough money to be financially secure. She
inserted the animal parts into her cervix and produced the first of
her animal children. Later the parts were merely concealed in her
vagina. Howard and Toft were hauled before a judge and Howard
was fined the then colossal sum of £800. Toft was allowed to go free.

The case was a debacle for the medical profession. Doctors rushed to put out pamphlets and statements claiming they had never been fooled by Toft, but it was too late for St André as his pro-Toft pamphlet had already been released. He placed an advertisement in the *Daily Journal* of 9 December 1726 which read:

> Having contributed, in some measure, to the Belief of an Imposter, in the Narrative lately published by me, of an extraordinary Delivery of Rabbits, performed by Mr. Howard, Surgeon, of Guildford; and having been since instrumental in the discovering of the same; so that I am now thoroughly convinc'd it is the most abominable Fraud: I think myself obliged, in strict regard to Truth, to acquaint the Publick thereof; and that I intend, in a short time, to publish a full Account of the Discovery, with some Considerations on the extraordinary Circumstances of this Case, which misled me in my Apprehensions thereof; and which I hope they will, in some measure, excuse the Mistakes made by myself, and others, who have visited the Woman concerned therein, will also be acceptable to the World, in separating the Innocent from those who have been guilty Actors of this Fraud.

Try as St André might to destroy all extant imprints of his work there were always copies floating about. His name became a byword for incompetence. A ballad was even written about the case.

> Monsieur St. A_d_é, that anatomist rare,
> Says all these same rabbits for preternatural were;
> And, faith, we must own there is something in that,
> For the first that came out, did prove a black cat.

St André lost his salary and was forbidden access to the king. He retired to the country and lived to the age of ninety-six – though he did not eat rabbit for the last fifty years of his life.

Hares have a longer heritage in Britain and feature in both feast and folklore throughout history. Bishop White Kennett wrote about a strange belief concerning hares in the eighteenth century. He claimed that 'When one keepes a hare alive and feedeth him till he have occasion to eat him, if he telles before he kills him that he will do so, the hare will thereupon be found dead, having killed himself'.[6]

Hares are less tractable than rabbits and their love of wild living has given them some bad associations. Witches were commonly thought to take the shape of hares. No sailor would dare board his ship if he had seen one on his way to the docks. One Cornish poacher was convinced that a hare he had met was the Devil himself and declared only silver bullets should be fired at white hares.

If you must eat some hare, you could make a sport of it. At Coleshill in Warwickshire the rector of the church would reward anyone who brought him a hare on Easter Monday with 100 eggs, a calf's head and a groat.[7] Others gave away hare meat at Easter.

Hare-Pie Scrambling is a sport carried out at Hallaton in Leicestershire.[8] It is said that two ladies had been wandering across a field one day when they were charged by a bull. At the very last moment a hare darted out and the bull was distracted. After making their escape the ladies donated a plot of land to the church on condition that two hare pies were given away each year. The pieces of these pies were dangled above a waiting crowd in a sack. When the pie fragments dropped those present would set to fighting over them.

If you do catch a hare, and have a naughty child, you might want to scoop out the hare's brains. When these were fed to an obstreperous young person they were thought to be good for manners. Certainly the threat of more hare brains would discourage further bad behaviour.

Fish Lore

While doctors today will tell you that it is good to include fish in your diet (high levels of mercury notwithstanding) they were not always thought to be healthy. In 1663 the governor of Massachusetts heard the following bit of medical news: 'I thought good to advertise you of a discourse I lately heard, that the Leprosie is caused by eating too much fish; for in Scotland where they eate much fish there is more Leapers then in all Europ besides; as it is said.'[1] John Evelyn had heard the same hypothesis in the Low Countries when he saw lepers living by a river in 1641.

The British have relied on their access to the sea for trade and food for millennia. For those lucky enough to live near the coast there was always a meal available in the waters. Fishing was a source of livelihood to many, and not only to the fishermen who braved the seas. Not all these jobs were pleasant. One of the most tedious jobs in history must have been sitting atop cliffs waiting to see signs of shoals of herrings migrating through coastal waters. In Cornwall it was a huer's job to watch for the migrating pilchards. When he spotted them he would lift his huge horn, around five feet long, and bellow, 'Hevva!' – Here they are! – to the fishermen below.[2] He would also signal the direction with a couple of bushes, originally bits of shrubbery covered in cloth.

Once the herring were landed they had to be preserved quickly and without the aid of refrigeration; this was mostly by salting and pickling. Herring girls travelled along the coast with the herring fleets to do this.[3] When the catch was brought to them they had to gut and clean the fish and place them into barrels. Workers were paid by the barrel so the job had to be done briskly and there was always the risk of a sharp knife cutting the girls' hands as they flashed through their work. After a day ankle-deep in fish guts in the cold air the herring girls who followed the fishing fleet were sometimes rejected by hotels because of the smell they brought with them. Preparing fish could be risky in other ways. In Scotland it was said that a fish hung up by moonlight would become poisonous.[4]

Despite the inconveniences of catching herrings they remained popular, particularly as they brought in much-needed trade revenue. Herrings were called silver darlings and the silver they sold for must have been most welcome. A family might thrive or starve depending on whether the herring came in large numbers. In predicting the haul some strange superstitions sprung up.

Herrings were considered somewhat mysterious. Because they eat small crustaceans it was sometimes hard to find any food in their stomachs. This led to the belief that they consumed nothing but the seawater they swam in.

It was said that 'a good year for fleas is a good year for herring'. One fisherman in Cromer, Norfolk, in the nineteenth century was convinced this was true: 'Times is as you may look in my shirt, and scarce see a flea, and then there won't be but few herring. But when you see my shirt alive with fleas, then there is certain to be a good tidy lot of fish.'[5] On Skye it was said that herring would never enter any part of the sea from where it was possible to see a grave.

Once you had your herring, though, you might want to give it something to wear. Herring were once a popular gift for 'first-footers' at Hogmanay. As the New Year began you would seek to bring good luck into your house by having a, preferably handsome, man cross your threshold first bringing gifts of food, drink and coal. In Dundee herring was a popular food to be presented with, but fish is not always the most appealing of presents. So the herrings were dressed up. They would be adorned with skirts, bonnets, wedding gowns, or kilts made of paper. These were known as Dundee Dressed Herring.[6]

Understandably fishermen were a superstitious bunch. Their livelihoods and indeed lives were at risk every time they boarded a boat. Some would never set out to sea on a Friday. Should a crew member be so foolish as to say 'good luck!' they were thought to have brought a curse down on the ship. Only punching the offender could ward off the doom. A dead wren was taken by the fishermen of the Isle of Man as an amulet against ill luck.[7] And it was always fisher*men* as women onboard were thought to be harbingers of disaster.

The salmon fishers of the River Tweed held a blessing ceremony around Valentine's Day, near the beginning of the salmon season.[8] The vicar of Berwick would go out on a boat and bless everything from the nets, to the salmon, to the river itself around midnight. Today the vicar merely wades a little way into the water to perform the blessing before the first fly of the year is cast.

The fish themselves could be marked by the Devil. It is said that the Devil was building the peninsula of Filey Brigg in Yorkshire when he dropped his hammer into the sea. Cursing, he reached in to grab it but ended up picking up a fish and exclaiming, 'Ha, dick!' This explains why to this day haddock are marked with two black spots – known as the Devil's thumbprint. Others preferred a more saintly explanation and claimed the spots came from the hand of St Peter (a fisherman) touching them.

Other saints have had run-ins with fish that left their mark. The twisted mouth of the flat flounder is said to have come from the fish having a sharp tongue. One day St Columbkille was wading into the sea when a flounder, perched on a rock, began to mock the holy man. Divine wrath soon fell on the fish and forever after the flounder's mouth was set at an awkward angle.[9]

Catching flounders used to take an unusual form in Scotland and Cumbria.[10] There you did not need a boat to catch them, just your two feet and perhaps a trident. Flounder tramping involves slowing treading your way through the sea at low tide until you step on one of the flat fish. Standing on a fish is a bit upsetting since it might try to wriggle free, but you just need to hold it down. Then you either shove your fingers in its gills and lift it up or stab it with your trident – taking care, one imagines, not to impale your own toes. A flounder-tramping championship was held at Palnackie in Dumfries and Galloway but this has been in abeyance since 2015.

Despite the inherent risks, fishing was an important industry. Fish offered a welcome variety in people's diet, especially during Lent when meat was not supposed to be eaten. Fish took the place of flesh. Of course there were ways around this ban on meat. Barnacle geese, thought to grow from a crustacean, were acceptable to church authorities. Similarly, the aquatic beaver and capybara were deemed to be fish for the purposes of Lent.

How you ate your fish was also important. In Wales it was said to be bad luck to eat a fish from the head downwards: you should start at the tail and move up. In Cornwall this was also true when deboning the fish. To start at the head was said to risk spooking the fish and driving shoals away from the shore.

Eating fish may be a delight but there is always the risk of getting a fishbone caught in your throat. Worry not, though, as there is a saint who can help. St Blaise, who died in AD 316, was a doctor in his youth and is today the patron saint of ear, nose and throat specialists. He earned this honour by helping a boy who was choking on a fishbone. Each year at St Etheldreda's Church in London there is a service known as the Blessing of the Throats on St Blaise's Day, 3 February.[11]

The danger of fishbones has been employed in darker rituals. Those who wished death on a person were advised to take a thin fishbone and poke it into their enemy's clothing. As well as probably making them smell a little, it was thought that as the bone dried out the victim would become ever more ill.

Eating fishbones deliberately was sometimes required by folklore. In the Outer Hebrides prophetic dreams could be brought on by eating an entire salted herring in three bites and then going quietly to bed. You were not even allowed a glass of water to help wash down the bones.[12]

There were a number of fishy cures available. To cure whooping cough the severed head of a trout should be put into the patient's mouth for them to breathe through.[13] Alternatively a live fish could be laid on the patient's chest where it flopped around until it died. When the fish expired so the cough would be gone. Milk in which a live trout had swum was also thought to be a good treatment as well because of the 'slime' of the trout being taken from its gills into the milk.[14]

Eels are some of the strangest fish to be found in Britain. They live in rivers but head out to sea to mate and spawn. Even today the exact location where eels breed is not known, though because small eels are found in the Sargasso Sea that is presumed to be where they go. Being unlike other fish in appearance and mode of living has given eels a special place in folklore.

To cure a wart you could cut the head off a live eel and rub the bloody end onto it.[15] The head should then be buried. By the time the head had rotted away the wart would be gone. Eel heads could be dangerous, however. In Scotland it was said that they caused insanity. One man was driven so mad after consuming an eel that he slaughtered his horse and was found eating its flesh. His brother shot him to halt his rampage.[16] That the madman attacked his horse might have been rational in its way as the most popular theory was that eels grew from horse hairs that had fallen in water and were left for nine days. This theory of the equine generation of eels led to particularly thin and threadlike eels being called horsehair eels.

This antipathy towards eels was widespread throughout Scotland. Many considered the snake-like form of the eel to be a mark of its satanic nature. It was thought to ruin a pan if you cooked an eel in it. The Scots were canny, though – they had no problem selling eels to their English neighbours.

Eel skin was supposed to be an amulet against cramps. When a person suffered a sprain they could call for the 'stamp-strainer' – a person who would stamp on eel skin before applying it to the wounded limb.[17] Sometimes the skin was lined with goose fat.

Lampreys, an eel-like fish, seem like something from a bizarre body horror film. In place of a traditional mouth they have a sucker filled with rows of rasping teeth. They use these to attach themselves to other fish then gnaw into their flesh to suck their blood. According to the Roman author Pliny the Elder, a man named Vedius Pollio kept a pool of lampreys and, should any of his slaves displease him, he would cast them into it.[18] Later authors said that Pollio then ate the lampreys that had feasted on human flesh.

Being vampiric monstrosities did not prevent the lamprey from gracing the dining tables of even the highest in the land. King Henry I of England was said by the historian Henry of Huntingdon to have had such an immoderate fondness for lampreys, even though they always made him ill, that he died of a 'surfeit' of them.[19]

This apparently did not put subsequent English monarchs off eating lampreys. Throughout the medieval period the city of Gloucester would send a lamprey pie to the king each Christmas.[20] When they failed to do so under King John they were fined the large sum of £26 13s. 4d. This tradition was allowed to lapse in 1836 as the cost of catching the increasingly rare lamprey and lavishly decorating a gilded pie was considered too great. Occasionally such pies are still presented to the Crown. For the coronation of Queen Elizabeth II in 1953 a large lamprey pie was baked, but the fish had to be sourced from elsewhere in the country due to their absence from the River Severn. When one was prepared for the Diamond Jubilee in 2012 the lampreys had to be brought from North America.

Alas, it seems that in recent years the pie was not even eaten by the monarch. When the council of Gloucester ordered a pie in the 2023, because of environmental concerns it contained no lampreys at all – it was merely decorated with lamprey motifs. The monarch did not even look at it. It was presented to the Lord Lieutenant and then given to a charity.

Dairy Lore

Milk, cream, cheese and butter are all simple foodstuffs that add much to our diet. They are also rich in protein and fat and so have always been important sources of nutrition. Best of all was that you did not have to kill the beasts that provided them.

Not all animals profited from their association with milk, however. Thanks to the belief of some that hares were witches in disguise, to see one in a field of cows was a terrible thing; it was thought they stole the milk. One enterprising Yorkshire witch was said to take the form of a cute hedgehog while out milking her neighbour's cows.[1] Alternatively hares might have been familiars for the witch out on a dairy raid. In Norway there are murals in churches that show demons holding a cow still while a hare suckles on its udder. The hare is then later seen regurgitating milk into a bucket for the benefit of a witch.

Witches could harm a dairy in other ways. In a witch trial case from Guernsey in 1581 the accused witches, Katherine Eustace and her daughter, were said to have put a curse on a cow.[2] Their accuser, Collas Cousin, is said to have turned away the pair when they came begging for milk. Later Cousin's cow began to produce blood instead of milk.

The ruining of farm animals and produce was a crime for which many witches were prosecuted. A cow drying up could spell ruin for a family on the verge of poverty anyway and some reason had to be found for the misfortune. A witch's covetous

eyes were an easy explanation, and an easy accusation to make
against an enemy.

Cow's milk was not the only milk that witches hungered after.
Witch's milk was the term for the fluid that comes from some
babies' nipples.[3] This neonatal galactorrhea can be caused by the
influence of the mother's hormones on the developing infant but
was in the past thought to be sought by witches as food for their
familiar spirits.

The fifteenth-century guide to witch hunting, the *Malleus
Maleficarum*, described in great detail how 'there is not even the
smallest farm where women do not injure each other's cows, by
drying up their milk, and very often killing them'.[4] It also informs
us of the most common way in which witches will plunder a
dairy.

> For on the more holy nights according to the instructions of the
> devil and for the greater offence to the Divine Majesty of God, a
> witch will sit down in a corner of her house with a pail between
> her legs, stick a knife or some instrument in the wall or a post,
> and make as if to milk it with her hands. Then she summons her
> familiar who always works with her in everything, and tells him
> that she wishes to milk a certain cow from a certain house, which
> is healthy and abounding in milk. And suddenly the devil takes
> the milk from the udder of that cow, and brings it to where the
> witch is sitting, as if it were flowing from the knife.

There is an interesting piece of theology behind why the Devil
and his servants would have to steal milk. Christianity believed
that the power of generating new materials or creation belonged
to God alone. The Devil could corrupt or take but he could not
make something from nothing. If he wanted to reward his followers he had to steal something that already existed.

Witches and the Devil were not the only milk thieves out
there. Cats may proverbially love to get the cream but they really

shouldn't: cats lack the enzyme lactase that breaks down the sugars in milk. Feeding milk or cream to a cat is good for nothing except vomiting and diarrhoea, yet in Scotland the fondness of cats for cream was so entrenched that a rather drastic remedy was created.

In the nineteenth century cats could be seen with their left ear missing, cut off to discourage them from stealing milk and cream.[5] This practice springs from the legend of a man who had been left in charge of the home while his wife was at confession. Spotting the family cat filching milk, he sprang on it and hurled it through a window which shattered and sliced off the cat's left ear. The man greeted his returning wife by brandishing the ear aloft as a sign of his successful guarding of the dairy. Apparently the cat never stole milk again and would even refuse it if offered.

If you don't want your cat to leave your house, though, it was said that you should butter the soles of its feet. This might actually work if your cat then has to spend a long time cleaning its paws.

Dairy products could be almost as harmful to humans in some cases. According to the fifteenth-century compendium of the lives of English saints, collected by John Capgrave, St Juthwara was undone by dairy and a stepmother's bitterness.[6] Juthwara was a saintly young woman of Dorset and a virgin. When her father remarried, Juthwara's new stepmother began to spread rumours that she was not really chaste. When Juthwara started to experience painful breasts her stepmother told her that soft cheeses applied to her bosom would ease her suffering so Juthwara tried it.

The stepmother told Juthwara's hot-headed brother that the girl was no virgin – all he had to do was check her clothing for signs of milk. Juthwara was leaving church one day when she was accosted by her brother. When the brother felt Juthwara's breasts he found them moist and asked her loudly who had made her pregnant. Juthwara denied she had ever had sex, but he did not believe her. The brother was so outraged by the shame Juthwara had brought on the family that he sliced her head off.

Being a saint, this was not the end for Juthwara. She picked up her own decapitated head and walked back into the church. A spring with healing powers is said to have gushed from the earth on the spot where her faithful head had fallen. In images Juthwara is usually pictured as a cephalophore – a saint carrying their own head – and her symbol is a wheel of cheese.

MILK

Milking cows has had such a notable effect on human history that is even written into our genes. Most people are lactose intolerant as adults as the gene that produces the enzyme lactase usually becomes inactive after infancy when humans stop breastfeeding. For around a third of people, however, mostly of European heritage, this gene remains and allows them to consume dairy products without the risk of a dicky tummy. The ability to consume high-calorie milk offered an advantage to surviving. The centrality of cow's milk to the European diet meant that having an ample supply of milk and dairy products was incredibly important.

To avoid witches making off with your milk you had to be very careful. No farm wanted to be the first to light their fire on 1 May because it was thought that a witch could capture the smoke from their chimney to work magic.[1] The first smoke on the day would allow a witch to carry off that farm's entire year of milk. In Scotland it was said that to stop witches coming after your milk you should put tar behind the ears and on the tails of your cattle on Beltane Eve, the night before 1 May. On St Kilda a small flower was placed into the bucket while milking to prevent the evil eye falling on it.[2]

When one farmer did find his cow was bewitched and no longer producing milk, a local wise man gave him advice on how to end the spell.[3] The farmer was to take what little remained of the cow's milk and put eleven pins that had never touched cloth into it. This mixture was then boiled and poured around a stone in the cow's field that the animal had become obsessed with. A nearby neighbour's wife soon fell dead and the cow's milk returned to full flow.

When a cow stopped giving milk in the Highlands of Scotland its owners were advised to take some of the cow's urine and place it in a bottle.[4] This should then be sealed tight so that not a drop escaped. The witch who had cursed the cow stopped 'making water', which caused such pain that she would lift her spell.

Having an ample supply of milk was not only good for the health, it could save your home from burning down. It was said that only milk could quench a fire that had been started by lightning. One report from Cambridgeshire records milk being employed for this purpose:

> In the yeare of our Lord 1601 and uppon ye 14 day beinge thursday ther was great thundringe and lightninge and descendinge from heaven kindled in a white-thorne bush neere to a muddwall in Brook-street westward from Thom his house, it burned and consumed ye bush and tooke into about on yeard then by milke brought in tyme it was quen it did noe more harm.[5]

If a cow was no longer producing milk or its udders were running dry, Scottish wives were advised to bake a bannock with a hole in the middle.[6] The cow should then be milked so that the liquid fell through the hole for nine consecutive days.

The Scots held that the milk from a red or brown cow was better than that from a black or white one. Yet in Wiltshire, a child fed from a white cow thrived more than on milk from any other colour of cow.

Some cows were said to produce a prodigious amount of milk, the best known being the Dun Cow of Warwickshire. This huge beast was owned by a giant and had the ability to fill whatever vessel it was milked into. The entire neighbourhood could have as much milk as it wanted, and was amply provided for, in some tellings, by her eighteen teats. One day an ill-disposed old woman decided to milk the cow into a sieve, an impossible vessel to fill. This so enraged the cow that it broke free and roamed the countryside, leaving destruction in its wake. The legendary knight Guy of Warwick rode out and slew the Dun Cow. One of the cow's ribs was displayed in Warwick Castle (in fact it was a whale bone) and one of its enormous horns was on show at Harwich Castle. (On closer examination, this horn turned out to be an elephant's tusk . . .) Other bones from the cow (if indeed that's what they were) could once be seen in churches and inns in several other places.[7]

In the North of England it was once common to find advertisements for the Dun Cow's milk. One from Yorkshire read:

> Oh, come you from the east,
> Oh, come you from the west,
> If ye will taste the Dun Cow's milk,
> Y'll say it is the best.[8]

Other versions of this legend were told around England. The name Medgelly's Cow is recorded from Shropshire in 1753 and was used to refer to any cow that gave a lot of milk.[9] It derives from the tale of a giant who kept a white cow in Medgel's Fold that could provide as much milk as was needed but was similarly tricked with a sieve. In the field there is a stone circle where the prodigious white cow is said to have appeared in a time of food shortage to give tremendous quantities of milk to the people living there. When a witch tried to milk the cow into a sieve the animal disappeared, and for her sins the witch was turned into one of the standing stones. A similar story is told about the Callanish Standing Stones on the Isle of Lewis where a white cow emerged from the sea to provide milk after a hungry mother prayed for help for her family. When a witch performed her trick with the sieve the cow waded back into the sea.

In Wales the name 'Penllyne Cow' was given to both a cow that gave huge quantities of milk and to an unusually generous person.[10] This is because a kindly woman provided a cow that would produce as much milk as was required, but would only give its milk to those who were in need.

When a miraculous cow known as the White Milch Cow appeared in Wales, it too could provide an infinite amount of milk. Not only was there plenty of milk to go around, the milk also had supernatural healing properties. The cow never stayed in one spot for long and on its wanderings made its way into the Valley of Towy. There the people decided not to milk the cow but to eat it. Just as they were about to kill the cow it disappeared, milk and all. A house in the area was known as Y Fuwch Laethwen-Lefrith – The Milk-white Milch Cow.[11]

Tales of the Dun Cow and its ilk have certain aspects that seem related to fairy cattle. Known as 'crodh sith' in Scotland, these cows could appear from nowhere and provide much-needed milk. In Skye folklore it was said that the fairy cows would swim to the island from Raasay to graze and return home when their fairy owner called them. To stop this the islanders would scatter earth gathered from a churchyard around the cattle to prevent them being recalled to their rightful, magical, owners. The fairy cows could then be kept by the islanders and apparently produced superior milk.

The Welsh had the legend of *gwartheg y llyn* – kine of the lake – which were cattle belonging to maidens who lived in a lake.[12] One farmer managed to lure one of these cows away when it fell for a bull in his herd. From that fairy cow's progeny came many cows which produced milk in never before seen quantities. When the owners of such cattle attempted to slaughter them they often returned to their lake, leading all their descendants with them and leaving the farmer poor and bereft.

When cows did provide milk it had to be kept very carefully. No loud noises were allowed in the room where it was stored, and the door could not be slammed in the dairy. In Devonshire it was said that you should never sweep the cobwebs from a dairy because the cows would give less milk and the calves would suffer mishaps.[13] Such folklore at least has the benefit of saving you from endless cleaning.

It is a commonly said that you should not cry over spilled milk, but you should be careful where you spill it. In Scotland it was feared that if milk was spilled near natural bodies of water it would be tasted by the 'Macha dhubh' – the Trout Mother.[14] If the Trout Mother got a taste of the milk, it was thought that it could cast an evil spell over the rest of the milk in the dairy. To stop this happening, if any milk does spill into a lake or river it should be followed by handfuls of mud to disguise the taste. If the Trout Mother does get a taste for your milk you can end the spell by forcing milk into the mouth of a live trout.

It was also thought that by examining your milk you could get a glimpse of the future. One mother learned that her son had drowned at sea when all the milk in her dairy began to ripple like waves on the water.[15] But you should not always infer death from choppy milk. In the coastal towns of Lincolnshire it was thought that milk would foam in the churn until high tide had passed.

Feeding a sick person milk, so long as they are not lactose intolerant, will probably do them some good. For some folklore cures the milk must be treated before the remedy will work. You could set a bowl of milk in front of a ferret, allow it to drink some, then retrieve the rest and give it to the child with whooping cough. According to lore the ferret would then take the whooping cough from the child. The ferret would die but the child would live. One vicar from the North of England recalled how 'A boy came into my kitchen the other day with a basin containing a gill of new milk, saying his mother hoped I would let my son's white ferret drink half of it, and then he would take the other half home to the bairn to cure its cough. I found the boy had been getting milk in the village for some days, and thus giving our ferret half of it.'[16] Some versions of this rite involve cutting a small piece of the child's hair, mixing it with the milk and feeding part of it to both child and ferret.

Should you need to cure yourself of a gallstone, one recipe was to take sheep's dung and boil it in milk until it was completely dispersed and then drink it.[17] Whether it was the dung or the milk that provided the healing is not recorded, though cow dung seems to have been a sovereign salve for all sorts of burns, lesions and other wounds.

There is a current trend to move away from animal milks for both health and ecological reasons. Everything from soy beans to hemp seeds to quinoa are being turned into milk alternatives. But if you want a miraculous milk alternative you only have to visit a certain well.

St Illtyd's Well in Wales is also known as the Butter Well because in 1185 milk flowed from it for several hours.[18] Centuries earlier St Illtyd had commanded the sea to stop inundating his home there and then struck the earth with his staff to draw forth a spring. For no apparent reason the well began to pour out milk in profusion and butter was made from the fatty cream that formed around the edges of the pool.

CREAM

A brownie, *or brùnaidh*, is a Scottish sprite that could be incredibly helpful around the house.[1] Brownies are often described as diminutive and somewhat ugly men with bushy beards and messy hair. They would emerge only at night and performed various tasks while the human occupants of the house slept. If, however, they thought there was too much mess or they discovered the servants of the house were doing a substandard job they would attack sleeping domestics by pinching them mercilessly. Though brownies were undoubtedly helpful there were misgivings about their nature as they were apparently offended by Christian symbols and images. For their service to the home they accepted no payment, but failure to leave a gift for them might drive them away. Their favourite food offering was a bowl of cream left beside the hearth.

In the 1920s Percy Shaw Jeffrey recorded an incident in Whitby whereby someone tried to shortchange a brownie-type spirit for its services.[2] A farmer named Gray had a servant, Ralph, who was caught in a snowstorm one day and froze to death. Soon afterwards, at night, noises could be heard coming from the barn as if someone was working hard. In the morning it was as if a dozen stout men had been labouring. To honour this invisible helper, Gray ordered cream to be set in the barn each night. When the farmer died this tradition was carried on by his son and the nightly workings continued, and then into the tenure of his grandson Jonathan.

Jonathan's first wife was happy to carry on paying in cream but when she died Jonathan married a more thrifty woman. She saw the expense of cream being sent to the barn every day as an intolerable luxury. When delivering cream to the barn she instead filled the bowl with thin milk. The spirit was not happy. No more work was ever done in the barn and the spirit migrated to the house, where he caused such howling, screaming, tantrums and poltergeist activities that Jonathan and his penny-pinching wife had to sell the house and move away.

BUTTER

If you go digging in a bog, as we all do from time to time, then you might discover something strangely recognisable. No, not the well-preserved bodies of sacrificial victims from millennia past, but the large quantities of butter that turn up in bogs from Ireland and Scotland. Usually buried in wooden containers, this ancient bog butter can still be eaten – though you probably shouldn't try it.[1] Putrid and pungent are two of the more polite words used by those who have bravely done so.

Butter is just as popular now as when our ancestors buried it in bogs, either as a method of preserving it or as an offering to the ancient gods. Every child knows that if you hold a buttercup under your chin and can see a yellow reflection, you love butter.

The first step in making butter is churning the milk. By agitating high-fat milk you cause the globules of fat in the liquid to begin to join together. With enough mixing the fat becomes solid and the liquid is taken off as buttermilk. Without the help of modern equipment, churning butter could be a long and labour-intensive process.

A children's nursery rhyme probably reflects their experiences of watching parents struggling to make the butter 'come'.

> Come, butter, come,
> Come, butter, come,
> Peter's waiting at the Gate,
> Waiting for a buttered cake,
> Come, butter, come.[2]

The reference may be to the apostle Peter. Certainly after a long time trying to get the butter to churn you'd be tempted to pray for a swift delivery from your labours in the dairy.

In Cornwall it was said that a red-haired person should never make butter. If they did, the butter would be tainted by a peculiar taste.[3]

If you found that your butter was not churning, you could try several tricks to help it along. Everyone who entered the dairy while the butter was being churned had to lay their hand on the churn or the butter would not come. The crank on a churn should only ever be turned in one direction otherwise you risked undoing all your hard work.[4] To help the butter form, a piece of silver was sometimes added to the churn.

One woman in Minnigaff, Scotland, could not get her butter to form at all until she placed a horseshoe under the churn: it worked immediately.[5] A northern butter tip very specifically says that the horseshoe worn by a two-year-old filly must be put inside the churn or witches will steal the milk straight out of it.[6]

Witches were often blamed if the butter failed to come. A hot iron thrown into the churn was thought to drive out any spell that was stopping the butter forming, and in Whitby a hot coal was placed under the churn to drive the witches out. In Scotland salt was placed on the lid of the churn for the same reason. Elsewhere a pinch of salt was placed inside the churn, which must have helped the flavour, while another pinch was thrown in the fire to burn the witch hindering the churning.[7] A red-hot poker could also be thrust into the churn.

Several stories of witches interfering with butter have been recorded. Welsh lore tells us of hags who were turned away when they came begging for a little butter and cursed the farm so that butter never churned again. In one case the spell was broken simply by requesting that the witch come and place her hand on the churn, then offering her some butter. When one farmer forced a witch to remove the spell from his churn she did so – but cursed the farmer instead so that he never again enjoyed good health. He did have plenty of butter, though, to ease his illness.

One woman from Leven in Fife, Scotland, who died in the 1840s recalled how, when she was young, her fisherman father would never enter the house by the front door if he returned in the evening. He claimed that witches would smear the handle of the door with butter at night and that even a single speck of this butter would put a curse on the next day's fishing.[8]

When not being used by witches, butter could produce a positive effect for fishermen. In Shetland if fishermen wanted to catch a turbot they would rub a bit of butter on the kabe, the peg against which the oar was rowed on their traditional clinker-built yoal boats.[9]

Butter has a long history of use in medicine. One folk remedy still has to be challenged by doctors today. If you sustain a burn, what should you do? Doctors would say that you run the affected area under cool, clean water. What they sometimes hear – and I have heard from someone who was with me when I burned myself flipping pancakes – is that you should apply butter to the burn.

This is one of those folk cures that at first seems as if it should have some benefit. Applying a nice cold bit of butter to a wound will feel soothing. Unfortunately, dairy in a wound rarely helps as it is a potential source of infection. At least one variant of this cure has died out. In Shropshire the remedy was to take goose dung and fry it in May butter. May butter was butter churned in May and kept throughout the year as a medicinal substance. In this case it was used to make the faecal folk cure for burns – one doctors would definitely not recommend.

In Essex a singular cure for whooping cough was collected from an old woman in the 1870s. She said that hair from the sick child's head should be cut off and mixed into a little ball of butter. This was then left on the doorstep for the first passing dog to eat. This would carry away the illness. The woman was certain it had worked. She tried it on one of her children and 'he never whooped again'.[10]

In Cumberland there was a jolly use for butter after the birth of a child. Rum butter was made by melting equal parts butter and sugar and mixing it with rum and cinnamon.[11] This was then allowed to set and served to the mother and her visitors on biscuits. A bowl of this confection was hidden in the house and any boys who visited took part in a hunt for the rum butter. If they found it they were allowed to wolf it down. It was thought that the first woman to cut the rum butter would be in need of rum butter herself before too long.

Giving away butter is always a pleasant thing. If two pats of butter are accidentally put on a plate it is a sign that a hungry visitor will join you for dinner. Those who received 'butter unasked for' accepted it gladly because it was a good luck charm. The lack of this butter cost one Scottish noble (most of) his head.

Hugh of the Little Head is one of the most strangely named and yet terrifying spectres one can encounter in the Highlands. It is said that Hugh lived in the fourteenth century and was the son of Hector the Stubborn. Hugh earned his name Little Head from his small intellect. A saying of the time was that you would find 'a big head on a wise man and a hen's head on a fool'.

One day before a battle Hugh encountered an elf maiden who was washing clothes in a stream. To keep her pendulous breasts out of the water she tossed them over her shoulders. Hugh spotted this and rushed over, clutched one of the breasts and placed the nipple in his mouth. This, he claimed, meant that she had nursed him and owed him her love. He then asked her to tell him if he was going to win the coming battle. She replied that he would if he and his army got 'butter without asking'.[12]

The next morning the woman managing the house brought breakfast but failed to bring butter to the table. Hugh did not allow his men to eat until the butter came and eventually he became so fed up with the woman's delay that he threw his shoe at her. This, understandably, did not make the woman more forthcoming with the butter. In frustration Hugh commanded his men to ride into battle hungry, and he and all his men perished. Hugh had his little head chopped in half with a single sword stroke. Yet instead of falling dead he leaped onto his horse and galloped off, perhaps being too simple to realise he should have expired. He is said still to be galloping to this day.

If you cannot bear to give away your hard-won butter, you are not alone. Butter making could be profitable for farmers. At the market in Wigton, Cumbria, the money raised from the sale of butter belonged not to the farmer but to his wife, and was for her use alone. Money made in this way was known as 'butter brass'.

CHEESE

Cheese, Clifton Fadiman wisely said, is milk's leap towards immortality. Milk may be delicious but, especially in the days before pasteurisation, it soured quickly. Turning your milk into cheese gave variety to the diet and was another way to make money without worrying your produce would spoil. Even if it did get a bit mouldy it might still be sellable. Some people's sense of taste is so degraded that they can even stomach blue cheese.

Getting a mouldy cheese was sometimes the aim of folklore. Tyromancy – divination using cheese – could be practised at almost any stage of cheese production. Watching the shapes that form as the cheese solidifies could allow a skilled tyromancer to predict the future. There was supposed to be a link between cheese making and the creation of the universe: just as a cheese emerges from the curds and whey, so the earth had formed from the primordial chaos. To find out which of several potential lovers you should pick, you could write their names on pieces of cheese. Whichever blossomed with mould first was the one you should choose.

Men may use cheese in their wooing of ladies. A popular quote from a book of folklore states boldly, 'You may fascinate a woman with a piece of cheese'. Alas, I can find no source for this idea before 1971. It may be worth trying the experiment. In 2021 a news story reported how a teenage girl on a date was given a 26lb wheel of cheese by a prospective farmer boyfriend.[1]

Once you had found a spouse you should serve a cheese at your wedding so that scrambling for the knife could take place.[2] The new bride would stab the cheese with her knife and there would be a spirited struggle to be the first man to get it loose. This occasionally meant guests got cut in the ensuing melee but the knife often went to the best man, probably due to his proximity to the cheese. If the best man failed to get the prize it was considered a sign that he faced seven years of bitterness in his marriage.

After the wedding, cheese played its part in sustenance and luck in childbirth. The Groaning Cheese, named for the groans of a woman in labour, was presented to the mother of a newborn child. In the borders of Scotland the cheese was given out to visitors but a special part was saved for young ladies.

The 'whang o' luck' was given to each unmarried female guest. In dialect a whang was something as tough as old leather, here meaning the rind of the cheese. The father of the baby was responsible for cutting them a piece – but he should do it carefully.[3] Should he cut himself and get blood on the cheese it presaged the early death of the child. The maids would then take this cheese home and place it under their pillows because it was said to encourage dreams of the man they would marry. Though perhaps *don't* have cheese in your bed if you want to charm a man into it.

In Durham the Groaning Cheese was put to a different use. It was eaten from the middle outwards so that a ring of the rind was left intact. On the day of the babe's christening it was thought lucky to pass it through the cheese.[4]

The Welsh had a cheese especially for the women. They would secretly make one the day the baby was born and conceal it from their menfolk. As soon as they could gather with the mother without men present, they would produce the cheese and copious amounts of beer and toast the successful birth.

When the baby was being taken to the church for baptism it was customary to give bread and cheese to the first person of the opposite sex to the child who was encountered. A parcel of bread and cheese was pinned to the christening gown of the child and handed to whomsoever was chanced on, sometimes with amusing results. One Scottish tale says that the first man met was a very grand duke. When the baby's nurse tried to give him the bread and cheese he haughtily refused, saying he was a member of the Church of England and did not observe such strange superstitions. The nurse would not be put off: 'I don't care if you're the King on his Throne, you'll take the bread and cheese.'[5]

There were other ways in which you might get some free cheese. In Aberdeen it was the custom for the wife of the owner of a new ship to offer bread and cheese to every sailor who came in after the ship's first return.[6] The canny husbands on such boats were said to delay their return for many hours to reduce the amount of cheese they had to give away. They could be seen bobbing on the water outside the port late into the night so that no boats came in after them.

The most famous way of getting free cheese in Britain involves hurling yourself down a hill in hot pursuit of a wheel of Double Gloucester. Every year several of these cheeses were rolled down Cooper's Hill in various races, while brave, or foolhardy, or hungry people plunge down the steep slope after them.[7] Since 2013 a foam cheese has been used for safety reasons – though the race remains one of terrifying tumbles. The first to reach the foot of the 200-yard slope wins the cheese and the glory.

The origins of this activity are imprecise. Some claim it can be traced back to before the Roman invasion of AD 43 and that the wheel of cheese represents the disk of the sun. There is, however, no written reference to cheese rolling before 1826. Locals claim to have family traditions concerning the event that date back much earlier than this. Whatever the origins, it is a hotly contested competition.

At Randwick in Gloucester the cheese rolling is a more sedate affair. A letter from 1827 describes how three large cheeses raised on litters and garlanded with flowers were borne through the streets.[8] On reaching the church the flowers were removed and the village children rolled the cheeses three times around the building. Once this was done the cheeses were carried away to be eaten at a communal meal.

At Stilton in Cambridgeshire, for around fifty years there was a cheese-rolling race through the streets. The village sign shows a man leaning down to push a cheese along the road. The race saw teams trying to roll their cheese around the course as quickly as possible. Sadly, in 2018 the event was cancelled due to lack of interest, the organisers lamenting that it was no longer seen as 'cool' to roll a cheese.[9]

Egg Lore

Chickens are wonderful creatures. With a minimum of fuss they peck around at grains and insects and turn those nutrients into a delicious egg. Many homes would have had a chicken or two to produce a steady source of protein-rich eggs. An egg for a hungry person was worth more than gold – to kill a hen was like killing the goose that laid the golden egg.

One of my favourite breakfasts as a child was a soft-boiled egg and soldiers: fingers of hot buttered toast dunked in a runny yolk. Everyone knows it as egg and soldiers, but this name has been claimed only to date back to 1965 in the famous Egg Marketing Board adverts that told people 'Happiness is egg shaped'. In it Tony Hancock asks, 'Where are me soldiers? You know I can't eat . . . oh there they are.' No written records can be found for boiled egg and soldiers that pre-date this advert. Where did the name come from?

We know for certain that lengths of toast were dipped in eggs before the advert aired. Lady Cynthia Asquith refers to 'the special "Egg-to-Your-Tea" with fingers of toast to dip in brown and take out yellow' as one of the treats to eat while travelling in her 1950 memoir.[1] Tellingly, the French, with their reputation for being gourmets, have two words for strips of bread eaten with egg – *une mouillette* and *une apprête*. When I posted the question on social media, several people remembered calling them soldiers in the 1950s, so the name must have been in the air when the advert was written. No doubt some parent decided to liven up their children's breakfast by referring to the regiments of straight-cut toast as soldiers.

Like all folklore and folk traditions that seem immortal, it may just be the mists of time lending them an air of antiquity. At the root of all the stories we tell, you will find one person who originated the idea – it is just that we seldom know who it was. For instance, who first decided that it was unlucky to wash in water in which eggs have been boiled?[2] Was it someone who did this and regretted smelling faintly of sulphur for the rest of the day? We just enjoy the product of their minds and thank them in their anonymity.

Folklore can give seemingly contradictory ideas about the nature of a condition. In Lancashire it was thought that water in which eggs had been boiled would bring out warts in profusion if you washed in it.[3] In Cambridgeshire, far from being the cause of warts, eggs were considered the best cure. Warts could be got rid of by either rubbing an eggshell on them or massaging them with egg white.

Eating eggs can be a cheap way of getting a good meal but that depends on the quantity you eat. According to lore recorded in *The Physicians of Myddvai*, advice collected from generations of Welsh doctors from the twelfth century onwards, you could neatly categorise your eating habits. 'One egg is economy, two is gentility, three is greediness, and a fourth is wastefulness.'

To get your eggs you must first get your hen. If you want to know how productive your hen will be you should, according to Highland lore, take the first egg it lays and give it to a young child. They then knock the egg on the hearth and count the number of taps it takes before the egg breaks.[4] The number they reach will tell you how many eggs it will lay. This seems a risky, not to say messy, prognostic process, given that children can sometimes be heavy-handed.

Welsh hens should never have an egg placed under them to incubate on a Friday.[5] As Friday was a day belonging to witches it was thought that the eggs would never hatch owing to the malign influence of hags. Alternatively, it was thought that any chicks that did emerge from the eggs would be pecked to death and eaten by the other chickens.

In Scotland women who owned hens had certain beliefs about how to ensure any chicks that hatched were healthy. The hen had to brood over an odd number of eggs or they would addle. It was also thought lucky to place the eggs under the hen when it was dark or else the resulting chicks would be blind.[6] To get hens from the eggs they would carry them to the hen house wrapped in an apron. For cocks they wore a man's hat while setting the eggs under the hen. In other places it was the working of the tide that decided the sex of chickens that would hatch. If you wanted hens, you set them under the chicken with the ebb tide; for male offspring it was the flood (rising) tide.

The first egg laid by a pullet (a young hen) is often very small and does not contain a yolk. These are sometimes called fairy eggs, cock eggs, or, in America, fart eggs.[7] Because of their diminutive size they were sometimes thought to have been laid by males. When considered as eggs laid by a cock they were a dangerous magical object. Such eggs, if placed under a toad, could hatch into a deadly cockatrice. To find these small eggs in your hen house could be a bad omen but any bad luck could be driven out by throwing the egg over the roof of your home so that it landed in the back garden.

Should you happen to find a toad incubating a chicken or duck egg and a monster hatches, you might want to try the solution used for the Wherwell Cockatrice.[8] In Hampshire, a duck laid an egg in the crypt of Wherwell Abbey, and a cockatrice with a rooster's body, serpent's head and bat's wings emerged. At first this prodigy seems not to have overly alarmed the community – until it grew large enough to carry off humans. Then they offered a plot of land to the person who could vanquish it. A clever servant lowered a polished steel mirror into the beast's lair and the

The monstrous cockatrice and basilisk could result from incubating
an egg laid by a rooster.

cockatrice was so convinced its reflection was real that it beat
itself senseless against it. While the monster lay dazed on the
ground the servant stabbed it to death with a spear.

Be sure to check the sex of the chicks that hatch from your
eggs carefully. In the North of England, for a hen to hatch a
brood of all-female offspring meant that there would soon be a
death in the family. If you use your eggs before they get a chance
to hatch then you should examine them for double yolks; this
means that there will be a birth in the house.[9]

To find out the sex of her child when a woman was pregnant,
all she needed was an egg and a little urine. The egg was broken
into a glass and, without puncturing the yolk, was mixed with
the urine. After being left overnight the melange was examined
to see whether the yolk stayed separate from the white or was
dispersed in it. If it had separated the child would be a boy; if
mixed it would be a girl.[10]

When a baby was born in Coxwold in Yorkshire it was

traditional for it to be given an egg and salt the first time it was taken to visit a neighbour. When this tradition was not observed it was not uncommon for the parents to feel hard done by.[11] The first egg the child received was emptied of its contents but the shell kept with the name of the donor written on it as a charm for the baby's health. In Guernsey, when a baby visited its nearest relatives an egg should be placed in its hands for good luck.

If you wanted to find out what your future spouse would do for their job, John Aubrey recorded a method in the seventeenth century. Young maids would take a freshly laid egg and break it into a pint glass, which they left out in the August sun. From the shapes that formed in the white they could try to discern what profession was foretold.[12] In Scotland a similar charm was employed using the first egg laid by a hen and pouring the white into a glass of water and trying to discern clues in the shapes that appeared.

To find out who your spouse would be, it was necessary to drip the white of an egg into water after drilling a hole in the shell with a pin. Some of this mixture was then taken into the mouth and held there while you went for a stroll. The first name you heard while doing this was the name of your intended.

In Ulster, when a study was made of folk remedies in the 1960s, urine was found to be a common cure for jaundice. Some patients were simply encouraged to drink their own urine but other cures involved peeing on an egg and then placing it into a stream or river while praying for a cure.[13] Whether the egg should be boiled or not is unrecorded.

Other cures involved similar passing of an illness into an egg for it to be carried away. In Devon one of the ways of ridding yourself of the ague was to take a freshly laid egg to a crossroads at midnight and bury it there.[14] This had to be repeated five times. At the end the ague would be dead and buried and you would be free of the illness.

In Worcestershire a wise man claimed he could cure a quinsy

(a sometimes dangerous abscess in the throat caused by tonsillitis) in the throat in a somewhat idiosyncratic way. The patient was forced to sit bolt upright in a chair while a poached egg was balanced on their head and roasted onions were garlanded around the neck. The healer then took an unknown powder and placed it into his pipe, which he then blew into the patient's throat.[15]

There are many fun activities that can be done with eggs – at least that is what my parents told me. One of the lesser known is egg shackling. At Stoke St Gregory Primary School in Somerset, this annual ritual is eagerly anticipated. Each child writes their name on an egg and they are placed in a garden sieve. This is then briskly shaken and the eggs rattle around against each other until they break. The last unbroken egg remaining is declared the winner and the owner of this egg gets a small cash prize.[16] The Victorians seem to have enjoyed this game and played it placing the eggs in a basket. Given the nature of the game, this would at least teach children the moral of never putting all your eggs in one basket.

Children with a taste for violence (which is perhaps most) could try their hand at 'blind egg'. Boys would steal eggs from birds' nests and line them up on the ground. One of them was then blindfolded and with stones tried to smash as many as possible. Sometimes the blindfolded child had to hop towards the eggs to see how many they could demolish.

Another game enjoyed by children is egg tapping, or egg jarping.[17] This game has been found in texts from Europe dating to the fourteenth century and sees competitors striking eggs against one another until one of them cracks. Several countries play this game around Easter and use brightly dyed eggs. In the UK there is a contest organised by the World Egg Jarping Association. Strict rules are enforced to ensure that jarpers do not tamper with their eggs to increase their strength. Originally the player with the unbroken egg got to keep all the eggs they had beaten but today an egg-shaped trophy is awarded instead.

Many cultures play a game involving tapping boiled eggs together.
The egg that breaks is the loser.

Most variations of this game – but not all – use boiled eggs, for obvious reasons. In a version played in one school the children used raw eggs and the school mistress caught the shattered eggs in a bowl. Once the children had left for the day she would pick the shells out and use the eggs to make her pancakes.

The most popular game involving eggs was, and remains, the rolling of eggs at Easter. In our house the boiled eggs were painted or decorated with felt-tip pens and taken to a steep slope. Whoever's egg managed to roll the furthest was the winner. When trying to interest my university friends with this on Arthur's Seat in Edinburgh, the contest was cancelled when the eggs rolled off a precipice, never to be seen again, as chasing them was considered too 'dangerous'.

The origins of this sport are lost to history but one of the largest egg-rolling events has been taking place in Avenham Park in

Preston since 1867. This Easter Sunday tradition was attended by a correspondent from the *Liverpool Mercury* who described the beauty of the newly opened park.

> The children at Eastertide are all supplied with what are called 'pace' eggs. These eggs are . . . rolled by the youngsters against each other, for the sole purpose, so far as I could guess, of seeing which would be soonest broken . . . altogether the scene was one of the strangest and yet most thoroughly happy and enjoyable that I have seen for years.[18]

Pace eggs were traditional fare at Easter. They derive their name from the Greek name for Easter – *pascha*. In the North of England you would be able to see pace egg plays, performed by pace eggers in costumes, in which a mock fight took place between a knight and a villain. After mock battles and singing the actors might be paid in boiled and decorated pace eggs. In Yorkshire one of the pace egging songs was recorded in the 1930s from a man who had been taught it by someone born in the early 1800s.

> Here's a few Jolly boys all in one mind
> We've come a paceggin, and we hope you'll prove kind.
> We hope you'll prove kind with your eggs and strong beer
> We'll come no more at you until the next year.
> Fol the diddle aye – Fol the day – Fol the diddle aye die dum![19]

The strong beer served to the pace eggers, the man recalled, was a drink made of eggs and beer flavoured with sugar, nutmeg and ginger and served hot.

Pace eggs could be highly decorated. Edward I is recorded as paying for eggs to be decorated with gold leaf for his household in 1290.[20] More usually they were dyed with onion skins, and you could use hot wax to protect the parts of the egg you did not want to dye in order to produce patterns. There is a collection of pace eggs in the Wordsworth Museum in Grasmere that was made by the Wordsworths' gardener in the 1870s that are covered with exquisite images of swans, birds and foliage. Most eggs, no matter how brilliant in appearance, must have been gratefully eaten by hungry mouths.

If pace eggers came to your door and you did not want to give any of your eggs away, the traditional response was: 'The cat has not laid yet.'[21]

In Cumberland eggs were given to all of your family and acquaintances around Easter, which tended to drive the price of eggs up at this time of year. These eggs were boiled and had names and dates written on them with a tallow candle which melted into the shell because of its heat. The eggs were then dipped in cochineal – a dye derived from crushed beetles – to make them a vivid red.[22] Alternatively the dye could be scraped off with a sharp knife to create a decoration.

It was thought in some places to mean good luck to eat an egg on Easter Sunday and burn the shell on Easter Monday.[23] In Warwickshire it was dreadfully bad luck to burn an eggshell as this could stop the hen that produced it ever laying again but this superstition was also known in other locations. Sir Charles Igglesden was staying at an inn in Rye in the early twentieth century when he heard the landlady recall the following:

Two years ago I had four hens laying at Christmas time, when eggs are worth having. And two gentlemen, who were snipe shooting, came in for breakfast. I boiled four eggs for them, two apiece. When they'd finished, what do you think they did? Threw the eggshells in the fire. They wanted their plates for jam. I didn't think anything of it at the time, but the next morning there wasn't a single egg laid – nor on the next day, nor the next week. The four laying hens moped. I gave them hot food, but all they did was to mope. And now, I'd like to ask you, didn't that prove that the superstition was right – never throw an eggshell in the fire?[24]

There was a long tradition of destroying eggshells in other ways. Sir Thomas Browne discussed how 'To break the egg shell after the meat is out, we are taught in our childhood, and practise it all our lives' in his *Vulgar Errors* of 1686.[25] He points out that Pliny the Elder had noted this belief in the first century AD. Browne says that eggshells were broken to stop witches harming people by writing their names on the shell.

The Discoverie of Witchcraft by Reginald Scot, published in 1584, discusses the widespread belief that witches were able to summon up storms at sea. They were also able to use discarded eggshells as boats and sail unscathed through such tempests. This was why after finishing your egg you should push your spoon through the base and ruin their 'vessel'. Why witches would have to steal the eggshells of others rather than simply source their own is not known.

Eggs could be a source of protection. Reginald Scot also says, 'To hang an egg laid on Ascension Day in the roof of a house

The phallic-looking stinkhorn fungus (*Phallus impudicus* – meaning 'shameless penis') grows from a round object called a 'witch's egg'.

preserveth the same from all hurts'.[26] Eggs laid on Good Friday never spoiled. Those on Maundy Thursday, if preserved in a house, protected the home against lightning. An egg laid at Whitsun could stop a fire if it was thrown into it.

Of course, not all eggs come from chickens. There is a separate strand of lore concerning duck eggs. It was thought that if duck eggs were brought into the house after sunset, they would be spoiled and never hatch.[27]

When one of your ducks produced dun or brown eggs, it was a terrible omen. Destroying the eggs was insufficient to ward off the danger – the duck itself had to be killed. In one example from Hoo in Kent, in the aftermath of a farmer's duck laying dun eggs all his cattle fell sick. The only solution was for the duck to be thrown alive into a hot oven.[28]

Bread Lore

'Man does not live by bread alone' – Matthew 4:4.

Whil Christ may here have been speaking of nourishment for the soul, for most people down the centuries bread was the very stuff of life. The traditional penny loaf in Britain would have made up the majority of calories a person consumed in a day. While the rich favoured bread made from wheat, the poor made do with the darker bread made from rye and other cereals. Two pounds of bread, just under a kilo, was thought to be the ideal amount for a peasant to eat. Bread was the glue that kept the spirit and the body united.

Bread came to symbolise everything important in life, specifically home, hearth and health. The smell of freshly baked bread in a house is said to be the most appealing for prospective buyers. Dr Andrew Boorde, a sixteenth-century Welsh physician and traveller, wrote in the *Dyetary of Health* an injunction to bakers on the importance of their work: 'Gentyll bakers, make good breade! For good breade doth comforte, confyrme, and doth stablysshe a mannes herte.'[1]

As the most common food in the country it inspired a great deal of folklore. Every child has surely been told to eat up the crusts of their sandwiches. Whether this will give them curly hair, a hairy chest, or make them grow up big and strong, however, is a matter of opinion.

Bread means communion – both holy and friendly. Part of the

Great Schism between the eastern and western churches was over whether the bread consecrated in the mass had to be leavened before it became the body of Christ. One Scottish ritual beloved of school children is to say 'bread and butter' if, when walking together, a lamp post comes between two friends. If you fail to say it, the friendship will be cut in two.

Even the humble bread roll can have folkloric resonances. The huffkins of Kent are soft bread rolls with a marked depression on the top. This dimple is said to have come about when a baker's wife, no doubt justly enraged by something her husband had done, stuck her thumb into the top of his rolls, hoping to spoil them. The baker carried them to market and found they sold perfectly well and so generations of Kentish folk have enjoyed this bread born from a marital dispute in the bakery. The dent on top invites one to fill it with jam or cherries.

While most people believe a dozen equals twelve, for bakers it means thirteen. It is said that the baker's dozen sprang from a thirteenth-century law known as the Assize of Bread and Ale which imposed strict fines on bakers who sold bread under the lawful weight. To ensure that they were not punished for selling less bread than mandated the bakers included a thirteenth loaf so there was no legal jeopardy. This extra bread was called the vantage loaf. Some researchers dispute this derivation of the baker's dozen, as few people would have been able to afford to buy so many loaves at once and inspectors only weighed a single loaf at a time to check it complied with the law.[2]

Even the act of handling bread can be fraught with danger. Some say that if you turn a loaf upside down there is bound to be a quarrel in the family. This tradition in Scotland is supposed to date from William Wallace's rebellion. Sir John Menteith betrayed Wallace to his English enemies and the signal he used was to turn a loaf of bread upside down. Sir Walter Scott employed this to assert that 'In after times it was considered ill breeding to turn a loaf when a Menteith should be in the company'.[3]

BAKING BREAD

Before you have a loaf to turn upside down you first have to bake one. Anyone who has worked with yeast knows how temperamental it can be. Today we know everything about baker's yeast, down to its DNA sequence, but in the past the ability of an invisible ingredient to transform flour into risen dough must have seemed miraculous. The barm, or foam, of a batch of beer might be used as a source of yeast or part of the last batch of bread dough could simply be held over.

To ensure that bread would rise in Yorkshire, well into the twentieth century housewives would take the proving dough and cut a deep cross into the top with a knife. This, they said, was to 'let the witch out'.[1] Staffordshire bakers thought it a bad idea to bake bread on Friday and the only way to make it rise and to prevent witchcraft on that day was to make a cross on it. In Oxfordshire a similar cross was made but in this case the cross was used to stop the Devil sitting on the bread and stopping it from rising. Of course, scoring a loaf has a practical use, too.

Some folklorists have connected the cross on top of British loaves with Roman bread that was similarly divided. A carbonised loaf preserved in Pompeii, and also seen in Roman frescoes, shows that loaves were cut into eight sections probably for the ease of breaking it rather than any ritual significance. The cuts then and now create weak points that allow the bread to rise in the oven in an orderly manner instead of simply exploding in unexpected directions. But practicality and folklore are not necessarily antagonistic. A cross would form on the top of a bucket of yeast if you set it out on Good Friday, according to the lore of the Kennet Valley.[2]

Yeast needs warmth in order to reach its full potential and make the dough rise. In Herefordshire a warm bed was thought to be the ideal place for this, but it had to be warmed by a living

Bread making is an ancient art, but that doesn't make it any easier to get right.

person.[3] A good excuse for a baker to go back to bed, probably the warmest place in most people's homes.

Nineteenth-century Warwickshire lore had it that rain falling on Holy Thursday was especially valuable to bakers. As soon as it started raining, housewives would dash out with buckets and saucepans to collect it. The rainwater could then be bottled and kept for the coming year. A spoonful of this special water added to the leaven, the yeast used to prepare the dough, would guarantee light bread.[4] Water used in baking in Stratford-upon-Avon sometimes had a red-hot poker plunged into it – to 'remove bitterness'.

In Scotland people thought the yeast had to be prepared within an hour of sunrise or the bread would be dense and heavy.[5] Another threat to rising bread in Scotland was if anyone were to sing nearby. Yeast can be devilishly tricky but it is rare to find it accused of being a music critic. In some parts of Scotland, though, it was not the bread but the baker that suffered; for as long as the baker sings is the length of time they will 'greet' – cry – for. Others claimed that the singing baker was sure to suffer a death in the family soon.

Those who could foresee a death in the family might take to baking bread to ward it off. The aroma of the bread in the oven was thought to distract evil spirits from hurting whoever was ill. Kneading dough is certainly a distraction from worrying about a loved one. If the worst did happen, though, and someone in your family died, under no circumstances should you attempt to bake with a corpse in your house. The reason for this Scottish superstition is not known but it would certainly be a kindness to provide the bereaved with some bread rather than forcing them to make it. Should you find yourself at a funeral with bread in your pocket you should probably avoid eating it – folklore has it that doing so will make your teeth hollow and fall from your skull.[6]

Bread used to come in two main forms depending on the grade of the flour used. While today we value brown and wholemeal bread as more healthy and wholesome, in the past people preferred white bread made from only the finest flour. In Gloucestershire it was believed that if the first butterfly of the year you saw was white, you would have the good fortune to have only white bread all year round. A brown butterfly foretold a drab twelve months of coarse brown bread.[7]

As every baker knows, once in the oven, the alchemy of the bread can be an uncertain thing. You might be tempted to open the door to test it, but this could be disastrous. A Shropshire saying has it that a woman 'who prods baking bread with a fork or knife will never be a happy maid or wife'. The true housewife will instinctively know when her bread is ready. As a poor househusband I sympathise with the young ladies who must have been upbraided for this lack of bready insight. Their choice of implement, a fork or knife, is also a bad one as it will create a large hole in the bread through which steam may escape. A skewer, if anything, should be used.

In Scotland, where thriftiness was much valued, it was

near-sacrilege to sweep flour or crumbs into the fire. Everything had to be brushed out of the door so that it might provide a feast for some of God's smaller creatures. If the young maiden of a northern Scottish family did let too much fall on the floor or burned the bread it was taken as being a grim outlook for her husband. The saying went:

Never mairry the lass,
It [that] burns the bread or spills the meal,
She'll ne'er dee weel t' child nor chiel [man].[8]

If too much flour or meal went astray when a woman was baking, the folk opinion of the wasteful baker was that 'She'll come to be glaid t'lick the mill-walls'. Young men were encouraged to find the 'savingest' – most thrifty – wife by watching them as they kneaded their bread. If a man should see her wasting any he was encouraged to find another potential wife as she would waste your household stores. Any woman who was dumped by such a man must have been thankful in the end that they did not have to live their life with a man always keeping an eye on them.

When the bread is taken out of the oven many things can be divined from the way it has baked. Should the top and bottom come apart while an unmarried lady is slicing it, it means she will not marry within the next year. A large hole in the middle was called a coffin and could mean a death in the family. Norfolk women were told to knead their dough exceedingly roughly to avoid both coffins and tight knots of unmixed dough in the loaf known as 'slut-farthings'. These were also sometimes called 'lazy-backs' as they suggested a lack of vigour in the kneading. A crack on the top (of the sort avoided by scoring with a cross) was thought to be a terrible omen for those who ate it. This belief once even made an appearance at an inquest.

In 1879 an inquest was held in Priorslee, Shropshire, to determine the cause of death of one Ana Woolly. Ana had left the house to fetch gin from the pub no more than a quarter of a mile away, yet her husband, George, was concerned for her safety. He went in search of her and found her body in a pool of water, along with two bottles of ale and a small bottle of rum. George had had a premonition of her demise when Ana pulled her bread from the oven that day and 'one of the loaves was cracked right across'. It was this 'that caused him to go out and look for her'. The jury passed no judgement on the omen but declared Ana's a case of accidental death.[9]

In one tragic case simply dreaming of bread was linked to death. An 1884 inquest in Walsall heard that a little girl named Brown had drowned in a canal. Her mother had refused to let her daughter go to school that day on account of a dream she had of baking bread. Having lost other children, their deaths also preceded by a dream of bread, she thought it safest to keep the girl at home. Instead of staying put, the girl wandered out of the house and fell into the canal.[10]

While bread can predict unhappy events it can sometimes also indicate happy arrivals. In several places when a large hole appears within a loaf of bread it is thought to be a sure sign that the baker will soon become pregnant. Bread could also be used more directly to help a woman fall pregnant: unwed daughters could sit on top of the oven while bread was baking in it to become more attractive to their desired lovers.

John Aubrey described a game called Cocklebread. 'Young wenches have a wanton sport which they call moulding of Cocklebread; viz. They gett upon a Table-board, and then gather up their knees and their coates with their hands as high as they can and then they wabble to and fro with their Buttocks as if they were kneading Dowgh with their A—, and they say these words, viz.:

My Dame is sick & gonne to bed,
And I'le go mowld my cocklebread.[11]

He thought it was just a fun, if shocking, sport but also suggested that in earlier times the women had actually used their buttocks to shape the dough before cooking cocklebread. If a portion of this was given to a man the girl fancied, he 'would adore the maid henceforth'. Perhaps the lucky gentleman simply enjoyed a well-made loaf – but magical properties have long been suggested for bread.

If they managed to attract their lover to the church, bread could help them conceive pretty children. A Welsh tradition saw the best man giving bread and butter to the bride to eat before the cutting of the cake at a wedding. It was thought that eating this would make the bride give birth to handsome lads and beautiful girls all blessed with small mouths – apparently something to be desired.[12]

MAGICAL LOAVES

Fossil echinoids are instantly recognisable. Small stony objects that fit in the palm of the hand, they are often heart-shaped or round and have five lines of dots radiating out from the centre. In Britain they turn up regularly on riverbanks, beaches and in fields. To the modern palaeontologist they are the earthly remains of ancient sea urchins and related creatures, but for our ancestors, who had no concept of the deep time that had gone before them, how were these stones to be explained?

One of the most popular names for them was Fairy or Pixie Loaves.[1] Looking, to the generous eye, like little loaves of bread, these fossils were said to be powerful amulets that caused bread to infallibly rise. Placing one next to the oven in a bakery or having one in the home was just part of sensible business and good home economics. There was sympathetic magic in their appearance that meant having one in the home would ensure the household never lacked for bread. In Essex they were known as

Echinoid fossils have been collected by humans for thousands of years. The prehistoric burial from Five Knolls Barrow Cemetery contained 200 such fossils.

Pharisee loaves and these loaves or stones ensured that their owner would always have food. These fossils could also be found on the windowsill in dairies into the twentieth century as they were thought to stop milk going sour.

Branscombe's Loaf is another stone associated with bread.[2] The tale goes that a thirteenth-century bishop of Exeter called Walter Branscombe was travelling home over Dartmoor one day when his stomach began to grumble. From nowhere the Devil, in disguise, appeared with a most appetising platter of bread and cheese. The holy but hungry man was on the point of accepting the Devil's cursed food when his servant spotted the cloven hooves of the Devil poking out of the bottom of his clothing. He knocked the bread from the bishop's hand and when it hit the ground it immediately turned into a large stone, known to this day as Branscombe's Loaf. The bishop should have learned from Jesus' own temptation in the wilderness – man cannot live by bread (and cheese) alone.

The Devil seems to have had a weakness for bread, as so many of us do, and a number of tales recounting his fiendish deeds relate to bread in some way. The walk up Rheidol Gorge in Wales can be a treacherous one, with steps of slippery slate that are often covered in wet leaves. The best way to get from one side to the other, avoiding the cascading River Mynach, is to take one of the three bridges across it. One of these bridges is the work of the Devil himself.

Legend has it that a local maid named Megan of Llandunach had been separated from her cow by the river. She was staring down into the gorge when a stranger appeared behind her. In return for building a bridge the mysterious man wanted only a small thing in return – the first creature to cross it. Megan needed her cow back but was suspicious of this kindly stranger. For a start his feet were cloven and his knees seemed to be on back to front. Promising to return with payment she went home and hatched a plan.

When she returned she was startled to find the stranger really had fulfilled his impossible part of the bargain: a bridge now crossed the once impassable gorge. Instead of praising her bene-factor she pretended to question its strength. From her pocket she pulled a crust of bread and from under her dress she revealed her dog. To test the bridge she tossed the bread across it and let the dog scamper after it. The Devil revealed his form and cursed her for tricking him – fortunately he did not claim the dog.[3]

In Aberdeenshire the Maiden Stone recounts another meeting between the Devil and a maid. The Maiden Stone is a 3m-high red granite monument covered in engravings left by the ancient Picts. To locals, however, it is no mere historical artefact. Once a stranger approached a maiden and made a wager with her. He would build a road to the top of the nearby craggy hill and complete it before she could bake a bannock – a flat bread that takes mere minutes on a fire. If he won, she would have to marry him; if she won, her village would eventually have a fine and serviceable road.

Of course the stranger used his diabolical powers to finish the road before the dough even had a chance to get warmed. The girl was terrified and fled from her devilish betrothed and as she ran she prayed to God for salvation just as the stranger grabbed her shoulder. For some reason God chose to 'rescue' her by turning her to stone. The spot where the Devil's hand was on her is now marked by a large notch on the stone.[4]

Consecrated bread, with its taste of the divine, was key in many magical and diabolic acts. Cornish lore recounts how a person might become a witch by stealing a piece of the communion bread. The would-be witch was to hide a morsel of the body of Christ, having stolen it from the hand of the priest. Then at midnight they were to carry the bread three times around the outside of the church, moving south to north and crossing eastwards three times. On the third pass a monstrous toad would appear and the bread should be fed to it. Once the toad's hunger was satisfied it would exhale three times onto the person who had fed it – who instantly became a witch with the power of the evil eye, able to curse those they looked at. Such people could be identified by black spots under their tongue.[5]

A report from Wales recorded how two ladies performed a similar rite.

> Sometime in the beginning of the last century [nineteenth century], two old dames attended the morning service at Llanddewi Brefi Church, and partook of the Holy Communion; but instead of eating the sacred bread like other communicants, they kept it in their mouths and went out. Then they walked round the Church outside nine times, and at the ninth time the Evil One came out from the Church wall in the form of a frog, to whom they gave the bread from their mouths, and by doing this wicked thing they were supposed to be selling themselves to Satan and become witches. It was also added that after this they were sometimes seen swimming in the river Teivi in form of hares![6]

The witch Maggie Osborne of Wigtownshire in Scotland was accused of feeding the diabolical toad in this way. Among the many crimes attached to her legend were killing a family in an avalanche, sinking a ship with a storm and using an army of angry cats to attempt to drown a serving girl in a vat of boiling beer. When the girl scalded one of the cats with the steaming liquid Maggie herself was later seen with a severe burn.[7]

Care is usually taken with consecrated bread, especially if too much has been accidentally blessed. What can you do if you have produced an overabundance of Christ's body? One of my friends attended a service where the vicar had been over-optimistic about the number of worshippers expected. Afterwards the faithful few were asked to eat far more bread than they might have wanted to: you cannot simply toss the Lord our Saviour into the bin.

Magic traditions often use what is near to hand. In Wales buttered bread falling from the table signified that rain was coming. Others recommended keeping bread handy to save you whenever you needed it. Keeping a crust of bread in your pocket was an easy talisman against ill fortune. A rhyme explained it this way:

> If ye fear to be affrighted
> When ye are, by chance, benighted;
> In your pocket for a trust
> Carry nothing but a crust,
> For that holy piece of bread
> Charms the danger and the dread.[8]

With bread ever-present in the cupboard anyone hoping to cast a charm or spell would always be able to find a crust for their magic. A widespread and surprisingly enduring spell involved using bread to locate the body of someone who had drowned.

In 1945 a young boy went missing and was thought to have drowned. The search included the use of a loaf of bread into which had been poured quicksilver – the liquid metallic element mercury. This weighted loaf was then placed in the water where the missing boy was thought to be. The general belief was that the bread would float towards the victim. It may be that the lively quickness of the mercury was irresistible to the dead person's spirit. In this case the loaf is said to have come very close to the body of the boy and so revealed his location. In 1767 a report of this method of body locating was included in the *Gentleman's Magazine* and there it was said the loaf sank at the spot where a child's body lay underwater.

Others were less persuaded of the efficacy of this weighty bread. One Northamptonshire inquest in the 1890s was told how 'A man named Edward Bird said that his employer (deceased's father) asked him one day last week to get a loaf and some quicksilver. Witness did so, and Mr Walker, who was at present an invalid, poured some quicksilver on the loaf, and told witness to throw it into Fawaley Pond, because on the day Miss Walker disappeared she told him that the bodies of drowning persons could be found by those means. He said if the loaf was thrown into the water it would float down to the spot where the body lay and then jump about.' This was done but we are informed that 'nothing extraordinary happened'.[9]

If you couldn't easily lay your hands on mercury or did not want to contaminate your water with it, another bread spell could be used to find a drowned person. In the north a lit candle could be placed on a loaf and then set adrift on the water. Again, it was said to float towards the body and to stay motionless over their resting place. Like the moving mercury the flickering of the candle's flame could be seen as a representation of the dead person's soul searching for its lost body.

Bread could also help in finding the living. If you were looking for a thief, you could go to a well in Lleyn in Wales, for example, and throw pieces of bread into the water. The name of the light-fingered under suspicion was then revealed. When the name of the guilty person was spoken out loud it was thought that the bread would sink.[10]

In Scotland on New Year's Day one of the methods of ridding a home of bad luck for the coming year was to give a dog a piece of your bread. Once this was done, the dog was quickly chased away – hopefully carrying any ill fortune with it. Shouting out 'Get away, you dog. Whatever death of men or loss of cattle happens in this house to the end of the year be on your head' hurried the unfortunate creature on its way.[11]

BREAD CURES

When I'm ill, for me nothing is as comforting as a slice of good bread and butter. Generally, though, this only cures me of the grumpiness that accompanies a cold. In the past there was a belief in the power of bread to cure diseases that would have us calling for a doctor. For those who could not afford to call in a professional, or where a professional was just as unable to offer effective help, bread was a useful ingredient in medicine. Sometimes you needed to add something to the bread to make it into a cure. To treat jaundice in Dorset it was thought that nine lice on your bread and butter would do the job.[1]

One of the most terrifying diseases in the past was rabies. A person bitten and infected by a rabid animal was sentenced to a painful and horrific death. Even today, once symptoms start to show there is very little doctors can do but minimise a victim's suffering, therefore anything is worth trying. One early remedy was to write on a piece of bread 'King of Glory come in Peace' and feed it to the afflicted.[2] Others suggested writing a spell on a piece of paper, wrapping it in white bread and feeding it to the patient.

Fits were so mysterious in the past that they were often thought to be a divine affliction, striking at random and with devastating results. One woman in a Hampshire village in the nineteenth century decided that simply reading the Bible wasn't enough to cure her fits. Every day she tore out a page from her Bible, placed it between two buttered slices of bread and ate it. Whether this helped is not recorded but one shocked contributor to *Notes and Queries* thought 'This was treating the Bible as a fetish with a vengeance!'[3]

In Strathclyde there was once a stone with a natural hole through it called Clach Thuill. A person suffering from tuberculosis could go to it and be passed through the stone three times while calling on the Father, Son and Holy Ghost for a cure. To be successful they also had to lay on the stone an offering meal of meat and bread. This was left for the birds, who in eating it would fly away with the patient's illness as well as their food.[4]

Sometimes it was not the bread that was effective in the cure but the person who sliced it. In Herefordshire a woman who had had two husbands with the same surname, but who were unrelated, was supposed to have the ability to cure whooping cough. She simply had to give a slice of bread and butter to the patient. Other cures for whooping cough involved taking hairs from the cross on a donkey's back and placing them between two slices of bread. Once this sandwich was eaten by the sick person they were sure to be cured.[5] An alternative cure from Staffordshire suggested that hair from the patient should be put in the bread, which was then fed to a dog, who would presumably have the illness passed to them.

In Scotland donkeys with bread could cure whooping cough in another way. A piece of the finest white bread had to be offered to the donkey and any crumbs that fell from its mouth were gathered up. These were mashed up with milk and fed to the child with a spoon made from the horn of a live animal.[6]

Oxfordshire did without the donkey entirely when dealing with whooping cough. To keep your family free of this bacterial infection all you had to do was go into the garden, dig a hole and bury a loaf of bread for a full day. When the bread was taken out, apparently 'quite moist and nice', everyone in the family ate some and the whole household would be whooping-cough free.[7] It might be that bacteria or fungi growing on this buried bread could offer some antibiotic assistance, but it seems more likely that you'd catch something rather than prevent it.

One of the best cures for whooping cough was thought to be bread baked on Good Friday. This might suggest that cures could only therefore be made around Easter, but Good Friday bread had some properties that made it useful all year round.

GOOD FRIDAY, GOOD BREAD

Good Friday was good for many reasons, but one such reason was that bread baked on that day would never, or only very slowly, go mouldy. In the New Forest bread made on this holy day was thought to be good for seven years.[1] This bread could then be kept in the home as a charm against general curses but brought out for illnesses, too.

Good Friday bread may not have gone 'ropey' but it would certainly have gone stale if kept for any length of time.[2] In Wales, Good Friday bread was known to go black from one year to the next. This meant you could not simply carve off a slice. To cure whooping cough or any other disease the loaf was taken and some of it grated into a drink. Even animals could be given this cure.

A Warwickshire lady told a correspondent of *Notes and Queries* in 1863 how Good Friday bread had saved her neighbour's infant from a 'bowel complaint' by grating some of the bread in brandy. The child drank this, was probably comforted for a while, and was wholly cured. When pressed by her interlocutor on what Good Friday bread was she told him. She had a loaf that was seven or eight years old. 'It is quite good, but very dry.' Her mother though had once kept a loaf for over twenty years.[3]

In the North of England, Good Friday bread was always given to sailors by their wives as a sure protective charm against shipwreck.

A loaf of bread baked on Good Friday in 1919 could still be

found on display in the Cambridge Folk Museum as late as 1969, apparently still free from mould. Even its curator had to admit, though, that it had gone somewhat dry and hard. When I checked with the museum in 2021 the curator was kind enough to inform me that it was still in one piece and not mouldy. I hope the same can be said about me when I'm over a hundred years old. In Cambridgeshire, Good Friday bread was thought of as helpful in cases of indigestion – unlikely though it may seem.

Norfolk folk also put great store by the powers of Good Friday bread. One village old maid had given up her neighbour as dead when she continued to suffer from diarrhoea – 'for she had already given her two doses of Good Friday bread without any benefit'.[4] Happily, there must have been some other form of divine intervention, for the neighbour afterwards recovered and lived a long life.

In Dorset you might once have found a Good Friday loaf hanging on the chimney in old farmhouses.[5] As well as being nigh-on indestructible these loaves were a sure charm for rustling up good bread. In a house with one of these talismans, the bread was always certain to rise and to taste delicious. It seems as if having once made a good loaf it was enough to keep that to encourage the rest of the year's bread to follow its example.

If you do keep a Good Friday loaf, you may wish to follow the custom in Cambridgeshire. There the loaf was kept for a year from the date of its baking, wrapped well in a tin. When the next Good Friday came around the tin would be opened and the loaf brought out. Invariably it would not have turned mouldy but would be incredibly hard to eat. To make it more appetising the loaf was moistened with water before being returned to the oven for a second baking. Then the bread was apparently quite tasty and a slice was enough to guarantee luck for the coming year. This bread was marked with a cross in the middle and that was the part that was eaten. The two ends of the bread that had no part of the holy cross were carried down to the river and thrown in to avert floods in the coming year.[6]

Northamptonshire folk seem to have had less faith in Good Friday bread. Anyone who made the mistake of baking on that day was taking their life in their hands for it was sure to cause the house to burn down.

BANNOCKS

Bannocks are a Scottish speciality and may be one of the most ancient forms of bread in Britain. They are quick breads made without yeast and gently fried on a griddle or pan. They could be made from almost any type of flour from oats to the ancient *bere*, a type of barley now only grown on a few islands. Many Scottish homes once had a bannockstane, a large, flat sandstone which was placed directly into the fire that bannocks were cooked on.

Lindow Man is the name given to a well-preserved body that was dug from a peat bog near Wilmslow in Cheshire. His remains date from the first century AD and it appears that he may have been a sacrificial victim. Lindow Man has injuries consistent with being stabbed, beaten and strangled before being deposited in the bog. In his stomach were the remains of burned barley.[1] Some have linked this to the bannocks which were served at Beltane in later centuries. There a bannock was covered in ashes and used to draw lots. Whoever picked the burned bannock from a bag of unburned ones had to undergo a mock sacrifice.[2] Did Lindow Man take part in a ritual of burned bannocks that had a very real, fatal outcome?

Most bannock folklore, however, did not have such a drastic conclusion. Bannocks in their simplicity lend themselves to lore. Everyone would have known how to make them and everyone had the ingredients for them. They could be used to teach habits of thriftiness. Any woman who threw away crumbs of dough or swept away leftover flour was considered a wastrel when such pickings could be turned into a hearty bannock. Allowing a bannock to fall on the floor was considered a very bad omen.

Little bannocks were made with any leftover flour and were known as *Siantachan a chlàir* – the charmer of the board.[3] If flour was left to go to waste, it was thought that the rest of the flour in the home would have all the goodness sucked out of it. Sometimes these little bannocks had a hole in the middle and were used as amulets to keep off the evil intentions of spirits and fairies. They were also placed next to women in their childbed.

It was thought that baking bannocks made it likely that a stranger would call, no doubt drawn by the delicious aroma. In one tale a mysterious stranger arrived and asked for a mouthful of dough. When presented with the bannock he asked for more, and more, and more, and was still not satisfied. It was only when he ate the tiny bannock made of leftovers that his hunger was sated and he left the house in peace.[4]

There were many types of bannock that the Scottish cook could try. These ranged from the sweet cryin'-bannock that was presented to the kimmers (the female friends who gathered after a birth) to the savoury cod liver bannock favoured on Barra. The teethin'-bannock was baked into a hard ring for babies to chew as their teeth started coming in. St Columba's bannock was made on the saint's day and had a silver coin baked in it. Whoever received the silver coin when the bannock was broken was considered lucky, though they always got the responsibility of looking after the lambs that season.[5]

In Scotland, Lammas, when the first fruits of the harvest were celebrated, was enjoyed with a special bannock that was prepared with flour from the first grain harvested that year.[6] The father of the house broke the bannock and fed it to his family in order of their age. Then he led the family in a procession around the fire the bannock had been baked in to ensure good health for the coming year.

On Beltane, children would gather on hilltops to bake bannocks. As well as the mock sacrifices that have been described, they would use their bannocks to predict the future. As the bannocks were baking, one side was marked with a cross. When ready, these were taken to a slope and allowed to roll down and it was observed which side the bannock fell. If they kept landing cross-side up, it foretold at least one more year of life, but, if cross-side down, the owner of the bannock could expect an early death.[7]

Pie Lore

Britain is a nation of pies. Other countries may have Champagne or Parmesan, products that are legally protected based on their area of origin, but we British have the Melton Mowbray pork pie. Some may dream of hearing their beloved comparing them to a summer's day but I think the tenderest expression in Britain is 'I love thee like puddings; if thou wert pie I'd eat thee'.

Pies were so popular in Cornwall and had such varied fillings that it was said the Devil feared to go into the county for fear of being turned into a pie. When you learn that the Cornish enjoyed Muggety Pie, made from a sheep's entrails and cream, you can understand the Devil's apprehensions.[1] If that doesn't tell you something about Britain then the range of folklore that bursts forth from pies like four and twenty blackbirds may enlighten you.

Perhaps the most famous Cornish dish is stargazy pie. It is immediately recognisable because it is baked with the heads of pilchards poking out of the crust. Supposedly it was made in commemoration of a heroic fisherman called Tom Bawcock who saved his village from starvation by venturing out in a storm and bringing home a massive catch.

The pies of Britain have some strange names. This is not so unusual. My nan was fond of something called a toenail pudding – a sweet jam pie with grated coconut on top instead of nail trimmings.

Pies can hide a multitude of surprises, pleasant or otherwise.

Live animals in pies occurred in real life, not just in nursery rhymes.

At the Painswick church clypping, whereby parishioners join hands to encircle the church, you may be lucky enough to sample a Puppy Dog Pie.[2]

The origins of this dog-unfriendly pie are unknown. One tale traces it to a man who had promised to bake a venison pie but was unable to kill a deer so he used his own dog. When this was discovered he was quite rightly ostracised. Another legend suggests that the first pie was made by two young women who discovered that their lovers were cheating on them. They did the obvious thing and slew their adulterous boyfriends' dogs and served them up in a pie. Today the puppy dogs of Painswick are safe as beef is used instead and the doggie element is represent by a ceramic dog baked into the middle. Other villages in the area would refer to those from Painswick as bow-wows on account of their fondness for these pies. In a similar way, the inhabitants of West Houghton in Lancashire were called 'cow 'yeds' because they ate a huge pie baked into the shape of a bull's head for the fair held on St Bartholomew's Day.[3]

In Lancashire Mother's Day was once known as Fag-Pie Sunday because fig pies were the traditional fare.[4] Other places enjoyed their fig pies at different times. At Wybunbury in Cheshire the Fig Pie Wakes has a festive air and sees locals rolling fig pies along the road to see whose travels the greatest distance.[5] This contest can be seen on a poster for the Wakes from 1819. The competition is taken seriously and all bakers of the pies must use the same recipe and bake pies of the same dimensions.

Other pies are remarkable for their size. The village of Denby in Derbyshire came together to celebrate that most British of events, the recovery of the monarch from madness. They toasted the return to health of George III in 1788 by baking a huge pie in the local pub which was then distributed to the villagers. Since then there have been other vast bakes in the village to mark special days. These have included the defeat of Napoleon and the repeal of the Corn Laws. The pies have tended towards ever greater size over the years. The Golden Jubilee pie of 1887 is said to have included: 1,581lb beef, 180lb mutton, 163lb veal, 180lb lamb, 250lb lean pork, 64 rabbits, 3 hares, 42 fowls, 40 pigeons, 12 grouse, 21 ducks, 4 plovers, 1 turkey, 5 geese, 2 wild ducks, 108 small birds and 40 stones of potatoes. Alas, the pie turned out to be rancid when it was cut open. The remains were quietly dumped into a rubbish tip. A Bicentenary Pie was baked in 1988 that included 3000kg of beef and was declared the largest pie ever made.[6] Luckily this one was edible.

Perhaps the best known British pie on the world stage is the strangely misnamed mince pie that is a feature of every Christmas. The sweet mince pie, stuffed with mincemeat made from dried fruit, developed from highly spiced meat pies of the Middle

Ages. *The Forme of Cury*, a fourteenth-century English cookbook supposedly by the master chef to Richard II, contains a meat tart full of the spices one might find in a mince pie.

Samuel Pepys mentions mince pies being served at other festive occasions. In 1662 he described how he went 'to dinner to Sir W. Pen's, it being a solemn feast day with him, his wedding day, and we had, besides a good chine of beef and other good cheer, eighteen mince pies in a dish, the number of the years that he hath been married'. These mince pies would still have had meat in them but were sweetened with sugar. Pepys was displeased to have to send out to buy a mince pie that same year as his wife was ill. When she recovered he thanked God that he 'at home found my wife making mince pies'.

By the eighteenth century the inclusion of meat, like beef tongue, was considered to be optional. The sweet mince pies had found their final form and soon became a staple of Christmas. Folklore was sprinkled over the pies like icing sugar.

In Wales it was said that you should not talk while eating a mince pie lest evil spectres enter your mouth.[7] Nor were you supposed to cut a mince pie in case you would let the good luck out. This makes sense. When I am eating mince pies I have neither the time to speak nor the will to have only half a pie.

Cake Lore

'Do you think because you are virtuous, that there shall be no more cakes and ale?' – Sir Toby Belch, *Twelfth Night*

Folklore and cake go hand in hand. Many people who love to natter about old ways and legends like to do it over a slice or two of cake. Many press reports of meetings of the Folklore Society in old newspapers end with remarks about how some member of the group, inevitably female, had provided the meeting with a supply of suitably folkloric treats.

One of the first bits of folklore that many children are introduced to comes with their birthday cake. Candles – one for each year of their life – are placed on the cake and lit, despite the risk of fire and bits of wax dripping onto the icing. The child then has to blow out the candles, ideally with a single breath, and to make a wish. There are many fanciful theories about the source of this tradition. Does it go back to the ancient religions where smoke from burned offerings pleased the gods? In all probability it is simply a fun activity for children, though as an adult these days I offer up my own prayer when offered a slice of cake that a child has blown spittle all over: that I may be spared some dreadful illness.

The children's rhyme Pat-a-Cake recalls a time when not every home had an oven.

Pat-a-cake, pat-a-cake, baker's man.
Bake me a cake as fast as you can.

Pat it, and prick it, and mark it with 'B'
And put it in the oven for Baby and me!

To have a cake required the use of the baker's oven, so marking your cake with a letter on top was an easy way to ensure you got your own back. There may also have been less than scrupulous bakers who were tempted to substitute substandard cakes for those of their customers, so marking them ensured you got the cake you desired. In an earlier version of the rhyme from the eighteenth century the instructions are slightly different.

Patty Cake, Patty Cake, Baker's Man;
That I will Master, As fast as I can;
Pat it and prick it, And mark it with a T,
And there will be enough for Tommy and me.[1]

At some point in the intervening years Tommy fell out of favour and, despite the dietary advice of neonatal nutritionists, Baby became the beneficiary of the cake. Lucky baby.

Sweet doughs and sponges can hold much more meaning than their airy structure might suggest. When starvation forces a family to abandon their children in deep, dark woods, Hansel and Gretel discover that an old lady has been hoarding enough gingerbread to build a house. Uneven distribution of wealth was just as much a concern of folk tales as it is for those looking askance at billionaires today.

Traditions like Thomasing were a way for poor people to get a chance to taste the sweeter life of their better-off neighbours. On St Thomas's Day, 21 December, in many places women would go from door to door begging for flour to make cakes and bread. By going in sizable groups they avoided the charge of begging because they were simply taking part in a larger activity. A shared shame is also a lessened one. The tradition took on many names including mumping, gathering, or gooding. Maureen Sutton recalled the tradition as it took place in Lincolnshire. 'Old women would come mumping and Mother would give them homemade cakes, half a cake or a whole one sometimes . . . They came very early, I was still in bed, before 7 o'clock. They used to sing, "Here we come a mumping."'[2]

Not everyone was as generous. 'This old lass went mumping for spuds, the farmer told her to clear off, so she said, "You might not get a good crop next year." The funny thing was, he didn't. Not many were as mean as that.'[3]

By the late twentieth century the tradition of Thomasing and mumping had died out in Britain. Many prosperous people found they did not want to have to distribute flour or goods by their own hands and instead donated money to their parish. This had the benefit of keeping their hands clean, their neighbours at arm's length and the dole of goods only going to the 'deserving' poor.

Getting a cake to bake properly is an art form. No one makes a cake as good as their mother's, which might suggest that each generation we are being exposed to progressively makes worse cakes. But there are some old wives' tales that might help you do your baking right. For instance, it is terribly bad luck to stir a cake batter with the left hand. To stir the cake widdershins, anti-clockwise, is also thought to spoil the baking.

In Durham it was said that if a housewife cut the first cake to come out of her oven all that followed would be dense and stodgy. To avoid this, canny northern housewives would break a piece off with their hands and eat that instead of cutting the cake.

Some folkloric cake advice is very time specific. While most people dislike rain on St Swithin's Day, as it is supposed to presage forty more days of rainy weather, one old lady of Somerset in the nineteenth century lived for it.[4] Should it happen to rain on that day she would rush out with pots and pans to collect the water. This was then used to make little cakes that she would give to her neighbours as medicine that they kept safe for the coming year. A bit of the cake in their food or drink was a sure cure for innumerable illnesses. If she failed to collect any rainwater, or if it was a fine St Swithin's Day, she was deeply upset because it meant the year was sure to be plagued by ill health.

Should you happen to know a married woman whose married name is the same as her maiden name, perhaps you should encourage her to make you a fruit cake. Cakes made by such nominatively conservative ladies have the power to cure whooping cough.[5] Unfortunately for the baker there were few rewards – paying them, or even offering to do so, would remove the medicinal powers of the cake.

KING ALFRED'S BAKING MISHAP

Every British child takes up cakes with their history lessons. The popularity of the image of Alfred the Great being told off by a common woman tells us about the British sensibility to power as much as it does our love of cakes.

As the story is commonly told, while Alfred was on the run after being defeated by the Vikings he had to flee for his life and stumbled into a lowly peasant's cottage seeking sanctuary. Staying there for several days reflecting on how the wheel of fortune turned, Alfred was still pondering this when the peasant woman put some cakes over the fire. Busying about her work, she left the king to watch the cakes but soon smelled burning. She roundly rebuked her noble kitchen assistant saying that he was not happy to watch the cakes but happy enough to eat them. The king took his chastisement calmly and ascribed it to a divine warning not to neglect the little things in life.

That is the story as most know it. Derived from *Asser's Life of King Alfred*, some people think it is a later interpolation of the text. One scholar, Rory McTurk, sees it as a borrowing from the very Norse that Alfred was fighting against.[1] In a saga that predates the tale of Alfred being written down, a Norseman called Ragnar is shown to have a loving nature when he is so distracted by the beauty of his prospective bride that he burns the loaves he

Kings getting involved in domestic mishaps are a common theme in folklore
as they remind us that no matter how high and mighty a person might
be, we all struggle with baking.

has been left to bake. Indeed, even the cakes that are usually said
to be burned by Alfred were probably small loaves of bread. The
Anglo-Saxons, according to the Venerable Bede, called February
Sol-Monath – Cake Month.[2] These cakes which Bede says were
offered up to the gods were probably similar to the hearth cakes
Alfred was supposed to be watching.

An ugly fungus called *Daldinia concentrica* is sometimes called
King Alfred's cake because its black nodules look like carbonised
buns.[3] Once on fire the fungus smoulders slowly for a long time,
giving off an acrid, pungent smoke even more depressing than
the smell of ruined cakes. Smouldering fungus could be placed in
a pocket and carried about in even the worst weather to kindle a
fire. This should not be tried at home, but the broken embers can
be blown on to light tinder if needs be.

Burning cakes have always been seen as a bit of a tragedy.
Imagine saving up the ingredients for a lovely cake only to find
them wasted on a scorched and inedible mess. In Peterhead it was

said that if cakes are burned in the baking, the baker will weep before they are eaten.[4] There's no use crying over a spoiled cake, but we all do it from time to time. In Pitsligo, burned cakes mean that the baker will be moved to anger before they are all used – more than just the anger at burning your cakes anyway.

WITCH CAKES

Sometimes folk tradition tells you that burning is an integral part of cake baking. If you want to catch a witch, burning a cake can be vital. In Lincolnshire it was said that to make a witch appear, a cake stuck full of pins should be burned on a griddle or pan over a fire. Quite what you should do with the witch once it arrives is not recorded.

If you want to make an effective witch cake, you may have to get creative with your ingredients. In the *Caledonian Mercury* of 1778 one writer records, 'As to the burning of cakes, made of the suspected person's water, I really do not put much faith in this, though Mr Forbes thinks it an infallible method of discovery'.[1]

Witch cakes containing urine played a starring role in the famous witch trials of Salem in 1692. Two young girls named Elizabeth Parris and Abigail Williams fell sick and started behaving erratically, apparently after dabbling with some folk magic. As the bizarre acts of the girls began to spread, some thought they detected witchcraft in the goings-on. It was suggested by a family friend called Mary Sibley that a witch cake might be the solution.[2]

She gave directions to the Parris family slave, John Indian, on how to prepare the cake. Urine was collected from the girls and mixed with rye flour. The resulting cake, probably with a biscuity texture, was fed to a dog. If this magic had worked the girls' symptoms should have been transferred to the dog, who may then have been able to locate the witch performing the curses. Unfortunately the dog proved unwilling or unable to point out the malefactor.

It seems that the use of urine-filled witch cakes had been imported to New England from Old England. From Yorkshire in 1683 there is a record of an even less appetising witch cake being used in a suspected case of bewitchment.[3] A doctor told an ailing man to prepare a cake made from his urine, hair and fragments of horseshoe baked with wheat flour. Once this cake was made the witch's spell could be broken by burning the cake in a fire.

Thankfully not all witch cakes required trips to the toilet. As late as 1913 the *Liverpool Echo* reported that 'Round about Flamborough Head "witch cakes" are to be met with in almost every cottage. These are circular-shaped, with a hole in the middle, and with spikes projecting on all sides. If you hang one up in your cottage and once a year burn it and put another in its place you will have good luck, we are told.'[4]

Lore had it that the cakes should be baked each year between 1 and 6 April and hung beside the main entrance to the house. The central hole in the cake allowed for string and rope to hang them up but also made the cakes resemble hagstones – stones

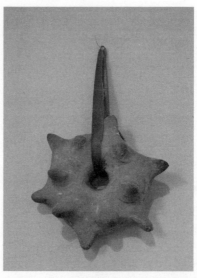

Hanging a witch cake is a very British form of apotropaic magic.

with a natural hole in them that are also said to ward off witch-craft. The spiky shape of the cakes probably served to prod and poke at any witchcraft that sought to enter the home. Such cakes can be found in the collections of many museums across the country, illustrating the widespread nature of this belief.[5]

PANCAKES

How do you solve a problem like pancakes? What type of a food are they? Opinions differ as to whether they are a specialised form of a flatbread or a very thin cake. Simply because they have the word cake in their name, and I like to eat mine sweet, I have placed them among the cakes. I hope my readers will not flip out over this.

Pancake Day can be a day of trepidation as well as one of deli-cious food. Will the pancakes stick to the pan? Will you drop them after you toss them in the air? Will you burn yourself? These risks apart, there is no better food day, in my opinion, than that produced on Pancake Day. There is an old saying about the joys of a pancake – 'If I were in bed with my hands full of pancakes I wouldn't get up for supper.' The only real question is whether you should put sugar on them before the lemon juice or lemon juice and then sugar. Any other accompaniment is an abomination.

People have worried that pancake making will die out for a long time. In a work of 1777, the antiquary John Brand revealed his own fears. 'The Custom of frying Pancakes (in turning of which in the Pan, there is usually a good deal of Pleasantry in the Kitchen) is still retained in many Families in the North, but seems, if the present fashionable Contempt of old Customs con-tinues, not likely to last another Century.'[1] The fact that you can buy pancake mix in a bottle at the supermarket around Pancake Day shows that these concerns were unfounded.

The eating of pancakes on Shrove Tuesday, or Goodish Tues-day as it is modestly known in Staffordshire, comes from it being the last day before Lent. They were the ideal way to use up rich milk, eggs and sugar before they were forbidden to Christians. The name Shrove Tuesday derives from people going to church on that day to have their sins forgiven, or shriven as it was known. There was one humorous tale that posits another explanation.

In John Taylor's satirical 1639 work titled '*Divers crabtree lectures Expressing the severall languages that shrews read to their husbands, either at morning, noone, or night. With a pleasant relation of a shrewes Munday, and shrewes Tuesday, and why they were so called. Also a lecture betweene a pedler and his wife in the canting language. With a new tricke to tame a shrew*', he includes the following story.[2]

A farmer returned home from a hard day in the fields and found his wife making pancakes. Nothing was right about them. He found the flour too coarse, the pancakes too thick and the taste of suet overpowering. She was none too pleased with this criticism of her cookery and so came up with a way to silence his carping. She said she would show him a trick. If the farmer stood outside the door with his back to the house and held out his plate she would toss a pancake up through the chimney and it would land on his plate. When he did so she gave him a whack across the skull with the hot pan and left the pancake hanging limply over his head. The farmer called his cackling wife 'an arrant Shrew' and said that the day would be forever known as 'Shrews Tuesday', which was corrupted into Shrove Tuesday. Knowing how I take any comment on the quality of my pancakes, I can well sympathise with the farmer's wife.

Because everyone makes pancakes everyone has their own bit of folklore as to their preparation. In my house it was well known that the first pancake is never any good. It turns out this is an old belief as many farmhouses would feed the first, the worst, pancake to the rooster or the dog.[3] In other houses, the first pancake had to be given to the laziest member of the household. In the past it was thought that any girl who could successfully toss a pancake would be married within the year.

Other pancake traditions were less amicable. The converse tradition for female tossers was that if they dropped the pancake they were hauled outside and had their faces blackened with ash from the fire. In Cheshire they encouraged people to eat their pancakes quickly. If you were unable to finish your pancake before the next one was served you would be dragged from the table and thrown on the dung heap outside. Or as they termed it, 'whummeled on to the muck-midden'.[4]

Things could be much worse. If a hen failed to lay an egg on Shrove Tuesday it was liable to be thrashed with a whip.[5] If the hen died from the whipping, it was given to the person who had delivered the blow. In Essex the task of beating a chicken fell to the ploughman. He was first blindfolded and then put in the hen house. If he could thrash a chicken to death its carcase was given to his companions and he was allowed to join the family for pancakes and dinner.

The crows of Eton didn't fare much better. Shrove Tuesday was a holiday for the boys and the cooks amused themselves by catching a crow and attaching a pancake to it. The bird was then hung from a door and it seems the boys would use it as target practice.[6] The crows at least might have survived.

One custom that is seldom remembered today is the Pancake Bell,[7] the church bell rung on Shrove Tuesday that summoned the faithful to confession. Commonly rung at 11 a.m., it indicated that the day's work had ended and became a symbol of the revelry that followed. It was not unknown for unscrupulous people to bribe those ringing the bell to do so much earlier than usual.

According to tradition, the first pancake race was run at the Buckinghamshire town of Olney in the fifteenth century. A housewife was so busy preparing her pancakes that she forgot the time. When she heard the pancake bell she rushed out of the door with her frying pan still in her hand. Today women who have lived and worked in Olney honour this tradition with a 380 m dash. The rules are that contestants must wear a skirt,

The sign for the village of Olney celebrates the famous pancake race
held there each year.

apron and headscarf, and that the pancake must be successfully
tossed at the beginning and end of the race.

Tossers should be careful. Part of the fun of Pancake Day
used to be that if you dropped the pancake while tossing you
had to eat it anyway. Writing in 1833, Mrs Bray found this a most
pleasing spectacle. 'The great sport of the day was to assemble
round the fire and each person to toss a cake before he had it for
his supper. The awkwardness of the tossers, who were compelled
to eat their share, even if it fell into the fire itself, afforded great
diversion.'[8]

The wisest people are those who let others make their pancakes. In the Bedfordshire village of Toddington, when the
pancake bell rings you can see small children lying down and
pressing their ears to the ground at Conger Hill.[9] The hill is
actually the man-made mound for an ancient castle and it is said
that when one of the owners of the castle wanted pancakes

Westminster School boys celebrate a pancake toss and scramble each year at Easter.

whenever he pleased he captured a witch who made the best pancakes in the area. He locked her in his dungeon and kept her there. It is said that the children who place their heads on the ground on Shrove Tuesday can still hear the sound of pancakes sizzling.

EASTER CAKES

As with bread baked on Good Friday, a special magic was associated with cakes produced on that day. In Cornwall farmhouses would place a cake on their bacon rack on Good Friday and preserve it throughout the year. The cake baked on Good Friday was thought to be 'of sovereign good in all manner of diseases that may afflict the family or the cattle'.[1] You did not have to worry about the cake being too stale to eat as it could be grated into a drink before being consumed.

Some believed that a cake made on Good Friday would never go mouldy. A person writing in 1847 noted that in Somerset a Good Friday bun could be found in many farmhouses. He was told that while cakes made on any other day were sure to go 'musty or sour', one made on Good Friday 'retained its sweetness for years'. The writer wanted to test this and asked a farmer to make him a cake to see how long it would last – even though it was not Good Friday. 'Certainly, but it won't keep good a week,' he was told. A year passed and the sceptical author found it 'in no respect the worse, except in extreme hardness; but I have some difficulty in persuading my friend, the farmer, that my cake is as good as his'.[2]

The cakes made by the wives of fishermen in Eastbourne were always kept from one Good Friday to the next. They believed that those cakes, if properly preserved, would protect their husbands at sea. If the cake should be lost, their husbands were at risk of being shipwrecked.[3] Hopefully the cakes did not include saffron because Cornish lore says that saffron cakes on a ship would drive the fish away.

Pax cakes, from the Latin for peace, were handed out by churches in Herefordshire after the Palm Sunday service. Each of the cakes, really more like shortbread, were marked with the image of a lamb. As the parishioners received the cake from the hands of the vicar they were told, 'Peace and good neighbourhood!' This tradition is said to date from the sixteenth century when ill feeling dominated several villages and Lady Scudamore left a bequest for the distribution of cakes in the hopes of creating a sense of community.[4]

On the Isle of Man, Good Friday was a day on which it was absolutely vital that no iron of any type touch the fire.[5] That meant no poker to stir the ashes or tongs used nearby. Not being able to use a griddle would make baking somewhat difficult, so the islanders developed a triangular cake known as Soddag. Instead of putting it on a griddle the cake was placed directly on the hearthstone.

The Kennet Valley provides a great example of how stories can build up around traditions. Easter has always been a time to celebrate with cakes and in the Kennet Valley it is said that the woman who bakes on Good Friday, and five subsequent Fridays, is blessed. Conversely, any woman who does her washing on Good Friday is accursed. It is said that when Jesus was being led to his crucifixion he called out to a woman for help. Since she was washing she refused him and splashed his face with soapy bubbles. When Jesus asked a woman who was baking for help she is said to have provided him with cakes.[6]

The Kennet Valley also offers an explanation as to why Shakespeare's Ophelia says, 'They say the owl was a baker's daughter'. According to legend, when Jesus visited a baker's shop to ask for something to eat the woman of the shop agreed to make him a cake – but without much enthusiasm. Every time she started to pour out flour she would scoop some back up and declare, 'Ooooh, that's too much'. Eventually she tested even Jesus' patience and he declared, 'Owl thou art and owl thou shalt be, And all the birds of earth shall peck at thee'. At this the woman was transformed into an owl and cursed always to be alone and to seek her food at night.[7]

It seems that Jesus was not alone in liking cakes. Whirlin cakes, a speciality of the Isle of Ely, got their name from an encounter with the Devil.[8] When a local woman prepared a batch for a mysterious stranger, actually the Devil abroad making mischief, he was so enchanted by them that he whistled up a whirlwind that carried all the cakes away. On the fifth Sunday in Lent whirlin cakes were made in memory of this.

Unlike the baker's daughter who became an owl, some were more than happy to share a cake at Easter. In Devonshire, Lent was a time for groups of children to visit their neighbours to go Lent Crocking. Usually the children would turn up at the most prosperous homes in the area and ask for housewife's crock – cake. Their best bet was to sing the Lent Crocking Song:

I see by the latch
There is something to catch
I see by the string
The good dame's within,
Give a cake, for I have none
At the door goes a stone;
Come give, and I'm gone.[9]

According to some, any house refusing to share cake could expect to have their door pelted with stones or bits of broken crockery. The sport then was for the children to escape from the irate homeowners without getting caught. Those too slow to escape could expect to be dragged into the kitchen and be put to work turning a spit over the hearth.

Elsewhere the boys would sing other songs to earn their keep.

Knick a knock upon the block;
Flour and lard is very dear,
Please we come a shroving here.
Your pan's hot, and my pan's cold,
(Hunger makes us shrovers bold)
Please to give poor shrovers something here.[10]

In Hertfordshire children were even luckier as Shrove Tuesday was known as Dough-Nut-Day. Little cakes were fried up in hog lard and liberally supplied to all the children of the area. The doughnut as we know it today may have originated in Hertford as one of the earliest recipes for 'dow nuts' appears in *The Receipt Book of Baroness Elizabeth Dimsdale*, from around 1800.

Sometimes even the fields would be treated to a bit of cake and ale. In Monmouthshire there was a ritual of 'walking the wheat' on Easter Sunday. The family of the farm would bake a cake and take it with them as they walked through the fields.

Some of the cake was eaten, some was buried and the rest thrown into the field. As they did so they chanted:

A bit for God, a bit for man,
And a bit for the fowls in the air.[11]

The tradition of a 'plow cake' was still being employed in Sussex in the 1920s when a heavy fruit cake was made and part of it buried in the fields to bring luck to the land.

Today if one cake is synonymous with Easter it is simnel cake. Indeed, it can be hard to find any of this delicious fruit cake baked with marzipan at any other time of the year. The cake we eat today is somewhat different from the original, which was boiled before being baked. The marzipan was also a later addition. The traditional eleven balls of marzipan on the top, said to represent the faithful apostles, seem to have first appeared in the Victorian age.

The name of the simnel cake probably derives from a French term but a legend of its origin was published in 1838 which credits it to a couple called Simon and Nell. While Simon argued that the best cake was one that was baked, Nell called for their cake to be boiled. Following a domestic dispute

SIMNEL CAKES.

The original form of the simnel cake did not feature the thirteen balls
said to represent those present at the Last Supper.

involving the throwing of furniture, a compromise was reached which saw the simnel cake was first boiled before baking.[12]

Some traditional Easter fare is best left untried. Gervase Markham in his 1615 book of recipes and remedies *The English Hus-wife* mentions a pudding for Good Friday. This was made using oats 'mixt with eggs, milk, suet, pennyroyal, boiled first in a linen bag, & then stript and buttered with sweet butter'. Pennyroyal is a plant long used in medicine, especially as a way of bringing on abortions, but is toxic to the liver and should never be consumed by anybody – unless they want to meet their maker face to face before Easter is over.

Other Good Friday cakes were made poisonous on purpose. When William Smith was put on trial in the 1750s he was accused of feeding a cake filled with arsenic to many of his neighbours, three of whom died. During the proceedings one of the would-be victims, a man named Trueman, explained to the judge why people would have been willing to accept any cake on Good Friday.

> My Lord I am a Butcher and I have had dealings with Mr Harper . . . and he invited me to dine upon a Good Friday Cake as we call it; for he was a right good neighbourly Man and he invited five other Neighbours . . . to eat of this Cake. Now you my worthy Lord must know, we have a Notion (which some Gentlemen who be here and come from that polite Town of London call a Superstition) in our Country, That if we do eat of a Cake made purposely on Good Friday we shall never want Money or Victuals all the Year round, which for as many years as I can remember has always fallen out true . . . But this Cake had such an odd Taste that I thought I should have choaked myself; whilst I was in this Agitation my good Lord, for I am somewhat pursy, Elizabeth Watt the Maid brought in the Roast Beef; I put the Mouthful I had taken of the Cake out, and made my Dinner, God be thanked for all his Mercies, on the Beef.[13]

Beef is often how the Lord shows his affection I am told.

WEDDING CAKES

The history of the wedding cake can be traced back through millennia. In ancient Rome the strictest form of marriage was known as *confarreattio*.[1] At these weddings a special cake, more like a wheat loaf, known as the *panis farreus*, was broken in half and the bride and groom each consumed a piece to signify them becoming one. The rite was only performed for patricians and only those whose parents had been joined in such a union were eligible for some of the highest priestly roles. Because divorce in such marriages was so difficult, few high-born Roman women were willing to undergo the ritual by the early days of the empire.

Cakes of some sort probably always formed a part of British wedding celebrations but in the sixteenth and seventeenth centuries it was more common for a wedding pie to be prepared. These could be enormous pastry constructions that were decorated all over with fanciful images. Inside there could be nested pies, smaller ones inside larger ones, each with various fillings. Thomas Dawson, in his 1596 book *The Good Huswife's Jewell*, gave a recipe for a 'Tarte to provoke courage in either a man or a woman' that would have been a delight at a wedding feast.

> Take a quart of good wine, and boyle therein two Burre rootes scraped cleane, two good Quinces, and a Potaton roote well pared and an ounce of Dates, and when all these are boyled verie tender, let them be drawne throgh a strainer wine and al, and then put in the yolks of eight Egs, and the braines of three or foure cocke Sparrowes, and straine them into the other, and a litle Rosewater, and seeth them all with Sugar, Sinamon and Ginger, and cloves and Mace, and put in a litle sweet Butter, and set it vpon a chafingdish of coales betweene two platters, and so let it boyle till it be something big.[2]

Robert May suggested a more complex wedding pie in 1660. His recipe 'To make an extraordinary Pie, or a Bride Pye of several Compounds, being several distinct Pies on one bottom' included dainties such as prawns, sweetbreads, marrow, lamb's testicles and oyster liquor – though thankfully each in their own pie. He set a little surprise in the middle of his pie that you do not often see at weddings these days.

> . . . you may bake the middle one full of flour, it being bak't and cold, take out the flour in the bottom, & **put in live birds, or a snake** [my emphasis], which will seem strange to the beholders, which cut up the pie at the Table.[3]

Wedding buns were also occasionally served in medieval England. These would be baked in profusion and stacked together to form as high a pile as possible. The bride and groom would then attempt to kiss each other over the tower of cakes. If they managed to lock lips without knocking the buns over, this presaged a prosperous union. John Aubrey mentions how when he was a little boy before the English civil war, he witnessed the bride and groom kissing over the 'bride-cakes'.[4]

In *The Compleat Cook* of 1658 we are informed of the 'The Countesse of RUTLAND'S Receipt of making the rare Banbury Cake which was so much praised at her Daughters (the right Honourable the Lady Chawerths) wedding'. This involves large quantities of spices, currants, sugar and 'a little Muske and Ambergreece'. Ambergris, the waxy substance from the stomach lining of the sperm whale, is not something you find in most supermarkets these days.

The multi-tiered wedding cakes of today are supposed to have originated from the infatuation of an apprentice with his master's daughter in the eighteenth century.[5] William Rich, or a Thomas Rich according to some sources, wanted to impress his future spouse by creating an impressive cake to present to her but was unsure what to do. He happened to espy the spire of St Bride's Church on Fleet Street, designed by Sir Christopher Wren as a series of four octagonal levels. Could the wedding cake really have been designed based on a church called St Bride's? It seems almost too romantic to believe.

Whatever the origin of modern wedding cakes, we do know that they have become associated with a great deal of superstition. The first slice of cake should be cut by the bride and groom at the same time to symbolise their working together and supporting each other. The enduring nature of the fruit cakes usually eaten at weddings was also loaded with symbolism.

The top tier of the wedding cake was supposed to be kept to be eaten at the christening of their first child.[6] Those who favour sponge cake at their weddings should probably not try this unless the mother is heavily pregnant and waddles down the aisle, as sponges become stale very quickly.

ST. BRIDE'S CHURCH, FLEET STREET, AFTER THE FIRE, 1824 (see page 56).

The tiered spire of St Bride's Church in London is said to have inspired the popular form of wedding cakes we see today.

In Yorkshire there was a curious tradition involving wedding cake that seems somewhat wasteful. As a correspondent for the *Manchester Chronicle* reported in 1853:

> Wedding Divination.—Being lately present on the occasion of a wedding, at a town in the East Riding Yorkshire, I was witness to the following custom, which seems to take rank as a genuine scrap of folk-lore. On the bride alighting from her carriage at her father's door, a plate covered with morsels of Bride-cake was flung from a window of the second storey upon the heads of the crowd congregated in the street below, and the divination, I was told, consists in observing the fate which attends its [the plate's] downfall. If it reaches the ground in safety, without being broken, the omen is a most unfavourable one. If, on the other hand, the plate be shattered to pieces, the better, and the auspices are looked upon as most happy.[7]

More than a plate could be broken. An old tradition holds that a specially made cake should be broken over the bride's head following the wedding. This was not done out of malice but to help unmarried women in attendance. In Tobias Smollett's *The Expedition of Humphry Clinker* he describes such an event. 'There he and his consort sat in state, like Saturn and Cybele, while the benediction posset was drank; and a cake being broken over the head of Mrs Tabitha Lismahago, the fragments were distributed among the bystanders, according to the custom of the antient Britons, on the supposition that every person who eat of this hallowed cake, should that night have a vision of the man or woman whom Heaven designed should be his or her wedded mate.'

In Scotland the cake broken over the bride was an elaborately decorated shortbread known as the infar-cake, or dreaming bread.[8] The fragments of this were apparently supremely suited to lovers' dreams. The person who managed to come away with the smallest piece of broken shortbread was deemed the luckiest as they had claimed the 'flame of the dreaming bread' which was even more powerful. Some areas of Scotland said that before the bride first enters her married home one of the guests must throw a piece of shortbread through the door.

Green has always been considered a peculiarly unlucky colour for weddings, but many people refuse to allow superstition to rule their lives. In 1934 the *Folkestone, Hythe, Sandgate & Cheriton Herald* reported on the marriage of Miss Constance Kerridge, who wore a green dress and had a green wedding cake. Apparently no bad luck occurred during the ceremony.

GROANING CAKES

Following the wedding it was hoped that children would soon follow. If they did, a groaning cake was called for. Nutrition is important for expectant mothers and those who have just given birth. The social aspect of a neighbourhood gathering to celebrate a birth, while also enjoying a nice cake, was also important.

The groaning cake, sometimes called the pepper cake or sickening cake, was usually a rich fruit cake and full of the calories that someone recovering from a delivery would need.[1] In Cambridgeshire it is said that the cake was liberally soused with gin and contained cannabis – probably equally welcome.

Once the cake was cut it was sometimes treasured by the young ladies present for its ability to provoke dreams of their future husband in much the same way as wedding cake. Sometimes the pieces of cake were placed in the midwife's apron and tossed in the air for the ladies to catch. These were then carried home and placed under the pillow.

A variation of this ritual was more complex but spared one the risk of crumbs in the bed. The lady would place a slice of the cake in the foot of her left stocking and then throw this over her shoulder.[2] Silently she would then have to walk backwards to bed and retire without a word if she wanted the dream to come.

In the North of England it was left for the doctor who had safely brought the baby into the world to cut and distribute the cake.[3] Should the doctor fail to do this it was said that the baby would grow up without any social charms. These cakes could be quite hefty and portions were given to all visitors up until the christening.

Those who happened to meet a party carrying a child to a christening might be given a piece of the cake, a somewhat unexpected bounty. Canon Humble described how 'I was once fortunate enough when a boy to receive the cake and cheese from a christening party going to St. Giles's church. I did not at once perceive what was meant when a great "hunch" of cake and some cheese were thrust in my hand, so I drew back. The nurse, however, insisted on my taking them, and I did so, bestowing them afterwards on the first poor boy I met.'[4]

The reason why the stranger had to take the cake was recorded in a report of this tradition written down in 1917. When a man out for a stroll had piece of cake offered to him, and was forced to sit on a stone while eating it, he was bemused to find himself being hailed as a hero for blessing a baby.[5]

The idea that the distribution of cake brought luck to a child was also found in Scotland. Here the cake was known as 'luck o' the bairn'. While in some places the cake had to be given to the first stranger of the opposite sex to the baby who was encountered, it was sometimes given to the first stranger, whoever they were – though a man was thought to give better luck. When one man discarded his portion of cake without eating, a scandal ensued as he was thought to have thrown away the baby's future luck.[6] Sometimes the cake was kept in a bag, but at other times the 'christening piece' was laid on the child's chest as it was carried to the church.

Cornish folk of St Ives prepared a saffron cake called a Cheeld's Fuggan which was given out on returning from the church after the christening. Who this cake was delivered up to seems to have been important, as one witness of the nineteenth century reported. 'It happened that, as most of the parishioners were at the service, no one was met until near home, almost a mile from the church, when a tipsy village carpenter rambled around a corner, right against our party, and received the cake. Regrets were expressed that the "cheeld's fuggan" should have fallen to the lot of this notoriously evil liver, and my idea was that it was a bad omen.[7] Happily, the writer says his brother, the baby being christened, grew up to be a respectable gentleman.

FARM CAKES

Of all the food folklore traditions in England perhaps the one I most wish to see involves a cake and a bull, as all good things do.[1] Herefordshire farmers would prepare a dense plum cake with a hole in the middle. This cake was then placed over a horn of the largest bull on the farm. According to accounts the animal was then prodded and 'tickled' to make him buck his head so that the cake was tossed from his horn. It was said that a bucket of cider sloshed into the bull's face might make him more active in throwing. How the cake was thrown was important: if the cake flew forwards the harvest would be bountiful, but if it fell backwards a meagre crop was predicted.

There were several songs associated with this ritual. One runs:

> Fill your cups my merry men all,
> For here's the best ox in the stall,
> Oh he's the best ox, of that there's no mistake,
> And so let us crown him with the 12th cake.

Another was sung by the servants of the farm as they surrounded the bull or cow:

> Here's a health to thee, Brownie,
> and to thy white horn,

God send thy master a good crop of corn.
Thee eat thy cake and I'll drink my beer,
God send thy master a happy New Year.

Sussex farmers seem to have been a generous bunch, giving their workers seed cake, a sponge flavoured with caraway seed.[2] This was not wholly charitable, however, as it was thought the cake made workers work harder and would stop them running off to other farmers before the harvest was complete.

Some animals on the farm could get a little taste of sweet cake from time to time. After a funeral some beekeepers observed the ritual of 'telling the bees' that there had recently been a death in the family. It was thought that if the bees were not told then they would fly away. As well as dressing the hive in black it was the custom to provide them with a slice of the funeral cake to keep them happy.[3] The bees did get to sample happier cakes as well. Sometimes they got a bit of wedding cake.

CHRISTMAS CAKES

Christmas is a time for feasting and getting as fat as the proverbial goose. Cakes feature heavily in all good festive seasons and Christmas is a particularly tasty time if you are a fan of heavy cakes and puddings.

The season begins on the last Sunday before Advent with Stir-up Sunday. The Book of Common Prayer says that on this day a prayer should be read in church that begins with the line 'Stir up, we beseech thee, O Lord, the wills of thy faithful people'.[1] This has been taken literally by families for centuries that this is the day the Christmas pudding should be prepared. The entire family is supposed to come together and take a turn in stirring the mixture which will be steamed into a Christmas pudding. As each person stirs they should make a wish for the following year. At this point a silver sixpence would also be added for some lucky person to discover when the pudding was served on Christmas Day. To find it was both lucky and financially rewarding – so long as you did not break a tooth.

Today if we are served Christmas cake we know what to expect: a dense fruit cake smothered with marzipan and a crisp layer of royal icing. There were other Christmas cakes that have fallen out of favour over the years.

The Suffolk kitchel cake was a small triangular cake made with sugar and dried fruit. These cakes were a traditional gift for god-parents at Christmas but children could also find themselves literally showered with them. In Harwich the new mayor would be installed on 21 December and he would don his crimson robes and ascend to a window of the guildhall.[2] From there he would scatter kitchels on the crowd below as the town crier declared: 'Catch a kitchel, if you can!' Today the ceremony is still per-formed, though it has moved to May.

In the North of England the most distinctive cake served over Christmas was the Yule-babby, also called Yule-dough, Yulldoo and Yill-Baby.[3] This anthropomorphic cake was shaped like an infant, and sometimes placed into a pie that served as the cradle. The cakes were handed out as gifts from bakers to their custom-ers. In Lancashire a Ewe-cake, possibly a corruption of Yule-cake, was given that was marked with the head of a lamb.

The Cornish would prepare special saffron-coloured buns stuffed with currants for Christmas. Every member of the family had to have their own. As each bun was prepared, a small bit of the dough from each was pinched off and shaped into a smaller bun that was then placed on top, creating a two-tier bun. This little bun was termed 'the Christmas'. To ensure good luck everyone would sample a morsel of every other person's bun – but not before Christmas Day itself or bad luck would follow.[4]

In Norfolk it was traditional to feed all the animals of the farm, from the cattle to the dogs, a little of the plum pudding before the family sat down to eat. This was thought to guarantee their luck for the following year.

Maids in Wales were told that if they sampled thirteen of the loaf cakes prepared at Christmas they were guaranteed to be married before the next festive season. That's my excuse for feasting on sweet treats, too.

SOUL CAKES

If you had a knock at the door during Allhallowtide, which begins on 31 October, you might have been faced by a group of people demanding a soul cake in the form of a song.

> Soul cakes, soul cakes,
> Pray you, good missis, a soul cake;
> One for Peter, and two for Paul,
> And three for the good man that made us all.

If this tradition of begging for sweet treats at Halloween strikes you as similar to our modern-day trick or treating, it has not escaped folklorists either. Soul cakes were not merely a way of getting a sugar rush; they originally had a religious purpose. The Soulers who came to the door would offer up a prayer for those the householder had lost, hopefully freeing the dead from Purgatory.

Thomas Blount, writing in 1674, mentioned how All Souls' Day, 2 November, was celebrated in Lancashire by the distribution of oat cakes by papists in Lancashire and Herefordshire. Those who received the cakes thanked their benefactors with the simple prayer 'God have your soul, bones and all'.[1]

These soul cakes seem to have taken several forms. Some mention them as simple buns but over time they developed into round shortbread-like cakes with raisins and currants mixed into the dough. They could be marked with a cross pressed into them with a knife before baking or have a cross of dried fruit arranged on top. In some places the soul cakes were not always eaten. Like hot cross buns, they were thought to be holy and so were imperishable and kept as good luck charms.[2]

FUNERAL CAKES

Funerals seem the wrong sort of place to serve a cake. It looks rather too much like celebration. The melancholy sight of a trestle table laden with limp supermarket sandwiches is a much better companion to a funeral. There was a time, however, when funerals were accompanied by a more generous spirit.

In Lancashire wealthier people were known to give a penny dole to all who attended. This could lead to some walking several miles to offer their condolences at a funeral for someone they had never met. One man in his sixties in 1867 recalled wistfully to a writer that in his boyhood funerals included 'a dow, gi'en to every lad and every wench as went, far and near – penny a-piece; and them as carrit a choilt [carried a child] had tuppence'.[1]

Sometimes funeral biscuits were given as mementos of the dead. They were wrapped in wax paper with the deceased's favourite hymn printed on it and often sealed with a blob of black wax. One of these wrappers from the funeral of Mrs Oliver in Yorkshire in 1828 survives and bears the following rhyme:

> Thee we adore, eternal Name,
> And humbly own to thee,
> How feeble is our mortal frame!
> What dying worms we be.
> Our waisting lives grow shorter still
> As days and months increase;
> And every beating pulse we tell
> Leaves but the number less

The year roll round and steals away,
The breath that first it gave;
Whate'er we do, where'er we be,
We're travelling to the grave.[2]

The biscuits, also known as arval bread, were also sent to those unable to get to the funeral so that they could take part in the mourning. Reference is made to them in the late eighteenth century but funeral biscuits as a business opportunity really took off with the death-obsessed Victorians, who loved nothing so much as flaunting a fatality. The *Englishwoman's Domestic Magazine* in 1877 remarked with remarkable sangfroid that the biscuits provided a useful message. 'The world must go round as usual, and folks must eat and drink even when their nearest and best are lying low. The manufacture of funeral biscuits is, we are all aware, quite a flourishing concern.'[3]

HOT CROSS BUNS

Hot cross buns!
Hot cross buns!
One a penny, two a penny,
Hot cross buns!
– Traditional rhyme

It used to be that the British marked the passing of winter into spring with reference to the growth of wild flowers, the songs of visiting birds and the (sometimes marginal) changes in the weather. Now most people only realise it is spring when the shops put out their first batches of hot cross buns. And where they lead, the delicious crack of thin chocolate in Easter eggs cannot be far behind.

The origins of hot cross buns are, perhaps naturally, hotly

debated among people who get hot under the collar about such things. Some believe that they were made with the dough left over when bread was made for the church altar during Easter services. The spices that give hot cross buns their moreish flavour would have been a rare treat for most people and so would have given Easter a profane and tasty appeal as well as the spiritual benefits it promised.

Hot cross buns procured in St Albans were prized in earlier days. Simply called Alban Buns, and with a cross pressed into their tops, most think that they were the original hot cross buns. As the *Herts Advertiser* of 1862 reported:

> It is said that in a copy of *Ye Booke of Saint Albans* it was reported that; 'In the year of Our Lord 1361 Thomas Rocliffe, a monk attached to the refectory at St Albans Monastery, caused a quantity of small sweet spiced cakes, marked with a cross, to be made; then he directed them to be given away to persons who applied at the door of the refectory on Good Friday in addition to the customary basin of sack (wine). These cakes so pleased the palates of the people who were the recipients that they became talked about, and various were the attempts to imitate the cakes of Father Rocliffe all over the country, but the recipe of which was kept within the walls of the Abbey.

The time-honoured custom has therefore been observed over the centuries, and will undoubtedly continue into posterity, bearing with it the religious remembrance it is intended to convey.[1]

They may have been overly sanguine about the religious significance of the hot cross bun surviving until today. Perhaps it was their religious imagery that saw hot cross buns fall foul of a decree issued in 1592 by the London Clerk of Markets which controlled the sale of bread:

> *Item*, That no Bakers, or other Person or Persons, shall at any Time, or Times hereafter, make, utter, or sell by Retail, within or

without their Houses, unto any the Queen's Subjects, any Spice Cakes, Buns, Bisket, or other Spice Bread, (being Bread out of Size, and not by Law allowed) except it be at Burials, or upon the *Friday* before *Easter*, or at *Christmas*; upon Pain of Forfeiture of all such Spice Bread to the Poor.[2]

The reason given by the statute is that such items fall outside the usual range of bread sizes permitted but it may have been because spiced bread and hot cross buns were a mark of popery. Yet they could not be banned entirely – at trying family times such as funerals, Good Friday meals or spending Christmases together, you could not deny people the joy of a little bun. So the hot cross bun was saved from the hot water.

Apart from the symbolism of the spices in the buns as representing the aromatics used to embalm Christ, the obvious, and eponymous, Christian element of the hot cross bun is the cross marked on the top. In some times this was a light indentation

The hot cross bun seller was once a common sight on the streets of Britain in the lead-up to Easter.

that allowed for easy tearing but is now made with a thick paste. The round shape is said to represent the world that Jesus watches over, the yeast of the bun how he rose from the dead.

Others in the nineteenth century were content with the natural variations in hot cross buns that occurred across the country. Those in Scotland who prefer their buns to be marked with the cross of St Andrew, or saltire, are encouraged to turn their circular buns by forty-five degrees. Sometimes the buns were, shockingly, triangular in shape!

Hot cross buns continue to play a role in the bun fights of modern life. In 2003 the *Daily Telegraph* reported a story about several boroughs of London refusing to give out hot cross buns to children for fear of offending non-Christians.[3] When those boroughs claimed they had no official policy on the weighty matter of buns the *Telegraph* issued an apology.

It is perhaps in the spirit of this sort of journalism that we should view the story in a 1902 *Lloyd's Weekly Newspaper* that reported an entrepreneurial baker who found a way to sell hot cross buns to his 'Mohammedan' customers. Feeling that Muslims were not buying his wares because of their overtly Christian symbolism he removed the cross and shaped his dough into crescents. These sold to his Islamic clientele like hot cakes . . . or hot cross buns.

If you ever find yourself caught without a hot cross bun you can always venture to the churchyard of St Bartholomew the Great in London. Here, on Good Friday, a dole is given out to twenty-one poor widows. For many years (no one can say how many) a ceremony has taken place whereby the widows would approach a large, flat gravestone to be met by the churchwarden. He placed silver sixpences around the edge of the tomb and each widow took her coin – it being a point of honour on the widows' part not to take the money directly from his hand.[4] It was reported in the nineteenth century that widows who were too stiff with age to bend down to pick up the sixpence were denied the money entirely.

Fearing that this act of charity was at risk of dying out, in 1877 Joshua Butterworth set up a trust and endowed it with money to provide for the widows. He also stipulated that children in the congregation were to be given hot cross buns. The charity continues to this day and thanks to Butterworth's largesse there are buns for everyone; children, widows and secular gawpers alike.

MAGIC BUNS

Rhymes have always been a part of the hot cross bun's magic. Sellers of these sweet breads used rhymes in their patter to draw in buyers. The one quoted at the beginning of this chapter, 'One-a-penny, two-a-penny' suggests a rather lax pricing system but has since been adopted by generations of British children.

Other rhymes speak more directly to the powers attributed to hot cross buns in folklore. Like most foods, hot cross buns can bring people together, and not just crowding around street sellers. One rhyme can be used to seal an unbreakable friendship. To stop any quarrels with a friend simply take a hot cross bun and ask your friend to share it while reciting this rhyme:

> Half for you, and half for me,
> Between us two, good luck shall be.[1]

Break the bun in two and your friendship will be solid for at least a year. So long as you both get equal shares of the bun, one assumes. Some sought more than mere friendship through buns. The *Illustrated London Magazine* in 1855 described how:

Young ladies are fond of preserving hot-cross buns. They puncture the date on its back with pins, and put it away, like a bag of lavender, in their drawers. 'Whoever keeps one of these mealy treasures for an entire twelvemonth is sure, it is said, to get married the next'; and yet we have known many a young lady, with a small pyramid of these buns, grown harder even than man's inconstancy, condemned to walk about with her finger still unfettered with a gold ring. There must have been some perverse ingredient kneaded, or rather some good ingredient wanted, in the manufacture of these faithless buns.

A rhyme recorded in *Poor Robin's Almanack* of 1733 describes a feature of hot cross buns that means you can probably ignore the sell-by dates most shops place on them.

> Good Friday comes this month – the old woman runs
> With one or two a-penny hot cross buns,
> Whose virtue is, if you believe what's said,
> They'll not grow mouldy like common bread.

The spices of the bun may have helped cover up any rotten flavour in them or may well have aided preservation. The tradition that these holy buns never go mouldy is one shared with all bread baked on Good Friday. Some claimed that the whole job of making the buns must be done on Good Friday itself – making the dough and baking – for them to be prevented from going mouldy. Others suggested baking them until they had a biscuit-like consistency if you planned to save them for the whole year. Like Jesus, whose body was thought not to have suffered decomposition after his death on Good Friday, the hot cross buns were thought to endure.[2] And like Good Friday bread, hot cross buns were thought to be a powerful medicine. No doubt this originated from the use of exotic spices as key ingredients in medicines in former times.

Hot cross buns that were preserved throughout the year could be given to the sick by grating them into water or brandy. Drinking this mixture was thought to cure most digestive problems. Though probably not nausea.

R. C. Nichols, writing in the *Folk-Lore Journal* in 1885, described

a hot cross bun cure being put to the test. 'The wife of my coach-
man, in Sussex, finding herself unwell a few weeks ago, was
"remembered" by her husband that she had "a bit of that Good
Friday bun, with a cross upon it . . ." in a drawer. This was accord-
ingly found, and enough of it grated in a nutmeg-grater to fill a
tea-spoon. This was mixed with brandy, and swallowed, with a
beneficial result – attributable, of course, solely to the bun.'[3]

To prevent mice eating your grain you should fry up hot cross
buns and use the grease to oil the axles of your wagon. This does
rather beg the question 'who fried a hot cross bun in the first
place to discover this?'

Once you had your lucky buns, you did not have to eat them
for them to have power. Simply hanging a bun in the home was
enough.[4] In places as far apart as Somerset and Yorkshire a hot
cross bun kept from one Good Friday to the next was a powerful
amulet against the house burning down. In Penrith hot cross buns
were hung in animal sheds to protect livestock from illness, and
homes from curses and evil spirits. Sailors thought a bun would
save their ships from wrecking and homes by the sea were often
decorated with old hot cross buns for this reason. Unfortunately
for one poor old woman, this charm proved sadly ineffective.

The Widow's Son pub in east London is said to have been
founded on the site of her home. Having already lost her husband she feared for the worst when her son, perhaps her only
living relative, declared that he was joining the navy. She did not
stand in his way but promised to bake him hot cross buns that
would be waiting for his return. Despite the supposed power of
hot cross buns against shipwreck, the son was never seen again,
presumed lost at sea.

The widow did not give up hope, however. Each year on Good
Friday she would religiously bake her hot cross buns and add
them to those already in nets hanging from the ceiling waiting
for her son to return.[5] Eventually the old woman died and her
house was rebuilt as a pub. Named in honour of her missing

child, the Widow's Son continued the tradition of adding to their collection of hot cross buns each year, and they still do.

No one knows for sure if there really was a widow who started this tradition, given that hanging buns in homes was widespread, but the pub has been known as the Widow's Son since it was built in 1848. References to the tradition in nineteenth-century newspapers suggest the hanging of hot cross buns at the site began in the 1830s. When Leopold Wagner wrote a book about the quaint customs of the city of London in 1921 he visited the pub to see its famous buns. Hanging in nets over the bar he found exactly eighty-four buns – perhaps giving a start date of 1837 if one had been added each year.[6] Charmingly the sign of the pub shows the son returning from his trip to discover the bulging sack of hot cross buns still waiting for him.

Hanging hot cross buns in various states of preservation or decrepitude is not unique to the Widow's Son. While many have disappeared altogether, some still exist and the tradition of adding to them survives. Each year the Bell Inn in Horndon-on-the-Hill in Essex sees a hot cross bun trussed up with string and dangled from a beam to join others from previous years, with the ceremonial hanging of the bun usually performed by the oldest villager available.

Unfortunately people are not as skilled at preserving themselves as they are at preserving hot cross buns. It seems that being selected to lead the ceremony at this pub is something of a poisoned chalice as often the person involved does not make it to the event in the following year. This has rather more to do with the nature of the human condition and ageing than with any sort of curse.

When Terry McNally was chosen to add the 110th bun to the rafters of the pub in 2016 some members of his family urged him not to do it.[7] Ignoring this warning, and perhaps hoping some of the magic of the buns would rub off on him, he put up his bun. It can still be seen today as, at the time of writing, can Terry himself.

Love Magic

Food folklore is often a form of domestic magic. Rituals, rites and superstitions involving food lend themselves to being tried at home. For hundreds of years the kitchen was the preserve of women. Of course there were those wealthy enough to delegate cooking and cleaning to others, but those others were often women, too, who had little choice but to work for their living. Other enterprising women escaped the home in various ways, but there has always been something feminine about food folklore that makes it a unique way of studying the lives of those who might otherwise be ignored by grand historical narratives. When considering the ways in which food was used in matters of love magic, we uncover the understandable concerns of ladies for whom happiness often depended on making the right matrimonial choice.

THE DUMB CAKE

The Dumb Cake gets its name from the unusual way in which it is made. Whoever is preparing it must do so in complete silence.[1] The exact recipe of the dumb cake varies, as do the specifics of how it should be made, but traditions of dumb baking are found throughout Britain.

Wales has a long history of *rhamanta* – the divination of romantic futures. One key ingredient was the first egg a hen laid. This was then broken in half to release the contents of the egg.

Half the shell was filled with salt and the other with flour. These were mixed with the egg into a dough and baked. A girl then ate half the cake and placed the other under her pillow.[2]

There were several days that were thought to be particularly propitious for making a dumb cake. One was 20 January, the night before St Agnes' Day. St Agnes may seem an odd choice for offering up love advice. She was martyred in the fourth century and legend has it that the authorities ordered she be raped before execution, but the men who attempted this were struck blind for their crimes. She has since been declared the patron saint of virgins, girls, and for some reason betrothed couples.

John Keats wrote 'The Eve of St. Agnes' in 1819, a poem that speaks of the long association between the day and prophetic visions:

> They told her how, upon St. Agnes Eve,
> Young virgins might have visions of delight,
> And soft adorings from their loves receive
> Upon the honey'd middle of the night,
> If ceremonies due they did aright;
> As, supperless to bed they must retire,
> And couch supine their beauties, lily white;
> Nor look behind, nor sideways, but require
> Of Heaven with upward eyes for all that they desire.

The Rev. M. C. F. Morris, writing in 1892, described a St Agnes' Day ritual.

What all the ingredients of the cake were I know not, but one principal one was salt. I remember being told some years ago, by an old inhabitant in one of the dales, about the composition of this mystic cake. It was somewhat as follows: In the first place four people had to assist in the making of it, each taking an equal share in the work, adding small portions of its component parts, stirring the pot, and so forth. During the whole time of its manufacture and consumption a strict silence has to be observed. Even when it is being taken out of the oven each of the interested parties must assist in the work. When made it is placed on the table in the middle of the room, and the four persons stand at the four corners of the room. When set on the table the cake is divided into equal portions and put upon four plates or vessels.

The spirit of the future husband of one of the four would then appear and taste from the plate of his future bride, being only visible to her whose husband he was destined to be. As a preliminary to this, every door of the house had to be thrown open. The traditional hour for making the feast was midnight.[3]

He also records that the spirits behind this ritual could be a little touchy. One anecdote tells that when it was performed on St Mark's Eve instead of St Agnes', the girls were startled by strange noises. The door then burst open and in flew a coffin that landed at the feet of one of them – she died within the year.

Sometimes it was thought that the girls had to prick the top of the dumb cake with their initials and those of the man they hoped to dream of with a pin. If the initials remained clearly legible after baking, the pair would marry before the year was out.

If you did not want to go to the bother of baking a cake, Northumberland offered a simpler, alternative recipe for St Agnes' Eve but it did involve a day of silence and fasting. The girl would take an egg and boil it. Then the yolk was removed from egg, the hole filled with salt and the egg eaten. After this, all you had to do was walk backwards to your bed while imploring the saint:

> Fair St. Agnes, play thy part,
> And send to me my own sweetheart,
> Not in his best or worst array,
> But in the clothes of every day,
> That to-morrow I may him ken,
> From among all other men.[4]

Another day that could produce the dreams that were sought was St Faith's Day, 6 October. Quite why Faith was chosen is a mystery as there was little romance in the accounts of her life up until her martyrdom. In the North of England girls would make a dumb cake and retire to bed while saying:

> O good St. Faith, be kind to-night,
> And bring to me my heart's delight;
> Let my future husband view,
> And be my visions chaste and true.[5]

One of the oddest forms of this magic is the Soddag Valloo made on the Isle of Man for Hop-tu-Naa, 31 October.[6] This cake was made by groups of girls working together in strict silence. The ingredients were flour, egg, eggshells, soot and prodigious quantities of salt – this was not a cake any but the most desperate would nibble on. Each girl having mixed the ingredients and had a hand in kneading the dough, the cake was then cooked on the hearth. After baking, the cake was broken up and a part handed to each girl, who would consume some before retiring to bed, still without speaking, to dream of her future lover.

Many of the recipes for dumb cakes mention the importance of unhealthy amounts of salt in the mixture. It may be that eating so much salt before one goes to sleep is bound to produce an interrupted night's slumber so you were more likely to remember your dream.

In Scotland the tradition was more usually performed with bannocks, which were called the sauty bannock or dreaming bannock.[7] Here the baking could become something of a game whereby those in attendance cracked jokes or made ribald comments in hopes of getting the silent baker to laugh or speak. If they succeeded, someone else had to try and bake the bannock in silence. Once it was made with all due solemnity, the bannock was broken and pieces given to everyone there to spark their dreams.

FINDING LOVE

There were other ways of bringing on love dreams. Some said that eating a salt herring roasted on a fire, bones and all, could do the trick. Others favoured a cabbage stalk. On St Thomas's Day an apple with two pins inserted in it crossways might be tried for bringing on dreams, and hopefully not stabbing the sleeping prognosticator. A hen's first egg, if eaten in bed, would also do the trick. The beds of those who were looking for love in the past seem to have been veritable pantries from the range of things they were placing under their pillows.

If someone found that the person they desired was too slow in accepting their wooing they could take an onion and poke it with pins before slowly roasting it. This was thought to 'prick the heart' of the victim towards making a move.

If you are in the happier position of having two potential lovers and unsure as to which to pick, onions could once again come to your rescue. Take two onions and carve the suitors' names into them. Whichever onion begins to grow first is the lover you should take.

If you need a stronger clue as to how your love life will turn out you can try a St Thomas Onion. On 20 December, the eve of St Thomas, a girl can take an onion, peel it and wrap it in a hand-kerchief. This is then placed under the pillow where she will sleep. A quick rhyming prayer is uttered before going to bed:

> Good St Thomas, do me right,
> And see my true love come tonight,
> That I may see him in the face,
> And him in my kind arms embrace.[1]

If the saint hears your plea, you will be granted a vision of your future spouse in a dream.

Young girls who wished to know more about their future husband were encouraged to wait until midnight to consume apples, the sinful fruit, in their bedroom. With a single candle burning behind them and a mirror before them, it was thought that as soon as the apple was eaten the face of the man she would marry would appear spectrally in the glass. In some versions of this love divination ritual, the apple eating had to be done while combing your hair. An alternative to combing was to cut the apple into nine pieces, of which only eight were to be eaten. By tossing the ninth over her left shoulder and turning quickly towards the mirror the girl would glimpse for a moment the form of her future husband.

Those unwilling or unable to wait up until midnight had only to get a knife and an apple. Using the blade she had to peel the apple in a single unbroken piece. Then a rhyme was said by the person invoking the magic:

St Simon and St Jude on you I intrude,
By this paring I hold to discover,
Without any delay to tell me this day,
The first letter of my own true lover.[2]

In turning around three times and throwing the peel over her left shoulder, the girl would be given the sometimes cryptic answer to her wishes. As it landed on the floor the peel was said to create the shape of her husband-to-be's initial, although this magic tends to favour those future husbands whose names begin with rounded letters. It would not do to cast the peel too hard – if it broke apart or no clear letter was discernible this meant that the girl would become a spinster.

If you do not want to give up any of the apple's edible parts, you can always turn to the pips. Take one pip and either whisper the name at the pip, or merely think of it in hope, and toss it into the fire. As you do so say:

If you love me, pop and fly,
If you hate me burn and die.

Alternatively, and with less risk of burning your finger, you can simply squeeze the pip between your finger and thumb and say:

Pippin, pippin, paradise,
Tell me where my love lies;
East, west, north, south,
Kirkby, Kendal, Cockermouth.[3]

The pip will squeak out of your fingertips and fly in the direction in which you will find your lover.

In Nottingham the lucky girl who found herself with two lovers could decide between them by taking two apple pips and naming each one after a beau. Placing one on each cheek the girl would say:

Pippin, pippin, I stick thee there,
That that is true thou may'st declare.[4]

She would then wait to see which pip would fall off first. The one that fell indicated the lover who would be more likely to abandon the girl. The one that stuck to the cheek would stick with the girl.

One of the most popular superstitions regarding wedding cake was that it had the ability to provide young ladies with a chance to dream of their own future spouse. A piece of the cake placed under the pillow was thought to prompt these prophetic visions.[5] Some said that the fragment of cake had to first be passed through the bride's wedding ring.

In Wales there was a competition of sorts to be the guest who gave a young lady her piece of cake to aid her dreams. Perhaps it was thought that she would remember you and so would feature you in her prophetic dream. It is said that particularly fair maidens would waddle away from a wedding holding in their skirts all the pieces of cake they had been given.[6] If a girl was particularly desperate to be married she was advised to keep a slice of wedding cake in her pocket as she would then be wed before the dress was ruined. Some would say that storing baked goods in one's clothing will tend to ruin them anyway.

One way of finding out who will be the next to marry is still performed at weddings, whereby the bride tosses her bouquet to the female guests. The one who catches it will be next in line. If the bride was willing to risk her wedding ring there was another technique. She would place her ring into a cake batter before baking and slices of the cake were handed out. Whoever got the ring would be the next to walk down the aisle. If a sixpence was placed in the cake as well, whoever got the coin would die an old maid.

This was not without risks. In 1855 it was reported that one young man had failed to notice the ring in the cake and swallowed it. Whether it was eventually returned to the bride is not known. Sometimes the ring purposely disappeared. When a Mrs Cook placed her ring into a wedding cake she marked the spot specially with two currants to ensure it was given to an unmarried lady. However, when the cake was cut the ring was nowhere to be seen. Suspicion fell on the servant, Ann Wilkinson, who had been in the kitchen at the time and she was hauled before a magistrate.

Folklore may help in matters of love, but tends to cut little mustard with a jury in matters of criminal theft.

Fairy Food Lore

The fairy cakes I made as a child usually had the top sliced off and cut in two to form charming little wings. That is the image most people have of fairies these days – cutesy little sprites fluttering at the bottom of the garden and dancing among bluebells. These are the fairies of infants' books and the Cottingley fairy photographs. The reality of fairies for most people across the centuries was of something far more uncanny and threatening. They lived in their own worlds where time behaved strangely, where babies could be whisked away never to be seen again, and where doing or saying the wrong thing could mean a terrible death.

One of the most common motifs in tales about fairies was food. Yet despite any encounter with the fair folk being potentially deadly, the rules of whether one should partake in their food are hazy. It would be perilous to accept their dishes but equally dangerous to refuse them. A spurned fairy is a terrible thing.

Most of the time fairy feasts are described as being made of the most ravishing ingredients but sometimes those humans who ate their meals found that what had once been a glorious meal turned into a nightmare. Robert Herrick's description of Oberon's Feast reveals what some fairies considered a good repast.

> . . . What would he more?
> But beards of mice, a newt's stewed thigh,
> A bloated earwig and a fly;

With the red-capp'd worm that's shut
Within the concave of a nut,
Brown as his tooth. A little moth
Late fatten'd in a piece of cloth:
With withered cherries, mandrakes' ears,
Moles' eyes; to these the slain stag's tears,
The unctuous dewlaps of a snail,
The broke-heart of a nightingale.[1]

In Scotland it was said that fairy food looked, smelled and even tasted delicious but that it would leave a person as hungry after the meal as they had been before. Worse still, if a Christian happened to say grace before the feast, all the food would be revealed as horse dung.[2]

The key to surviving a meal with a fairy is that if you are in the fairy world you should never accept their food lest you risk never returning to the mortal realm. In this fairy food seems to work the same as the pomegranate that trapped Persephone in the underworld in Greek mythology. If, however, you are offered fairy food in the human world you should always accept it.

There could be benefits to accepting fairy food. One young man of Nithsdale in Scotland was crossing a stream one day when he stumbled on a table set with a rich meal. Tinkling fairy voices sang to him and bade him join their dance and share their feast. He accepted a cup of wine and drank it and was allowed to depart in peace; forever after he had the gift of second sight.[3]

Fairies sometimes had a taste for human food, too. Robert Kirk, a Scottish clergyman, wrote a book in 1691 called *The Secret Commonwealth* which discussed the various species and types of fairy-being. One of them was the joint-eater who steals away the 'foyson', the nourishment of food, from those they latch onto. Kirk describes them 'feeding on the Pith or Quintessence of what the Man eats; and that therefore he continues Lean like a Hawke or Heron, notwithstanding his devouring Appetite'.[4]

While the food offered by a fairy tale character may seem delectable, it often comes with strings attached.

The Irish version of the joint-eater is called the *Alp-luachra* and it takes the form of a newt which crawls inside a person and steals the goodness from any food their host consumes. The cure for such a magical parasite is to eat lots of salt and lie down beside a stream with your mouth open. As the *Alp-luachra* grows thirsty it will slither out your mouth and into the water.[5]

A tale from Fife in Scotland tells of how a dairy maid had just finished churning the butter and was taking it to the well to wash it. As she lowered the butter into the water a tiny hand emerged and snatched it down into the depths, from which it never re-appeared. The fairy left the maid with only a rhyme: 'Your butter's awa', To feast our band, In the fairy land.' At least that is what the maid said when it was noticed that all the butter was missing.[6]

Fairies could also play havoc with the preparation of food in a human home. In Carmarthenshire it was said that if bread failed to rise, or turned out tough, it was the work of the fairies. The only way to stop them was to sacrifice an old slipper to the fire.[7]

Alternatively a cross could be marked on the top of a loaf to rid the fairies of their power over the bread. This may relate to the folk idea that the fairies were the souls of druids, or at least those who had been virtuous pagans. It was said that they were too good to be sent to Hell yet as non-Christians could not enter Heaven.

If you wanted help with your bread, a fairy might be of assistance. One farmer's wife in Bedrule in Scotland was worried when the harvest was not in and she had nearly run out of oatmeal. She was just baking her last loaf to feed her family and all the farm hands when a tiny person dressed all in green entered her kitchen and asked if they might borrow a cup of flour. Sensing this was a special being, she dared not refuse. When the fairy returned the flour, though finer barley meal, the wife made another loaf with it and this loaf turned out perfectly. Not only was it delicious but no matter how much was consumed some of it always remained and it did not go stale. That one loaf sustained everyone on the farm until the harvest was brought in.[8]

There are other similar stories from Scotland that involve miraculous meal given by the fairies. In many of them the barley meal that is returned by the fairy never runs out no matter how much is used, though sometimes the infinite flour fails when a careless family member speaks disparagingly of fairies.

It is strange that fairies would want to borrow oatmeal as in the Scottish isles oatmeal was used as protection against the power of fairies.[9] It was thought that it was not fit food for them and so they avoided it. If your child was out at night, you might fill their pockets with oatmeal to prevent them being spirited away. On the islands of Mull and Tiree, in 1900, there were still people who could remember old men sprinkling themselves with oatmeal before they went out of an evening.

The anger of fairies could often be assuaged with an offering of food. At Minch Moor, also in Scotland, there is a spring marked with two stones. This is known as the Cheese Well and anyone hoping to cross the moor safely would be wise to leave a little offering of cheese on the stone for the fairies.[10] Today most people leave a handful of coins instead, which one presumes the fairies use to buy their own cheese.

The knockers were spirits that populated the mines of Cornwall and could either help or hinder those working in perilous conditions underground. It was traditional for miners to leave a bit of their food in the mine for the knockers and those who did not might live to regret it. The expression 'stiff as Barker's knee' was proverbial and said to derive from the name of a miner who failed to offer up part of his meal and so the knockers hurled all their tools at him and left poor Barker lame for the rest of his life.[11] Cornish fishermen would always leave a fish on the shore to propitiate the monstrous (though occasionally helpful) Bucca, while farm workers spilled a few drops of their beer at lunch for the same reason.

The brownies which inhabited Portway Inn in Staunton on Wye in Herefordshire were said to be fond of stealing keys from the family who lived there.[12] In order for the keys to be returned they would set a piece of cake on the hearth and close their eyes. Soon they would hear the key being thrown onto the ground and when they opened their eyes the cake would be gone. Fairies seem to have a fondness for cake as Jersey housemaids unable to finish the day's work would set out a slice before they went to bed. In the morning the cake had been eaten and their chores completed.

Never count your cakes as they come out of the oven as doing so marks them down as belonging to the fairies. Cakes that have been counted have a way of disappearing, it is said. This sounds like an excellent excuse if a baker asks you why there are not as many cakes on a plate as when they left you alone with them.

Drink Lore

In the past people actually had good reason to avoid drinking water. If you lived in a city the chances were that your source of water could also be the cause of your death. The Thames running through London was famously little more than a sewer for hundreds of years; even today, after heavy rain much of the overflow from London's sewers ends up in the river. As well as human waste, the Thames carried away the effluence of industry and carcases of dead animals. In London the physician John Snow showed in the nineteenth century that drinking water from a public water pump infected by sewage could lead to disease outbreaks when he locked up one of the pumps in Soho.

Even healthy drinks such as milk could be risky. In the Georgian era, milk sellers plied their trade by the leave of the home secretary to milk their cows in St James's Park. This gave fashionable Londoners access to a pastoral idyll, but the truth could be somewhat less enchanting. The milk was sometimes diluted with water drawn from streams, ponds, or the river. In 1850 an investigation of London's milk by H. Hodson Rugg found milk that had been mixed with powdered chalk to improve its colour, the toxic sugar of lead to improve its taste and even mashed sheep's brains.[1]

Beer was brewed and drunk not because it was necessarily safer than water but because it was a relatively cheap way to get some nutrition. Everyone would have enjoyed a refreshing beer throughout the day. Even children were given small beer, one with a lower amount of alcohol, to preserve their health.

The ubiquity of drinking alcohol, and the merriment of being always slightly drunk, must have had an influence on history. William Pitt the Younger was prime minister at a crucial period during the Regency crisis sparked by George III's mental instability and the Napoleonic Wars. Yet he was also known as a 'three bottle man' because of the quantity of port he drank every day.

Curing a loved one of alcoholism might make the difference between a violent, poverty-stricken life and one of relative happiness, so people turned to some unusual folklore remedies. Wives were advised to put a live eel (presumably a small one) into their husband's drink to stop them becoming drunkards.[2] John Swan in his *Speculum Mundi*, published in 1635, states that 'the eggs of an owle, broken and put into the cup of a drunkard, will so work with him that he will suddenly loathe his good liquor, and be displeased with drinking'.

If that fails you can always use the method devised to prevent someone getting drunk in the first place. If you roast the lungs of a hog and eat them, and nothing else throughout the day, then no matter how much you imbibe it will be impossible to get drunk.[3] Or at least that is what was said. It may be that after feasting on hog's offal you do not feel like drinking much. According to Welsh belief you could mitigate the rest of the year's drink by going without on Good Friday.

WATER

Water may not have been the preferred drink at British meals in the past, but it did find its place on the table. Finger bowls, used to clean the fingers of grease and other dirt, were employed for sanitation and occasionally subtle acts of treason. When the Stuart kings were thrown out of Britain their Jacobite supporters found ways to make clear where their loyalties lay. The Stuart who claimed the throne at any given time was known as the 'King over the water' so when Jacobites raised a loyal toast to the Crown they often held their drink over the finger bowl so that they could literally toast the king over the water.

Water also found its way into many medical bits of lore. Rickets could be cured by dosing the patient with water that a blacksmith had used to quench a red-hot iron.[1] If a baby was suffering from colic or an overabundance of flatulence, they might be fed cinder tea – water that hot coals had been plunged into.[2] Perhaps the carbon in the coal was dispersed into the water and really did have a curative effect.

There were thought to be many ways of using water to bring about cures. On Tiree, water that had been taken from nine waves and boiled in a pot containing nine pebbles was considered the perfect cure for jaundice.[3] The patient did not drink this water (perhaps best as it was seawater), but their shirt was soaked in it and placed on the patient while still wet.

Given its ritual significance, the most potent water was that which had been used in a baptism. This was supposed to be particularly good for eye remedies, though in Scotland it was said that eyes washed in baptismal water would never be able to see the spirits of the dead.[4] The Cornish preferred to steal font water and sprinkle it over anything with a bad reputation. People, homes and animals were all doused in this way to remove the evil attached to them.

In Wales, and particularly Pembrokeshire, New Year's Day saw bands of children roaming the streets with sprigs of holly that they used to sparge (sprinkle) people with water drawn from a well. Once their faces had been thus anointed with this lustration the children would sing a song in hopes of a few pennies or other treats.

> Here we bring new water from the well so clear,
> For to worship God with, this happy New Year.

Chorus:
Sing levy-dew, sing levy-dew, the water and the wine,
The seven bright gold wires and the bugles that do shine.

Sing reign of Fair Maid, with gold upon her toe;
Open you the West Door and turn the Old Year go.

Sing reign of Fair Maid, with gold upon her chin;
Open you the East Door and let the New Year in.[5]

Whether or not wet people felt more charitable is not recorded. The levy-dew mentioned in the song may be a corruption of 'Llef i Dduw' which in Welsh means 'a cry to God'. Those met in the street had it lucky as in Carmarthenshire it was traditional for young men to burst into a young maid's bedroom and sprinkle her with water while she was still in bed. Not the best way to be woken when you're hung over. At least when I was woken by one of the Up Helly Aa Guizer Jarls while visiting Shetland, he was shoving a bottle of whisky in my face and commanding me to drink.

The Scots had a similar tradition involving water at New Year. Water was drawn from a stream that was crossed by both the living and the dead, usually on the way to church and burial. Known as 'saining', this ritual involved sprinkling the home with water from the 'dead and living ford' to purify the house for the coming year.[6] The person who fetched the water from the stream was always told to be especially careful as if any of the water, or even the vessel holding it, touched the ground before it was sprinkled, all the power of the water would be lost.

The Scots also had a very sneaky Christmas Eve water tradition. 'Creaming the well' involved creeping onto your neighbour's land and being the first person to draw off some of the water.[7] If you felt your neighbour was unfairly more successful than you, then by stealing the cream of the well you were bringing their

In Derbyshire there is a tradition of well dressing that sees wells decorated with
colourful mosaics made from natural materials each year.

luck into your own home. This rite was thought to be supremely
useful if your neighbour's cows were producing more milk than
your own. The purloined water would be fed to the cattle and all
the implements used to milk them were cleaned in the water.

Some said that the cream of the well had to be stolen as early
as possible on New Year's Day. If an unmarried girl captured the
cream, even from her own family's well, she could look forward
to a wedding before the coming year was out. If you feared
some other rascal stealing your luck with the well water, you
could collect it at precisely midnight and keep it in a bottle in
the house.

At the well of St Keyne in Cornwall it was said that if a couple
drank their first glass of water after their wedding they would be
assured of marital bliss. Other traditions about the well suggested that the first of the pair to drink from the well would be
the master in the marriage. Robert Southey wrote a poem about
this well:

If the Husband of this gifted Well
Shall drink before his Wife,
A happy man thenceforth is he,
For he shall be Master for life.

But if the Wife should drink of it first,—
God help the Husband then!
The Stranger stoopt to the Well of St. Keyne,
And drank of the water again.[8]

There are too many wells with storied pasts and famous legends to include in this book. Dropping coins into a well for luck is too common, and too ancient a tradition, to cover in depth.

Archaeological digs at the sites of wells, springs and rivers have turned up expensive metal objects from jewellery to swords to shields. These items were often ritually broken before being left as offerings. The exact meaning of these sacrificed prized possessions will probably never be known but the practice underlines how important water was as both a source of life and liminal space.

BEER

Beer and ale were not drinks that could be stored for long periods because they quickly went sour. If you wanted a drink, you had either to make it yourself or have someone nearby who did so. For much of British history the job of brewing beer was women's work. Alewives in the Middle Ages dominated the brewing industry, such as it was. A law passed under Edward III in the fourteenth century set out the punishments that men could face if their wives sold substandard ale.[1] Following the Black Death women were squeezed out of the brewing industry. Though brewing had once been common practice for both unmarried and married women as a way to

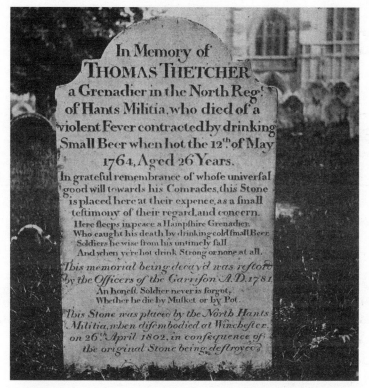

While drinking 'small beer' was thought to be safer than water, the grave of
Thomas Thetcher blamed drinking beer in hot weather for his death.

supplement income, those women who remained in brewing tended
to be widows who were managing their dead husband's business.

Individual brewers no doubt had their own recipe and traditions to ensure that their beer turned out well. Barrels were
sometimes made with an iron cross on the top to ensure the brew
did not spoil. In Kent iron was laid over beer when thunder was
in the air to keep it from souring. If your beer was 'going hard' –
apparently something to be avoided – you could plunge a red-hot
poker into the barrel.[2]

When making beer or ale the cereal grains are mashed and
steeped in water. The liquid which drains off this is known as

wort. The wort is then boiled. By observing this process a couple could tell whether their marriage would be happy or not. If the bubbles roiled on the far side of the pot it was unlucky, but if on the side nearest the couple all would be well.[3]

Beer may not be considered the healthiest of drinks today but it was part of several health-giving rites in the past. If you were suffering from warts, the foam that formed on top of beer as it brewed was the treatment of choice. This should be skimmed from the liquid and applied directly to the wart, and then left there, not wiped off, for three consecutive days. Rosemary was thought to be a cure for drunkenness so was sometimes added to ale while being brewed for both flavour and health.

John Aubrey recorded a strange visitor who offered up beer as part of a cure.

> In Staffordshire, lived a poor old man, who had been a long time lame. One Sunday, in the afternoon, he being alone, one knocked at his door: he bade him open it, and come in. The Stranger desired a cup of beer; the lame man desired him to take a dish and draw some, for he was not able to do it himself. The Stranger asked the poor old man how long he had been ill? The poor man told him. Said the Stranger, 'I can cure you. Take two or three balm leaves steeped in your beer for a fortnight or three weeks, and you will be restored to your health; but constantly and zealously serve God.' The poor man did so, and became perfectly well. This Stranger was in a purple-shag gown, such as was not seen or known in those parts. And no body in the street after even song did see any one in such a coloured habit. Doctor Gilbert Sheldon, since Archbishop of Canterbury, was then in the Moorlands, and justified the truth of this to Elias Ashmole, Esq., from whom I had this account, and he hath inserted it in some of his memoirs, which are in the Mussuem at Oxford.[4]

Holy days were often holidays when beer was appreciated by workers. In Cornwall miners called the day after St Paul's Day

(24 January), Paul Pitcher Day.[5] They would gather around a ceramic water jug and pitch stones at it until the jug shattered. This was the sign to take up another large jug and convey it to the pub. The water jug then became an ale jug and much merriment was had. In Wales there was a custom of 'tooling'. Workers would turn up at a farm where beer was brewed and say that they had left the tools of their trade behind the barrel of beer. When the tools could not be found a cup of beer was provided.

Even churches, not usually known for an alcoholic atmosphere, found uses for ale. At Whitsuntide a strong ale was served that had been especially brewed. The parish would then gather for a feast where ale was sold. The money that was raised was put towards repairs for the local church.

Beer remains one of the most popular drinks in Britain and folklore is still accruing to it. Peeling the label off a bottle of beer is, according to the lore endlessly repeated by students, a sign that you are sexually frustrated. Given the hormones and confusing relationships experienced by university students away from home for the first time, it is probably a good bet that you are frustrated whether you peel or not.

WINE

'Never put new wine in old bottles'
English proverb, derived from the Gospel of Luke

Wine played a central role in Eucharist services where the blood and body of Christ were offered to worshippers in the form of wine and bread. The rarity of wine in northern Europe meant that for centuries it was only the priest who drank the wine from the chalice while his flock ate the bread. Just as with consecrated bread, which must be eaten and not thrown away, so consecrated wine must be drunk. In some high church services in the Church of England, after the vicar has polished off the wine in the chalice they will pour in a little water, swirl it and consume that to make sure not a drop of the sanguinary beverage is wasted.

The holy nature of sacramental wine lends itself to cures. A drop of consecrated wine was given to babies that were failing to thrive by parents in Surrey.[1]

In 1 Timothy, St Paul writes, 'Drink no longer water, but use a little wine for thy stomach's sake and thine often infirmities'. Scientific research suggests a bit of wine is really good for your health. At university I was told by a doctor that a bottle of red wine was better for you than sleeping pills if you couldn't sleep. Wine has always been used in folk cures as it does have immediate and noticeable effects – even if only to get you drunk.

Dysentery or, as the ancients colourfully knew it, the bloody flux, was a major cause of death in former days. The loose bowels and bloody mucus it produced made death by dehydration a real risk. The cures for dysentery were as extreme as the condition they sought to treat. One method involved mixing powdered human bones into red wine and feeding it to the patient.[2]

The ague, or recurrent fevers, was common in the past. A cure for the ague was published in 1611 in *A Closet for Ladies and Gentlewomen*.

> Make a posset with white wine and take away the curd. Take horse-dung from a stone horse [a stallion, stone being a common word for testicles] as hotte as you can get it from the horse and strain it with the posset drink, and put a little mithridate and cardus benedictus [blessed thistle] and unicorn's horne – and if you have no unicorn's horne then put ivorie or seahorse tooth and give it to the sicke to drink fasting in the morning. Use this two or three mornings.

Should you try to make this recipe for yourself be warned that neither unicorns nor seahorse teeth will be available. Seahorses have no teeth. In the past hippopotamuses were sometimes referred to as sea horses and they do have teeth. Big ones.

Wine could be the most fitting drink for toasting someone who had died. It was once thought that consuming wine over the dead body could remit some of their sins. When one man refused the proffered drink, on the grounds that he never consumed wine, the brother of the deceased grew indignant. 'But you must drink, sir, it is like the Sacrament. It is to kill the sins of my sister!' Another account says that each drop of wine drunk over the body is a sin taken from the soul of the dead and carried away by the mourner.

TEA

Man cannot live on alcoholic drinks alone, more's the pity. For those who regard the corrosive power of water on iron, or the questionable things fish do in water, as adverse to health, the advent of tea in Britain was a godsend. When tea first arrived in the seventeenth century it was a costly and rare drink that was often thought of as a medicine.

The origin myth of tea in China was also tied to the divine and the health-giving. It was apparently in the third millennium BC while the emperor of China, Shennong – the Divine Farmer – was sitting in his garden that the drinking of tea first took place. A chance gust of wind blew some tea leaves from a fire into his cup of boiling water. As it infused its flavour the emperor drank and found that it was good. It was supposed to offer protection against seventy poisonous substances.[1]

An alternative legend says that tea came into existence when Bodhidharma, the Indian monk who brought Buddhism to China, became frustrated by his inability to stay awake while meditating. After falling asleep once too often, the monk tore off his own eye-lids and threw them onto the ground. From them sprang the first tea bushes.[2] Tea does indeed tend to help one stay awake and the caffeine it provides must have been helpful to monks who found the search for enlightenment a little soporific.

Portuguese explorers and traders were the first to bring tea in large quantities to Europe. Charles II's queen, Catherine of Braganza, was Portuguese and is said to have made the drinking of tea popular in the English court. While men were busy doing business and swapping news in coffee houses, tea was a more domestic drink that was enjoyed by fine ladies. When Thomas Garraway, owner of a famous coffee house, announced that he was also selling tea, he published an advertisement proclaiming its health benefits in 1688:

It maketh the Body clean and lusty.

It helpeth the Head-ach, giddiness and heaviness thereof.

It removeth the Obstructions of the Spleen.

It is very good against the Stone and Gravel, cleansing the Kidneys and Vriters, being drank with Virgins Honey instead of Sugar.

It taketh away the difficulty of breathing, opening Obstructions.

It is good against Lipitude Distillations, and cleareth the Sight.

It removeth Lassitude, and cleanseth and purineth adult Humors and a hot Liver.

It is good against Crudities, strengthening the weakness of the Ventricle or Stomack, causing good Appetite and Digestion, and particularly for Men of a Corpulent Body, and such as are great eaters of Flesh.

It vanquisheth heavy Dreams, easeth the Brain, and strengtheneth the Memory.

It overcometh superfluous Sleep, and prevents Sleepiness in general, a draught of the Infusion being taken, so that, without trouble, whole nights may be spent in Study without hurt to the Body, in that it moderately heateth and bindeth the mouth of the Stomach.

It prevents and cures Agues, Surfets and Feavers, by infusing a fit quantity of the Leaf, thereby provoking a most gentle Vomit

and breathing of the Pores, and hath been given with wonderful
success.

It (being prepared and drank with Milk and Water) strengtheneth the inward parts, and prevents Consumptions, and
powerfully asswageth the pains of the Bowels, or griping of the
Guts and Looseness.

It is good for Colds, Dropsies, and Scurveys, if properly infused,
purging the Blood by Sweat and Urine, and expelleth Infection.

It drives away all pains in the Collick proceeding from Wind,
and purgeth safely the Gall.[3]

With such apparently miraculous powers, no wonder tea was
highly prized as a medicine. It was also highly prized because of
the vast cost of importing it. Early tea caddies had locks to prevent the precious leaves from being pilfered.

Not everyone was quick to understand how tea should be taken.
A folk tale from Scotland says that a boy from the Highlands went
to do business in Edinburgh at a time before tea was common and
managed to procure a pound of it. Proud of his purchase, he sent
it home to his mother – who promptly boiled it up, poured away
the water and enjoyed the tea leaves mixed with butter.[4]

Once tea had caught on in Britain it became so associated with
the British as to be almost a stereotype. And with some justifica-
tion. During the eighteenth century, some in government were
concerned about the amount of silver pouring out of the country
to pay China for tea. Millions of pounds of tea were legally
imported annually, and millions more smuggled in to avoid the
high import taxes. Even today the writer has turned a prodigious
number of cups of tea into the words you are now reading.

The ubiquity of tea and the rituals around its social brewing
and consumption lent itself to the developing of many superstitions around it. In Scotland it was said that you should never stir
a cup of tea with anything other than a spoon for fear of stirring
up trouble. In England, to stir the tea in the teapot at all was

thought unlucky. If you put your milk into your tea before the sugar you risked losing the heart of your loved one. Bubbles on tea when poured from the pot were a sign that kisses would come to the pourer.[5]

Two people pouring from one teapot at the same sitting was also deeply unlucky according to some. A variant of this was that if two ladies pour from the same teapot then one of the pair is bound to become pregnant soon.[6] Another way a woman could suffer from tea was if she let a man pour her two cups of tea. She would then be certain to fall victim to his wicked wiles.

Leaving the lid off the teapot was to invite a stranger into the house. A person staying in the Welsh town of Lampeter was served tea from a pot without the lid and the lady serving him declared that 'a stranger is sure to come'. When they finished the tea without anyone entering, he dismissed it as superstition – until a stranger waltzed in.[7] If too many cups of tea were poured, an unwelcome visitor was expected to come to the house.

The most famous use of tea in folklore must be tasseomancy – the reading of tea leaves to unveil secrets and the future. By examining the shapes and positions of loose tea leaves in a cup after drinking, those with the skill and knowledge could interpret them. This tradition probably grew out of earlier ways of predicting the future by examining coffee grounds in a cup, which developed during the time of the Ottoman Empire.

The exact process of reading the leaves changes depending on the practitioner. In Wales, once the cup had been drunk it was thought helpful to rotate it three times in the left hand and then turn it upside down in the saucer to allow the tea to drain, but with the leaves left in place. The shapes formed and their position determined the meaning.

According to Welsh lore a perfectly clean bottom was good luck, but if the leaves all clumped there it was a terrible omen.[8] A ring of leaves could be a sign that a marriage was in the offing if it formed at the rim of the cup; conversely, a ring around the bottom

Reading tea leaves or coffee grounds at the bottom of a cup, sometimes called cup tossing, was a popular method of predicting the future for hundreds of years.

of the cup meant ill fortune in matters of love. Other symbols such as crosses, coffins and animals all had their own interpretation. As with so many types of predictive rite it is the element of chance that allows the gods, the spirits, or the universe to pass their messages.

In an early case of the commercialisation of folklore, special cups and saucers marked to make the reading of tea leaves easier were sold by potteries in the nineteenth century and can still be found today.

Free Food and Doles

There's no such thing as a free lunch, they say. Britain, however, has a long history of giving away food and drink and the ceremonies that surround these doles of food can be spectacularly bizarre.

At St Briavels Church in Gloucestershire, each year on Whit Sunday a preacher is invited to deliver a sermon. At the end of the service, if the congregation is pleased, they all cheer and a purse of £1 6s. 8d. (in old money) is given as payment. This is called the Whittington purse in memory of William Whittington who bequeathed money to the parish in 1625 for this purpose.[1] It is after this service that people can get a free meal – as long as they are a good catch. A procession of the congregation wends its way to the towering Pound Wall. Two people climb the wall with baskets containing small cubes of cheese and bread, which they then shower down on those waiting below. Today some enterprising members of the crowd use upturned umbrellas to gather some of the falling largesse. In the past these bits of free food were preserved as good luck charms and were thought to offer prophetic dreams if placed under the pillow.

In Abington there is a 400-year-old tradition of distributing buns from the county hall. These fruited buns are thrown into the marketplace by the mayor and other notables in their finery and are eagerly snatched up by the crowd below. These distributions tend to be held on significant events such as royal jubilees and coronations. Up to 5,000 buns have been tossed at each of the throwings.[2]

Doles where food is scattered to a crowd are known as scrambles because of the rush they create to grab as many bits of food as possible. The riotous behaviour that these doles provoked was not welcomed by the authorities. In 1645 parliament issued an ordinance banning the giving away of two large cakes at Twickenham church at Easter because the mad rush to rip away a bit of cake was profaning the Lord's day.[3] Instead loaves of bread were handed out with more decorum. You cannot keep a good tradition down and even this charity morphed into the Vicar's Bread Charity, which saw loaves of bread thrown from the bell tower for which the children of the parish scrambled.

Bread doles were relatively common in churches as benefactors would leave money in their wills for the relief of the poor. At St Mary's Church in Warwick two bread racks still hang on the walls of the church marked with the names of Joseph Blissett, Rev. John Smith and Ann Johnson, along with the sums of money spent for the bread. Photographs from the early twentieth century show people still queuing up for their loaf of bread from these racks. Today, like many such charities, the bequests have been combined with other charitable funds and are dispersed in other ways.

Sometimes food was offered up to the church. At St Paul's Cathedral the Baud family had, since 1247, held land that was owned by the cathedral. Their rent was to be paid twice a year, once in the form of a buck and once in the form of a doe. The deer would be carried in procession up to the high altar of the cathedral before being removed and cooked on the orders of the Dean. The head and antlers were mounted on a pole and walked in a circuit around the exterior of the cathedral. This tradition is said to have taken place until the reign of Elizabeth I.[4]

There are still religious bodies that maintain the tradition of giving out free food. In Winchester a hungry visitor can ask politely for sustenance at the Hospital of St Cross and Almshouse of Noble Poverty and they will receive the Wayfarer's Dole. A small mug of beer and a piece of bread have been given out to those in need there since the twelfth century. The tradition is said to have begun with a monk from France who was in the habit of giving out bread and wine, but it soon became anglicised with beer substituted for continental vino.[5]

Charity can carry a stigma that can, quite wrongly, embarrass those who accept it. In one photograph of the bread dole at Aymestry church in Herefordshire in the early twentieth century a lady can be seen carrying off a large bag stuffed with bread. The caption beneath it reads 'The Lady with the bag insists she is laden with the loaves of absent neighbours!' There could also be real danger in accepting charity. The Restoration dramatist Thomas Otway fell into absolute poverty and was spared from starvation only by a gift of money to buy food. He is said to have eaten the bread he bought so quickly that he choked to death on it.

Many charities today are revivals of past customs that had been forgotten. There is always the risk that a bequest could be lost or squandered. Equally, there have always been those who were willing to add their own money to a good cause. Farthing Loaf Day in Kidderminster was started when an unmarried lady left 40s. to provide an annual feast for her neighbours in hopes of fostering harmony in the community. Unfortunately, bad investments drained the fund but it was rescued in 1776 by John Brecknell who left £150. He commanded that instead of just bread, the charity should provide a plum cake for every child and beer and a pipe of tobacco for the men alongside the loaves. The toast of the day was 'Peace and good neighbourhood!'[6]

The most famous British giveaway is undoubtedly the Tichborne Dole which takes place in Hampshire.[7] This dole occurs on 25 March each year, Lady Day, and is supposed to date from the eleventh century. It was while Lady Mabella Tichborne was suffering from a wasting disease that she asked her husband Sir Roger to institute a charity in her name. Being a bit of a miser, he agreed only with a spiteful proviso – he was to give away as much land to support the charity as his dying wife was able to circle while carrying a burning torch. Lady Mabella rose from her deathbed and managed to crawl around a 23-acre field that is known as The Crawls to this day.

To ensure that the charity was never forgotten, Lady Mabella is said to have issued a curse against it being discontinued. If it was ever allowed to lapse, the Tichborne family would produce seven sons in one generation but seven daughters in the next, and the family name would become extinct.[8] In 1797 the dole had become too rowdy and the event was banned. Sir Henry Tichborne was the lord of the manor at this time and he was the oldest of seven brothers. He had seven daughters. Fear of the curse is said to have prompted him to reinstate the dole. The last heir to the baronetcy was lost in a shipwreck in 1854, and an imposter appeared in 1866 to claim the title and lands. He was tried, found guilty and served ten years in prison for perjury.

The dole continues to this day. Flour is blessed by the parish priest and given out to people who live in Tichborne and Cheriton. Every adult is given a gallon of flour and children receive half that amount. A 1671 painting of the dole shows large crowds

This 1671 painting shows the Tichborne dole being given out as loaves of bread to all who needed it.

surrounding the Tichborne family as baskets of bread are brought forward to be handed out.

It was not always bread that was left to the poor. Herring seems to have been a popular gift. One member of the fishmongers' guild left two pounds annually for the purchase of herring, and an extra sum to transport the fish to his town. In the village of Felstead, Essex, seven barrels of white herring were donated by Lord Rich to be given to ninety-two of the poorest homes in the area. Those who disgraced themselves, or entered the workhouse, were forbidden from receiving this largesse.

John Aubrey records that in Oxfordshire children on their Easter break from school would call at country houses and clack on their doors with little pieces of wood. They would then chant:

> Herrings, herrings, white and red,
> Ten a penny, Lent's dead;
> Rise, dame, and give an egg,
> Or else a piece of bacon.
> One for Peter, two for Paul,
> Three for Jack a Lent's all
> Away, Lent, away![9]

The householder was then expected to offer up an egg and a piece of bacon. If they did so the children would thank the benefactor, saying, 'Here sits a good wife, Pray God save her life; Set her upon a hod, And drive her to God'. Those who neglected to give any charity would be cursed as a 'bad wife' and a hope that she would be sent to the Devil. For good measure the children would push earth into the keyhole.

Bell-ringers of Harlington in Middlesex feasted on a leg of pork every 5 November as a way of tempting them to sign on for another year of service.

Not all doles were peaceful, or dull. In 1661 George Staverton gave £6 yearly so that a bull might be baited in Wokingham. The flesh, hide and offal were to be sold and the money bestowed on poor local children. A bull was baited until 1823 after which it was professionally butchered and the meat given directly to the poor.

In Hornchurch, on Christmas Day there was a wrestling match that was watched over by a boar's head decorated with bay leaves.[10] The boar that was sacrificed belonged to the parish and the head was awarded to the victor of the bout. The rest was then carried to the nearby pub and provided a feast for the combatants.

The case of the Biddenden Maids is one that is hard to classify. Is it a food dole if the foodstuffs are inedible? Regardless, it is too fascinating not to include.

As you enter the village of Biddenden in Kent you are greeted by a sign which shows two ladies, said to be twins, joined at the hip and shoulder. These are the celebrated Maids of Biddenden, Mary and Eliza Chalkhurst, who are said to have been born there in 1100.[11] When they died in 1134 they bequeathed a portion of

The Biddenden Maids given out each year are biscuit-like plaques representing the conjoined twins who initiated the dole.

land, known afterwards as the Bread and Cheese Lands, to support a charity in memory of them that gave away bread, cheese and ale at Easter. That the ladies existed is supported by the hard biscuits that are stamped with their image each year.

That is how the story goes, at least. Sources tell us that a distribution of bread at Easter was known in the village in the seventeenth century, being suppressed in 1605 because of the indecorous behaviour of those who partook too liberally of the beer and cakes.[12] In the middle of the century one of the vicars of the village tried to claim that the Bread and Cheese Lands were actually meant for the use of the church, and more particularly himself. Two government committees found against him and the charity continued in their ownership of the lands.

It was only in the 1770s that the charity began to give away the Biddenden Maid biscuits which popularised the image of the sisters as conjoined twins. Was this simply a case of a bad biscuit pressing? Were the sisters merely supposed to be standing beside each other? It is very unlikely that conjoined twins should be joined at the hip and shoulder. Some nineteenth-century antiquaries suggested instead that the sisters, whose names only appear relatively late, were joined at the hip only and walked with their arms around each other's shoulders for comfort. Whatever the truth, the biscuits are made of flour and water and it is probably best not to try and eat them. They are still distributed today as souvenirs.

The Cheese and Bread Lands have since been sold for housing but this has been a boon for the charity. With the funds derived from the sale, food and tea is given to pensioners at Easter and a cash sum at Christmas. And the biscuits, too, of course.

Conclusion

This book began with salt and it's appropriate that it should finish with salt.

During the archaeological excavations of graves at St James's Gardens in London and Park Street in Birmingham as a result of the construction of the HS2 railway line, a strange thing was discovered. Several of the graves, dating from the eighteenth and nineteenth centuries, were found to contain ceramic plates of the sort people would have eaten from every day.[1] Grave goods are common from early burials, but these hardly seem the sort of things that most of us would want to accompany us into the afterlife. The explanation for these plates is salt.

Salt plates were once a common part of a ritual concerning the burial of the dead. A coroner, writing in 1920, noted that 'almost universal amongst the poorest classes in the country is the placing of a saucer of salt on a dead man's breast'. In the late eighteenth century John Brand said that salt was used because, like the immortal soul, it was incorruptible and because it protected the dead from the machinations of the Devil. He, apparently, 'loveth no salt with his meat'.

In Scotland the laying of a plate of salt onto the corpse was known as 'dishaloof'. An old lady would wave a candle three times around the body and then place three piles of salt on the plate while saying:

> Thrice the torchie, thrice the saltie,
> Thrice the dishies toom for loffie

These three times three ye must wave round
The corpse, until it sleep sound.
Sleep sound and wake nane,
Till to heaven the soul's gane.
If ye want that soul to dee
Fetch the torch frae th' Elleree;
Gin ye want that soul to live,
Between the dishes place a sieve,
An it sail have a fair, fair shrive.[2]

With rituals such as this we have to ask whether they were really for the dead or for the comfort of the living. Probably both. Belief in the afterlife offers comfort for the bereaved and they would do anything to ensure the postmortem happiness of those they lost. But the placing of salt on a corpse was an activity for the living. Families, friends and neighbours came together in a time of grief. In poor homes the offering of salt may have been the only affordable gift they could give to their loved one. That such a simple thing as salt could carry so many meanings and hold such hopes is testament to the human striving for connection.

Studying folklore has taught me that there is power in the community that it brings together. Traditions help to unite people. There can sometimes be a troubling tendency with folk beliefs to think of them as exclusive to one group or ethnicity. At its most basic level folklore transcends boundaries. It should be shared if it is to be enjoyed and come to life. Exclusion is not only unhelpful, it is damaging to one's ability to truly get to grips with folklore. Superstitions and traditions are carried with us wherever we go because they are so deeply ingrained in our natures. The study of folklore should be international because the spread of beliefs connects us to our shared past.

This book has been a long time baking in the oven of my brain. Reading about the delectable food of the past has made me hungry to discover more. It has also made me literally hungry.

I'm just glad they don't weigh authors at the beginning and the end of writing a book. When a new mayor is chosen at High Wycombe in Buckinghamshire they are weighed at the start and at the end of their term. When just about to leave office they are publicly seated on a large brass scale and the results announced. If they have lost a few pounds during their service, they can expect a hearty cheer from the crowd because they must have been working hard on the public's behalf. If they have gained weight, it is assumed they have been slothful and dining at the public expense and they are booed from the scales. At least I can claim that eating has been part of the research for my book.

I hope that the next time you spill some salt you take a pinch of it and consider all those who have come before and done the same thing as you are about to do.

Acknowledgements

We might see books as the products of lone authors toiling away and trying to force words from their brains. Picture the poor, pale author trying desperately to convert tea into page count by some strange alchemy. But it turns out that no book is born in isolation. There are many people who need to be thanked for getting me to this point, not least those who have supported it financially to make it a reality.

First I would like to thank Mathew Clayton, who took a chance on a strange little book about strange little titbits of food folklore. Thank you for all your encouragement and help when things looked tough. Everyone at Unbound has been superb. I owe you a cake. Hayley Shepherd did a wonderful job of holding my hand through the difficult first edit and improved this book in so many ways. Richard Collins kneaded the dough of the manuscript to help it rise into a well-baked loaf. Marissa Constantinou has been a wonderful editor in all the ways it is possible to be. You should not judge a book by its cover but since Mark Ecob did such a wonderful job designing the cover for this one I hope the contents live up to it.

Dee Dee Chainey and Willow Winsham created #Folklore-Thursday on Twitter and brought together a huge group whose passion for myth, legend and all things weird was an inspiration. You were also kind enough to have me as a host so many times. Without you and everyone who participated this book would never have happened.

The British Library is one of the glories of life. For no charge

I was able to get out any number of little read and little consulted books that were full of exciting bits of lore. The staff were knowledgeable, kind and patient. Thank you all.

Aunt Karen was one of the first people to support this book, and made me feel welcome in her home by thrusting Billy the duck into my hands the moment we met. It was an honour to know you and you will be sorely missed.

Claude Tarazi was also a very enthusiastic supporter of this project. I thank him for his incredible help with various stages of this project; it really might not have happened without him. May your cakes ever come out well baked and unbewitched.

My friends have helped keep me sane during the production of this book. Nic and Jayne, Olly and Jess, Beth, Anna and Sarah, Hannah and Jamie, Sal – you are amazing. I will try not to bombard you with too many disgusting food facts in future.

My family has been so supportive and kind, and always bring a smile to my face. I'll never be able to thank you enough for all you have done. Mum and Dad – you've given me too much for me to ever repay, not least encouraging my love of reading. Sorry to add yet another book to your shelves. Anna, Luke, Shaun, Danni, Ella, Aden, Tilly and Max – thanks for tolerating your weird brother and uncle; I'll buy you a cake.

Finally, I need to thank my wonderful fiancé Michael Cragg. You've been a perfect darling and calmed me down when it seemed as if this book would never get made. I really could not have done this, or anything really, without your love and terrible puns. I can't wait to kiss you over a pile of bride cakes. I promise never to feed a urine-soaked witch cake to our dog. Love you.

Picture Credits

p. 45 'Chestnutting', After Winslow Homer via The Met, Harris Brisbane Dick Fund, 1930.
metmuseum.org/art/collection/search/369654

p. 49 *The book of days: a miscellany of popular antiquities* via Wikimedia Commons.
commons.wikimedia.org/wiki/File:Trial_of_a_sow_and_pigs_at_Lavegny.png

p. 52 The Wellcome Collection via Wikimedia Commons.
commons.wikimedia.org/wiki/File:The_Dunmow_Flitch;_a_procession_of_people_follow_the_winning_Wellcome_V0039124.jpg

p. 54 History and Art Collection / Alamy Stock Photo.

p. 61 Library of Congress via Wikimedia Commons.
commons.wikimedia.org/wiki/File:%22Good_luck%22_LCCN2016652341.jpg

p. 71 The Wellcome Collection via Wikimedia Commons.
commons.wikimedia.org/wiki/File:Mary_Toft_(Tofts)_appearing_to_give_birth_to_rabbits_in_the_Wellcome_V0014994.jpg

p. 102 Statens Museum for Kunst (National Gallery of Denmark) via Wikimedia Commons.
commons.wikimedia.org/wiki/File:Melchior_Lorck,_Basilisk_(1548).jpg

p. 105 *Die Gartenlaube* via Wikipedia.
no.m.wikipedia.org/wiki/Fil:Die_Gartenlaube_(1894)_b_188_1.jpg

p. 108 User: Dohduhdah via Wikimedia Commons.
commons.wikimedia.org/wiki/File:Phallus_impudicus.jpg

p. 113 Kröller-Müller Museum, The Yorck Project via Wikimedia
Commons.
commons.wikimedia.org/wiki/File:Jean-François_Millet_
(II)_005.jpg

p. 118 Author's own photograph.

p. 131 *Mother Goose's Melodies* via Wikimedia Commons.
commons.wikimedia.org/wiki/File:Four_and_Twenty_
Blackbirds.png

p. 138 Walker Art Library / Alamy Stock Photo

p. 140 Author's own photograph.

p. 144 User: Uksignpix via Wikimedia Commons.
commons.wikimedia.org/wiki/File:UK_Olney_(Pancake_Sign).jpg

p. 145 Chronicle / Alamy Stock Photo

p. 149 History and Art Collection / Alamy Stock Photo

p. 153 The British Library via Wikipedia.
en.m.wikipedia.org/wiki/File:ONL_(1887)_1.060_-_St_Bride's_
Church,_Fleet_Street,_after_the_Fire,_1824.jpg

p. 164 User: Theornamentalist via Wikimedia Commons.
commons.wikimedia.org/wiki/File:Nursery_rhymes_
pg_16.jpg

p. 180 *The Violet Fairy Book* via Wikimedia Commons. commons.wikimedia.org/wiki/File:The_violet_fairy_book_ (1906)_(14566680270).jpg

p. 187 User: WhaleyTim via Wikimedia Commons. commons.wikimedia.org/wiki/File:Well_Dressing_Tissing ton_Derbyshire_UK_2007.jpg

p. 189 Winchester: tombstone of Thomas Thetcher, who 'died of a violent fever contracted by drinking small beer', 1764. Photograph, 18--. Wellcome Collection.

p. 197 Nicholas Joseph Crowley via Wikimedia Commons. wikipedia.org/wiki/File:Cup_tossing.jpg

p. 201 The Picture Art Collection / Alamy Stock Photo

p. 203 The Wellcome Collection via Wikimedia Commons. commons.wikimedia.org/wiki/File:Biddenden_Maids_cake_ and_newspaper_cutting,_England_Wellcome_L0057057.jpg

Notes

Vegetable Lore

1 William Henderson, *Notes on the folk-lore of the northern counties of England and the borders* (London: Publications of the Folk-lore Society, 1866), p. 81.

ONIONS AND GARLIC

1 Onion, *Plant Lore*. www.plant-lore.com/onion/
2 *Notes and Queries*, Eleventh Series, Vol. XII (London: Oxford University Press, 1915), p. 101.
3 Eddie W. Wilson, 'The Onion in Folk Belief', *Western Folklore,* Vol. 12, No. 2 (April 1953), p. 103.
4 Linda-May Ballard, 'An Approach to Traditional Cures in Ulster', *Ulster Medical Journal*, Vol. 78, No. 1 (January 2009), pp. 26–33.
5 Chris Wingfield, 'Tylor's Onion: a curious case of bewitched onions from Somerset.' web.prm.ox.ac.uk/england/englishness-tylors-onion.html
6 Thomas Firminger Thiselton-Dyer, *The Folk-lore of Plants* (New York: D. Appleton and Company, 1889). www.gutenberg.org/files/10118/10118.txt
7 Nicholas Culpeper, *The Complete Herbal* (London: Thomas Kelly, 1850), p. 82.
8 Linda-May Ballard, 'An Approach to Traditional Cures in Ulster', *Ulster Medical Journal*, Vol. 78, No. 1 (January 2009), pp. 26–33.

LEEKS

1 William Shakespeare, *The Life of King Henry the Fifth* in *Complete Works*, edited by Jonathan Bate and Eric Rasmussen (London: The RSC Shakespeare, 2022), p. 1072.

2 St David's Day, National Museum of Wales. museum.wales/articles/1183/St-Davids-Day

3 Nicholas Culpeper, *The Complete Herbal* (London: Thomas Kelly, 1850), p. 341.

POTATOES

1 Potato used as a cure for rheumatism. Object identification number 1897.83.3. objects.prm.ox.ac.uk/pages/PRMUID110796.html

2 Carly Stern, 'Mother is branded "insane" after revealing she made her sick son wear a POTATO necklace to cure his 102.3-degree fever.' *Daily Mail*, 2020. www.dailymail.co.uk/femail/article-7845463/Mother-ridiculed-making-necklace-chopped-POTATOES-cure-sons-fever.html

3 Jessica Session, 'Sock Potato Flu Hack! Fever is gone, I believe toxins were drawn out. Pretty cool!'. www.tiktok.com/@jessica_session/video/7164978709768850730

4 Linda-May Ballard, 'An Approach to Traditional Cures in Ulster', *Ulster Medical Journal*, Vol. 78, No. 1 (January 2009), pp. 26–33.

5 Michael Walters, 'Curing of warts', *Folklore*, Vol. 103, No. 1 (1992), p. 114.

BEANS

1 Ben Jonson, 'The Green Children of Woolpit', *Historic UK*. www.historic-uk.com/CultureUK/The-Green-Children-of-Woolpit/

2 John Clark, 'Martin and the Green Children', *Folklore*, Vol. 117, No. 2 (August 2006), pp. 207–14.

3 Roy Vickery, *Garlands, Conkers and Mother-Die: British and Irish Plant-Lore* (London: Bloomsbury Continuum, 2010).

4 Nicholas Culpeper, *The Complete Herbal* (London: Thomas Kelly, 1850), p. 19.

5 R. E. Martin, 'The Legends, folklore and dialect of Leicestershire with an introduction on the general history of the county', 1933. www.le.ac.uk/lahs/downloads/MartinlegendsPagesfromVolume17.pdf

6 Elizabeth Mary Wright, *Rustic Speech and Folk-Lore* (London: Oxford University Press, 1913), p. 250.

PEAS

1 J. B. Partridge, 'Folklore of Durham', *Folklore*, Vol. 26, No. 2 (1915), p. 212.

2 Thomas Firminger Thiselton-Dyer, *British Popular Customs, Present and Past Illustrating the Social and Domestic Manners of the*

People. Arranged According to the Calendar of the Year (London: G. Bell, 1900), p. 122.

3 Elizabeth Mary Wright, *Rustic Speech and Folk-Lore* (London: Oxford University Press, 1913), p. 224.

4 Sitala Peek, 'Knocker uppers: Waking up the workers in industrial Britain', BBC Website, 2016. www.bbc.co.uk/news/uk-england-35840393

CABBAGES AND SPROUTS

1 Nicholas Culpeper, *The Complete Herbal* (London: Thomas Kelly, 1850), p. 37.

2 Edward Berdoe, *The Origin and Growth of the Healing Art* (London: Swan Sonnenschein & Co., 1893), p. 284.

3 Boh Boi, Serena Ko and Desley Gail, 'The effectiveness of cabbage leaf application (treatment) on pain and hardness in breast engorgement and its effect on the duration of breastfeeding', *JBI Libr Syst Rev*, Vol. 10. pp. 1185–1213, 2012.

4 Hew D. V. Prendergast and Naomi Rumball, 'Walking Sticks as Seed Savers: The Case of the Jersey Kale [Brassica oleracea L. Convar. Acephala (DC.) Alef. Var. Viridis L.]', *Economic Botany*, Vol. 54, No. 2 (2000), pp. 141–3.

5 Mark Hay, 'Scottish Singles Used to Spend Halloween Picking Kale', *Atlas Obscura*. www.atlasobscura.com/articles/kale-halloween-traditions

CARROTS

1 K. Annabelle Smith, 'A WWII Propaganda Campaign Popularized the Myth That Carrots Can Help You See in The Dark', *Smithsonian Magazine*, 2013. www.smithsonianmag.com/arts-culture/a-wwii-propaganda-campaign-popularized-the-myth-that-carrots-help-you-see-in-the-dark-28812484/

2 W. J. Hoffman, 'Folk-Medicine of the Pennsylvania Germans', *Proceedings of the American Philosophical Society*, Vol. 26, No. 129 (1889), pp. 329–52.

TURNIPS, SWEDES AND MANGELWURZELS

1 James Tapper, 'Thérèse Coffey's "eat turnips" message leaves bitter taste after UK's biggest grower gives up', *Guardian*, 2023.

2 Suetonius, *The Twelve Caesars*, translated by Robert Graves (London: Penguin Books, 1957), p. 275.

3 An Old Irish Cure for Whooping Cough. www.duchas.ie/en/cbes/5008883/4963620/5078287
4 L. Winstanley and H. J. Rose, 'Welsh Folklore Items, III', *Folklore*, Vol. 39, No. 2 (1928), pp. 171–8.
5 K. Palmer, 'Punkies', *Folklore*, Vol. 83, No. 3 (1972), pp. 240–44.

PARSLEY

1 Parsley, *Plant Lore*. www.plant-lore.com/parsley/
2 Alan Titchmarsh, 'The old wives', tales of gardening that are total rubbish – and the ones with a grain of truth', *Country Life*. www.countrylife.co.uk/gardens/gardening-tips/alan-titchmarsh-on-gardening-wisdom-i-confess-to-growing-tagetes-with-my-tomatoes-239245
3 Angelina Parker, 'Oxfordshire Village Folklore, II', *Folklore*, Vol. 34, No. 4 (1923), pp. 322–33.
4 Beatrix A. Wherry, 'Miscellaneous Notes from Monmouthshire', *Folklore*, Vol. 16, No. 1 (1905), pp. 63–7.

Fruit Lore

1 Translation of Chaucer's 'The Reeve's Tale'. Based on work from the Harvard Chaucer Site, and Librarius website.
2 Alys Fowler, 'Medlars', *Guardian*, 2010. www.theguardian.com/lifeandstyle/2010/nov/27/alys-fowler-medlars
3 Greig Watson, 'King John: Dysentery and the death that changed history', BBC Website. <www.bbc.co.uk/news/uk-england-nottinghamshire-37641202>

APPLES

1 'The Amazing World of Apple Varieties', *The Orchard Project*. www.theorchardproject.org.uk/blog/the-amazing-world-of-apple-varieties/
2 M. A. Courtney, *Cornish Feasts and Folk-lore* (Penzance: Beare and Son, 1890), pp. 2–3.
3 Ronald Hutton, *The Stations of the Sun* (Oxford: Oxford University Press, 1996), p. 67.
4 Arthur Machen, *Dog and Duck* (London: A. A. Knopf, 1924).

5   M. L. Stanton, J. B. Partridge and F. S. Potter, 'Worcestershire Folk-lore', *Folklore*, Vol. 26, No. 1 (1915), pp. 94–7.

6   Elizabeth Mary Wright, *Rustic Speech and Folk-Lore* (London: Oxford University Press, 1913), p. 300.

7   John Brand, *Observations on Popular Antiquities: Chiefly Illustrating the Origin of our Vulgar Customs, Ceremonies, and Superstitions*, Vol. 2, edited by Henry Ellis (London: 1849), p. 273.

8   Steven Roud, *The English Year* (London: Penguin Books, 2008).

9   G. F. Northall, *English folk-rhymes: a collection of traditional verses relating to places and persons, customs, superstitions, etc.* (London: Kegan, Paul, Trench, Trubner & Co., 1892), p. 159.

10 'Marldon Apple Pie Fair', Marldon Local History Group. marldonlocalhistorygroup.com/apple-pie-fair/

11 Egremont Crab Fair. www.egremontcrabfair.com/

12 William Hone, *The Every-Day Book and Table Book*, Vol. I (London: Thomas Tegg, 1830), p. 1338.

13 John Noake, *The rambler in Worcestershire; or, Stray notes on churches and congregations* (Worcester, 1848), pp. 203–5.

14 Elizabeth Mary Wright, *Rustic Speech and Folk-Lore* (London: Oxford University Press, 1913), p. 238.

15 Edgar MacCulloch, *Guernsey Folk-lore* (London: Elliot Stock, 1903), p. 395.

PEARS

1   John Harland and T. T. Wilkinson (eds), *Lancashire Folk-lore: Illustrative of the Superstitious Beliefs and Practices, Local Customs of the People of the County Palatine* (London: Frederick Warne and Co., 1867), p. 69.

2   Joan Morgan, *The Book of Pears* (London: Chelsea Green Publishing, 2015), p. 45.

3   'Tarte of Wardens', *Medieval Cookery*. medievalcookery.com/recipes/tartwardens.html

4   John Gerard, *The Herball, Or Generall Historie of Plantes*. Accessed online. www.exclassics.com/herbal/herbalv50630.htm

ORANGES AND LEMONS

1   Alas Pennington-Bickford lived just long enough to see his beloved church gutted by Luftwaffe bombs in 1941. His parishioners say he died of a broken heart five weeks later. His wife then killed herself afterwards

by leaping from a window having told her cook, 'I prayed every night that God might take me too', *Time*, 'The Bells of St. Clement's', 29 September 1941.

2 'Oranges and Lemons – Fruits of St Clement's', *Geography*, Vol. 15, No. 6 (1930), p. 480.

3 Arthur Mursell, *Lectures to Working Men* (Manchester: John Heywood, 1859), p. 74.

4 Rita Swift, 'Orange Rolling on Dunstable Downs', *Dunstable History*. www.dunstablehistory.co.uk/archives/MNO/Orange%20rolling.htm

5 'Good Friday on the Downs', *Dunstable Gazette*, 18 April 1900.

6 Nicola Davis, 'Can you smell what I smell? How scents linked to Christmas have changed', *Guardian*, 2022.

7 R. Chambers (ed.), *The Book of Days* (London: W. & R. Chambers, 1863), pp. 290–91

CHERRIES

1 'Wild Cherry', *Oxford University Plants*. herbaria.plants.ox.ac.uk/bol/plants400/Profiles/op/Prunusa

2 Francis James Child, *The English and Scottish Popular Ballards*, Vol II (New York: Dover Publications Inc., 1965), pp. 1–6.

3 'Celebrate the Cherry', *Bucks Free Press*, 2002. www.bucksfreepress.co.uk/news/199213.celebrate-the-cherry/

4 John Nicholson, *Folk Lore of East Yorkshire* (London: Simpkin, Marshall, Hamilton, Kent, & Co., 1890), p. 48.

5 James Hardy, 'Popular History of the Cuckoo', *The Folk-Lore Record*, Vol. 2 (1879), pp. 47–91.

6 Ibid.

PLUMS

1 L. Valentine, *Aunt Louisa's Nursery Rhymes* (London: Frederick Warne & Co., 1894).

2 Valerie Elliott, 'Saving damsons in distress . . . meet the melodious Plum Charmer of Pershore.' *Daily Mail*, 2012. www.dailymail.co.uk/news/article-2170385/Paul-Johnson-Saving-damsons-distress--meet-melodious-Plum-Charmer-Pershore.html

3 J. G. Whitehead, M. Terry and Barbara Aitken, 'Scraps of English Folklore, XII (North Bedfordshire, Suffolk, London and Surrey)', *Folklore*, Vol. 37, No. 1 (1926), pp. 76–80.

BERRIES

1 'Notes, Queries, Notices, and News'. *The Folk-Lore Journal*, Vol. 1, No. 11 (1883), pp. 363–5.

2 Caleb Threlkeld, *Synopsis Stirpium Hibernicarum* (Dublin: S. Powell, 1727).

3 Jeremy Harte, 'Michaelmas: The Day the Devil Spits on the Blackberries?', *Folklore Thursday*. folklorethursday.com/folklife/michaelmas-the-devils-blackberry-day/

4 Samuel X. Radbill, 'Whooping cough in fact and fancy', *Bulletin of the History of Medicine*, Vol. 13, No. 1 (1943), pp. 33–53.

5 Liz Locke, Pauline Greenhill and Theresa A. Vaughan (eds), *Encyclopedia of Women's Folklore and Folklife: M–Z* (Westport: Greenwood Press, 2009), p. 478.

6 Steve Roud, *The Penguin Guide to the Superstitions of Britain and Ireland* (London: Penguin Books, 2006).

7 Elizabeth Mary Wright, *Rustic Speech and Folk-Lore* (London: Oxford University Press, 1913), p. 198.

8 'Gooseberry', *Plant Lore*. www.plant-lore.com/gooseberry/

9 Steve Roud, *The Penguin Guide to the Superstitions of Britain and Ireland* (London: Penguin Books, 2006)

10 Linda-May Ballard, 'An Approach to Traditional Cures in Ulster', *Ulster Medical Journal*, Vol. 78, No. 1 (January 2009), pp. 26–33.

RAISINS

1 'Does Eating Gin-Soaked Raisins Help Relieve Arthritis?' Healthline. www.healthline.com/nutrition/gin-soaked-raisins-for-arthritis

2 Lewis Carroll, *Through the Looking-Glass, and What Alice Found There* (1872).

NUTS

1 Evelyn Carrington, 'Singing Games', *The Folk-lore Record*, Vol. III, Part II (London: The Folklore Society, 1881).

2 James Henry Dixon, *Chronicles and Stories of the Craven Dales* (London: Simpkin, Marshall & Co., 1881), pp. 144–5.

3 C. S. Burne, 'Scraps of Folklore Collected by John Philipps Emslie', *Folklore*, Vol. 26, No. 2 (1915), pp. 153–70.

4 Meg Elizabeth Atkins, *Haunted Warwickshire* (London: Hale, 2009), p. 90.

5 John Brand, *Observations on Popular Antiquities: Chiefly Illustrating the Origin of our Vulgar Customs, Ceremonies, and Superstitions*, Vol. 2, edited by Henry Ellis (London: Henry G. Bohn, 1849).

6 Nut Amulet, Object no. 18.96.6. National Museum of Wales. museum. wales/collections/online/object/8ae3639d-3331-3309-ba39-721ba069158f/ Nut-amulet/

7 Dorothy Blakey-Smith (ed.), *The Reminiscences of Doctor John Sebastian Helmcken* (Vancouver: UBC Press, 2011), p. 20.

8 Elizabeth Mary Wright, *Rustic Speech and Folk-Lore* (London: Oxford University Press, 1913), pp. 234–5.

9 Edward Wedlake Brayley, *A Topographical History of Surrey*, Vol. III (London: David Bogue, 1841), pp. 41–2.

10 E. Wright, L. F. Ramsey, Christobel M. Hood, and H. B. Seabrooke, 'Scraps of English Folklore, XV', *Folklore*, Vol. 37, No. 4 (1927), pp. 364–71.

Meat and Animal Lore

1 Alfred Adams, 'Folklore notes from Cornwall', *Folklore*, Vol. 30, No. 2, 1919. pp. 130–31.

BEEF

1 William Henderson, *Notes on the folk-lore of the northern counties and the borders* (London: W. Satchell, Peyton and Co., 1879) p. 75.

2 Ibid.

3 John Gregorson Campbell, *Superstitions of the Highlands & Islands of Scotland* (Glasgow: James MacLehose and Sons, 1900), p. 240.

4 M. A. Courtney, *Cornish Feasts and Folk-lore* (Penzance: Beare and Son, 1890), p. 149.

5 J. B. Partridge, 'Notes on English Folklore', *Folklore*, Vol. 28, No. 3 (1917), pp. 311–15.

6 H. Laing Gordon, *Sir James Young Simpson and Chloroform* (London: T. Fisher Unwin, 1897), p. 5.

7 Bull's heart pierced with nails and thorns. Pitt Rivers Museum. Object no. 1917.53.600

PORK

1   Thomas Barlow, *The triall of a black-pudding. Or, The unlawfulness of eating blood proved by Scriptures, before the law, under the law, and after the law. By a well wisher to ancient truth* (London: F:N, 1652)

2   Jenna Campbell, 'The World Black Pudding Throwing Championships is back for 2022 – here's everything you need to know', *Manchester Evening Herald*, 2022. www.manchestereveningnews.co.uk/whats-on/food-drink-news/world-black-pudding-throwing-championships-24954316

3   E. J. Ladbury, Charlotte S. Burne and S. O. Addy, 'Scraps of English Folklore, III', *Folklore*, Vol. 20, No. 3 (1909), pp. 342–9.

4   Thomas Firminger Thiselton-Dyer, *Domestic Folklore* (London: Cassell, Petter, Galpin & Co., 1881), p. 109.

5   C. H. Evelyn White (ed.), *East Anglian, Or, Notes and Queries on Subjects Connected with the Counties of Suffolk, Cambridge, Essex and Norfolk*, Vol. 5 (London: Elliot Stock, 1893), p. 214.

6   Mrs Murray-Aynsley, 'Scraps of English Folklore, XVI. Herefordshire', *Folklore*, Vol. 39, No. 4 (1928), pp. 381–92.

7   Francis W. Steer, *The History of the Dunmow Flitch Ceremony* (Essex Record Office Publications, 1951).

8   *The Cabinet: Or, Monthly Report of Polite Literature*, Vol. 3 (London: Mathews and Leigh, 1808), pp. 244–8.

9   James Hardy, 'Wart and Wen Cures', *The Folk-Lore Record*, Vol. 1 (1878), pp. 216–28.

10 Ibid. Quoting Francis Bacon, *Sylva Sylvarum* (London, 1651), p. 216.

11 M. A. Courtney, *Cornish Feasts and Folk-lore* (Penzance: Beare and Son, 1890), p. 141.

12 'Pig Face Day at Avening.' www.cotswolds.info/strange-things/pig-face-day-avening.shtml

13 David Bressan, 'The Strange History of the Myth of Entombed Animals', *Forbes*, 2015. www.forbes.com/sites/davidbressan/2015/10/31/the-strange-history-of-the-myth-of-entombed-animals/

14 Francis Grose, *A Provincial Glossary: With a Collection of Local Proverbs, and Popular Superstitions* (London: S. Hooper, 1787).

LAMB AND MUTTON

1   Percy Manning, 'Some Oxfordshire Seasonal Festivals: With Notes on Morris-Dancing in Oxfordshire', *Folklore*, Vol. 8, No. 4, (1897), pp. 304–24.

2 Norman Lockyer, *Stonehenge and Other British Stone Monuments Astronomically Considered* (London: Macmillan and Co., 1906), p. 196.

3 'Custom demised: Eton Ram Hunting, Berkshire', Calendar Customs. traditionalcustomsandceremonies.wordpress.com/2016/08/31/custom-demised-eton-ram-hunting-berkshire/

4 William J. Thoms, 'Divination by the Blade-Bone', *The Folk-Lore Record*, Vol. 1 (1878). pp. 176–9.

5 George Henderson, *Survivals in Belief Among the Celts* (Glasgow: James MacLehose and Sons, 1911), p. 230.

6 John Gregorson Campbell, *Superstitions of the Highlands and Islands of Scotland* (Glasgow: James MacLehose and Sons, 1900), pp. 264–6.

7 *The Universal Fortune Teller: Being Sure and Certain Directions for Discovering the Secrets of Futurity* (London: W. S. Fortey, 1860).

8 Curative Charm, museum number 13.2. Horniman Museum.

9 John Abercromby, 'Traditions, Customs, and Superstitions of the Lewis', *Folklore*, Vol. 6, No. 2 (1895), pp. 162–71.

10 *Booke of Curtassye* (Sloane MS 1986), British Museum.

11 One example is in the Kelvingrove Museum, Glasgow.

12 Ann Ewbank, 'The Myth and Mystery of Scotland's Haggis', *Atlas Obscura*. www.atlasobscura.com/articles/what-is-haggis

FOWLS

1 John Aubrey, *Remaines of Gentilisms and Judaisme* (London: W. Satchell, Peyton, and Co., 1881), pp. 92–3.

2 Angelina Parker, 'Oxfordshire Village Folklore (1840–1900)', *Folklore*, Vol. 24, No. 1 (1913), pp. 74–91.

3 Marie Trevalyan, *Folk-lore and Folk-Stories of Wales* (London: Elliot Stock, 1909), p. 327.

4 Andrew Forgrave, 'Barbaric "hen thrashing" and other bizarre Pancake Day customs in North Wales', North Wales Live. www.dailypost.co.uk/news/north-wales-news/barbaric-hen-thrashing-bizarre-pancake-26293783

5 Thomas Firminger Thiselton-Dyer, *Domestic Folklore* (London: Cassell, Petter, Galpin & Co., 1881), pp. 138–9.

6 Raphael Holinshed, *Chronicles of England, Scotland and Ireland*, Vol. III (London: J. Johnson, 1807). Accessed via Project Gutenberg. www.gutenberg.org/files/46672/46672-h/46672-h.htm

7 'Adlestrop', *British Folklore*. britishfolklore.com/adlestrop

8 'The Folk-Lore of Drayton. Part II. Minerals-Animals-Portents (Continued)', *The Folk-Lore Journal*, Vol. 2, No. 9 (1884), pp. 266–77.

9 John Harland and T. T. Wilkinson (eds), *Lancashire Folk-lore: Illustrative of the Superstitious Beliefs and Practices, Local Customs of the People of the County Palatine* (London: Frederick Warne and Co., 1867), pp. 120–21.

10 John Chipperfield, 'Ducking and Diving In', *Oxford Mail*, 2014. www. oxfordmail.co.uk/news/11321920.ducking-diving/

11 Donald MacLeod, 'Oxford Dons Go Quackers', *Guardian*, 2001. www.theguardian.com/education/2001/jan/12/highereducation. donaldmacleod

12 'Hunting the Mallard at All Soul's College Oxford', Traditional Customs and Ceremonies. traditionalcustomsandceremonies.wordpress. com/2019/01/31/custom-occasional-hunting-the-mallard-at-all-souls-college-oxford/

13 John Rutty, *An Essay Towards a Natural History of the County of Dublin* (Dublin: W. Sleaty, 1772), p. 331.

14 John Timbs, *London and Westminster: City and Suburb, Strange Events, Characteristics, and Changes, of Metropolitan Life*, Vol. 1 (London: Richard Bentley, 1868), pp. 79–83.

RABBITS AND HARES

1 Esther Addley, 'Ben-Fur: Romans brought rabbits to Britain, experts discover', *Guardian*, 2019. www.theguardian.com/lifeandstyle/2019/ apr/18/ben-fur-romans-brought-rabbits-to-britain-experts-discover

2 'Notes', *The Folk-Lore Record*, Vol. 1 (1878), pp. 235–45.

3 Glennda Leslie, 'Cheat and Imposter: Debate Following the Case of the Rabbit Breeder', *The Eighteenth Century*, Vol. 27, No. 3 (1986), pp. 269–86.

4 Quoted on 'The Rabbit Woman', Early Eighteenth Century Newspaper Reports. rictornorton.co.uk/grubstreet/rabbit.htm

5 Nathaniel St André, *A Short Narrative of an Extraordinary Delivery of Rabbets, Perform'd by Mr. John Howard Surgeon at Guilford* (London: John Clarke, 1727).

6 George Henderson, *Survivals in Belief Among the Celts* (Glasgow: James MacLehose and Sons, 1911), p. 104.

7 Charles J. Billson, 'The Easter Hare', *Folklore*, Vol. 3, No. 4 (1892), pp. 441–66.

8 Ibid.

Fish Lore

1 *Winthrop Family Papers*, Vol. III (Boston: Massachusetts Historical Society, 1943), p. 113.

2 Lauren Hogan, 'Curator's Choice: Huer's Horn', National Maritime Museum Cornwall. nmmc.co.uk/2018/07/curators-choice-huers-horn/

3 Christopher Unsworth, *The British Herring Industry: The Steam Drifter Years 1900–1960* (London: Amberley Publishing, 2013).

4 Walter Gregor, *Notes on the Folk-Lore of the North-East of Scotland* (London: Elliot Stock, 1881), p. 152.

5 Arthur Michael Samuel, *The Herring: Its Effect on British History* (London: John Murray, 1918), p. 42.

6 James Simpson, 'Bid to revive Dundee tradition of gifting "dressed herring"', *The Courier*. www.thecourier.co.uk/fp/news/dundee/2544191/bid-revive-dundee-tradition-gifting-dressed-herring/

7 C. I. Paton, 'Manx Calendar Customs (Continued)', *Folklore*, Vol. 52, No. 2 (1941), pp. 120–35.

8 E. F. Coote Lake, 'Folk Life and Traditions', *Folklore*, Vol. 60, No. 2 (1949), pp. 300–302.

9 A. Goodrich-Freer, 'More Folklore from the Hebrides', *Folklore*, Vol. 13, No. 1 (1902), pp. 29–62.

10 'Cruelty flatly denied by flounder-trampers', *The Herald*, 1997. www.heraldscotland.com/news/12312834.cruelty-flatly-denied-by-flounder-trampers/

11 'St Etheldreda's Church, Ely Place', Hidden London. hidden-london.com/nuggets/st-etheldredas-church

12 Alexander Polson, *Our Highland Folklore Heritage* (Edinburgh: G. Souter, 1926), p. 11.

13 William Henderson, *Notes on the folk-lore of the northern counties and the borders* (London: W. Satchell, Peyton and Co., 1879), pp. 140–41.

14 Jonathan Ceredig Davies, *Folk-lore of West and Mid-Wales* (Aberystwyth: Welsh Gazette, 1911), p. 283.

15 James Hardy, 'Wart and Wen Cures', *The Folk-Lore Record*, Vol. 1 (1878), pp. 216–28.

16 A. Goodrich-Freer, 'More Folklore from the Hebrides', *Folklore*, Vol. 13, No. 1 (1902), pp. 29–62.

17 William Henderson, *Notes on the folk-lore of the northern counties and the borders* (London: W. Satchell, Peyton and Co., 1879), p. 123.

18 Pliny the Elder, *Natural History*, Book 9, Chapter 39.

19 Marc Morris, 'A Surfeit of Lampreys'. www.marcmorris.org.uk/2013/12/ a-surfeit-of-lampreys.html

20 Ed Stilliard, 'Gloucester to give Lamprey pie to King Charles III for his coronation', *Gloucester Live*. www.gloucestershirelive.co.uk/news/ gloucester-news/gloucester-give-lamprey-pie-king-8003538

Dairy Lore

1 Owen Davies, *Witchcraft, Magic and Culture, 1736–1951* (Manchester University Press, 1999), p. 190.

2 Edgar MacCulloch, *Guernsey Folk-lore* (London: Elliot Stock, 1903), pp. 306–7.

3 D. J. Madlon-Kay, '"Witch's milk". Galactorrhea in the newborn', *American Journal of Diseases in Children*, Vol. 140, No. 3 (1986), pp. 252–3.

4 *Malleus Malificarum*, part 2, chapter 14. Via Sacred Texts. www.sacred-texts.com/pag/mm/mm02a14a.htm

5 Alexander Stewart, *'Twixt Ben Nevis and Glencoe: the natural history, legends, and folk-lore of the West Highlands* (Edinburgh: W. Paterson, 1885), pp. 235–7.

6 Carl Horstman (ed.), *Nova Legenda Anglie*, Vol. II (Oxford: Clarendon Press, 1901), pp. 98–100.

MILK

1 A. H. Singleton, 'Dairy Folklore, and Other Notes from Meath and Tipperary', *Folklore*, Vol. 15, No. 4 (1904), pp. 457–62.

2 J. Sands, 'Notes and Queries', *The Folk-Lore Journal*, Vol. 2, No. 12 (1884), pp. 377–82.

3 'Some Cow Charms', *Aberdeen Evening Express*, 28 June 1879.

4 William Henderson, *Notes on the folk-lore of the northern counties and the borders* (London: W. Satchell, Peyton and Co., 1879), p. 112.

5 John Cyprian Rust, 'Notes and Queries', *The Folk-Lore Journal*, Vol. 6, No. 3 (1888), pp. 209–12.

6 Alexander Stewart, *'Twixt Ben Nevis and Glencoe: the natural history, legends, and folk-lore of the West Highlands* (Edinburgh: W. Paterson, 1885), pp. 260–61.

7 *An historical account of the Church of St. Mary Redcliffe. Extracted from the Rev. J. Evans's History of Bristol. With an appendix, containing some*

particulars relative to 'the Dun Cow,' one of the Ribs of which is preserved in the church, (Bristol: John Evans & Co, 1815).

8 Charles Hardwick, *Traditions, Superstitions, and Folk-lore (Chiefly Lincolnshire and the North of England)* (London: Simpkin, Marshall, and Co., 1872).

9 Edward Peacock, 'Notes and Queries', *The Folk-Lore Journal*, Vol. 6, No. 4 (1888), pp. 271–7.

10 Marie Trevalyan, *Folk-lore and Folk-Stories of Wales* (London: Elliot Stock, 1909), p. 334.

11 Wirt Sikes, *British Goblins: Welsh Folk-lore, Fairy Mythology, Legends and Traditions* (London: William Clowes and Sons, 1879), p. 38.

12 Ibid., pp. 36–7.

13 *Report and Transactions*, Vols 67–68, The Devonshire Association for the Advancement of Science, Literature and Art (1935), p. 132.

14 Malcolm MacPhail, 'Folklore from the Hebrides. III', *Folklore*, Vol. 9, No. 1 (1898), pp. 84–93.

15 M. A. Courtney, *Cornish Feasts and Folk-lore* (Penzance: Beare and Son, 1890), p. 133.

16 William Henderson, *Notes on the folk-lore of the northern counties and the borders* (London: W. Satchell, Peyton and Co., 1879), pp. 112–13.

17 Mrs Gutch, *County Folklore*, Vol. VI (London: D. Nutt, 1912), p. 70.

18 Wirt Sikes, *British Goblins: Welsh Folk-lore, Fairy Mythology, Legends and Traditions* (London: William Clowes and Sons, 1879), p. 357.

CREAM

1 Dee Dee Chainey, *A Treasury of British Folklore* (London: National Trust Books, 2018), pp. 82–3.

2 Percy Shaw Jeffrey, *Whitby Lore and Legend* (Horne, 1923).

BUTTER

1 Kristina Killgrove, 'I Can't Believe It's 3,000-Year-Old Butter!', *Forbes*, 2019. www.forbes.com/sites/kristinakillgrove/2019/03/15/i-cant-believe-its-3000-year-old-butter/

2 Sarah Hewett, *Nummits and crummits: Devonshire customs, characteristics, and folk-lore* (London: T. Burleigh, 1900), p. 67.

3 This bit of lore is widely stated online, and appears among my research notes but alas I cannot find a source for it. I am certain it did not come to me in a dream.

4 *Whitby Gazette*, 6 April 1917.

5 *Scotsman*, 21 January 1897.

6 *Sheffield Evening Telegraph*, 20 April 1899.

7 *Dalkeith Advertiser*, 5 August 1943.

8 John Ewart Simpkins, *County Folk-Lore* – Volume VII – *Examples of Printed Folk-Lore Concerning Fife with Some Notes on Clackmannan and Kinross-Shires* (London: Sidgwick, 1914), p. 125.

9 *Shetland Times*, 5 February 1876.

10 M. F. Irvine, 'Essex', *Folklore*, Vol. 21, No. 2 (1910), pp. 223–4.

11 T. W. Carrick, 'Scraps of English Folklore, XVIII. Cumberland', *Folklore*, Vol. 40, No. 3 (1929), pp. 278–90.

12 John Gregorson Campbell, *Superstitions of the Highlands & Islands of Scotland* (Glasgow: James MacLehose and Sons, 1900), pp. 252–3.

CHEESE

1 Rebecca Flood, 'Woman Gifted 26lb Wheel of Cheese on a Date and People Say He's a Keeper', *Newsweek*. www.newsweek.com/woman-gifted-26lb-wheel-cheese-date-keeper-1583767

2 Thomas Firminger Thiselton-Dyer, *Domestic Folklore* (London: Cassell, Petter, Galpin & Co., 1881), pp. 45–6.

3 William Henderson, *Notes on the folk-lore of the northern counties of England and the borders* (London: Publications of the Folk-lore Society, 1879), p. 3.

4 John Brand, *Observations on Popular Antiquities: Chiefly Illustrating the Origin of our Vulgar Customs, Ceremonies, and Superstitions*, Vol. 2, edited by Henry Ellis (London: Henry G. Bohn, 1849), p. 71.

5 *Brechin Advertiser*, 20 August 1935.

6 *Aberdeen Press and Journal*, 26 May 1877.

7 E. F. Coote Lake, 'Folk Life and Traditions', *Folklore*, Vol. 70, No. 4 (1959), pp. 550–53.

8 William Hone, *The Every-Day Book and Table Book*, Vol. I (London: Thomas Tegg, 1830), p. 553.

9 'Stilton cheese rolling cancelled as "no longer seen as cool"', BBC News. www.bbc.co.uk/news/uk-england-cambridgeshire-42788965

Egg Lore

1 Cynthia Asquith, *Haply I May Remember* (London: J. Barrie, 1950), p. 117.

2 John Gregorson Campbell, *Superstitions of the Highlands & Islands of Scotland* (Glasgow: James MacLehose and Sons, 1900), p. 252.

3 John Harland and T. T. Wilkinson (eds), *Lancashire Folk-lore: Illustrative of the Superstitious Beliefs and Practices, Local Customs of the People of the County Palatine* (London: Frederick Warne and Co., 1867), p. 121.

4 John Gregorson Campbell, *Superstitions of the Highlands & Islands of Scotland* (Glasgow: James MacLehose and Sons, 1900), p. 252.

5 Marie Trevalyan, *Folk-lore and Folk-Stories of Wales* (London: Elliot Stock, 1909).

6 Thomas Firminger Thiselton-Dyer, *Domestic Folklore* (London: Cassell, Petter, Galpin & Co., 1881), pp. 108–9.

7 K. A. Rookledge and P. J. Heald, 'Dwarf Eggs and the Timing of Ovulation in the Domestic Fowl', *Nature*, Vol. 210 (1966), p. 1371.

8 George Long, *The Mills of Man* (London: Herbert Joseph, 1931), pp. 153–5.

9 William Henderson, *Notes on the folk-lore of the northern counties and the borders* (London: W. Satchell, Peyton and Co., 1879), p. 45.

10 L. F. Newman, 'Some Notes on the Folklore of Poultry', *Folklore*, Vol. 53, No. 2 (1942), pp. 104–11.

11 F. York Powell and Hugh C. Fairfax-Cholmeley, 'Jottings from Easingwold, Yorkshire', *Folklore*, Vol. 5, No. 4 (1894), pp. 341–2.

12 John Aubrey, *Miscellanies Upon Various Subjects*. Accessed via The Gutenberg Project. www.gutenberg.org/ebooks/4254

13 Linda-May Ballard, 'An Approach to Traditional Cures in Ulster', *Ulster Medical Journal*, Vol. 78, No. 1 (January 2009), pp. 26–33.

14 Ralph Whitlock, *The Folklore of Devon* (Totowa: Rowman & Littlefield, 1977), p. 167.

15 Elizabeth Mary Wright, *Rustic Speech and Folk-Lore* (London: Oxford University Press, 1913), p. 245.

16 Nick Wakefield, 'Unusual "egg shackling" tradition takes place at Stoke St Gregory School', *Somerset County Gazette*. www.somersetcountygazette. co.uk/news/10216641.unusual-egg-shackling-tradition-takes-place-at-stoke-st-gregory-school/

17 Pamela Hutchinson, 'Egg jarping: when hard-boiled eggs come to blows', *Guardian*, 2012. www.theguardian.com/lifeandstyle/shor tcuts/2012/apr/08/egg-jarping-hardboiled-eggs-blows

18 'A History of Preston's Annual Egg Rolling', *Visit Preston*. www.visit preston.com/article/3060/A-History-of-Preston-s-Annual-Egg-Rolling

19 Edward Meryon Wilson, 'An Unpublished Version of the Pace-Eggers' Play', *Folklore*, Vol. 49, No. 1 (1938), pp. 36–46.

20 'A Hunt for Medieval Easter Eggs', The British Library Blog. blogs. bl.uk/digitisedmanuscripts/2017/04/a-hunt-for-medieval-easter-eggs. html

21 Trefor M. Owen, *Welsh Folk Customs* (Cardiff: J. D. Lewin and Sons, 1959), p. 86.

22 William Hone, *The Every-Day Book and Table Book*, Vol. I (London: Thomas Tegg, 1830), pp. 425–8.

23 *Framlingham Weekly News*, 18 April 1936.

24 Charles Igglesden, *Those Superstitions* (London: Jarrolds, 1931), p. 82.

25 Thomas Browne, *The Works of Sir Thomas Browne,* Vol. II (Edinburgh: T. and A. Constable, 1904), p. 265.

26 Anna Barrows, *Eggs: Facts and Fancies About Them* (Boston: D. Dolthrop, 1890), p. 18.

27 Edwin Radford and Mona Radford, *Encyclopedia of Superstitions* (1949).

28 Ibid.

Bread Lore

1 Andrew Boorde, *A Compendyous Regyment, or A Dyetary of Health*. In Early English Text Society, extra series X (London: N. Trubner and Co., 1870), p. 261.

2 James Davis, 'Baking for the Common Good: A Reassessment of the Assize of Bread in Medieval England', *Economic History Review*, Vol. 57, No. 3 (2004), pp. 465–502.

3 Walter Scott, *Tales of a Grandfather* (Edinburgh: Robert Cadell, 1836).

BAKING BREAD

1 *Whitby Gazette*, 6 April 1917.

2 L. Salmon, 'Folklore in the Kennet Valley', *Folklore*, Vol. 13, No. 4 (1902), pp. 418–29.

3 Ella M. Leather, 'Herefordshire', *Folklore*, Vol. 24, No. 2 (1913), pp. 238–9.

4 *Royal Cornwall Gazette*, 13 May 1869.

5 *Whitby Gazette*, 6 April 1917.

6 Leo Kanner, *Folklore of the Teeth* (Detroit: Singing Tree Press, 1968), p. 67.

7 Edwin Radford and Mona Radford, *Encyclopedia of Superstitions* (New York: The Philosophical Library, 1949).

8 Walter Gregor, 'Bread', *The Folk-Lore Journal*, Vol. 7, No. 3 (1889), pp. 195–8.

9 'Superstition in Shropshire', *Edinburgh Evening News*, 24 January 1879.

10 *Scotsman*, 5 September 1884.

11 John Aubrey, *Remaines of Gentilisme and Judaisme* (London: W. Satchell, Peyton, and Co., 1881), pp. 43–4.

12 Edwin Radford and Mona Radford, *Encyclopedia of Superstitions* (New York: The Philosophical Library, 1949).

MAGICAL LOAVES

1 Kenneth Page Oakley, *Decorative and Symbolic Uses of Fossils* (Pitt Rivers Museum, 1975).

2 'Branscombe's Loaf and Cheese', *Visit Dartmoor*. visitdartmoor.co.uk/myths-and-legends

3 William Jenkyn Thomas, *The Welsh Fairy Book* (London: T. Fisher Unwin, 1907), pp. 292–6.

4 'Maiden Stone', *Historic Environment Scotland*. www.historicenvironment.scot/visit-a-place/places/maiden-stone/history/

5 M. A. Courtney, *Cornish Feasts and Folk-lore* (Penzance: Beare and Son, 1890), p. 145.

6 Jonathan Ceredig Davies, *Folk-lore of West and Mid-Wales* (Aberystwyth: Welsh Gazette, 1911), p. 231.

7 J. Maxwell Wood, *Witchcraft and Superstitious Record in the South-Western District of Scotland* (Dumfries: J. Maxwell and Son, 1911), pp. 11–14.

8 C. J. S. Thompson, *The Hand of Destiny* (London: Rider & Co., 1932), p. 117.

9 *Notes and Queries* (1898), p. 463.

10 John Rhys, *Celtic Folklore: Welsh and Manx*, Vol. II (Oxford: Clarendon Press, 1901), p. 690.

11 Edwin Radford and Mona Radford, *Encyclopedia of Superstitions* (New York: The Philosophical Library, 1949).

BREAD CURES

1 Edwin Radford and Mona Radford, *Encyclopedia of Superstitions* (New York: The Philosophical Library, 1949).

2 William Thomas Fernie, *Animal Simples* (London: Simpkin, Marshall, Hamilton, Kent & Co., 1899), p. 119.

3 Jonathan Bouchier, 'Bible Eating: An Extraordinary Superstition', *Notes and Queries*, 1902.

4 Edwin Radford and Mona Radford, *Encyclopedia of Superstitions* (New York: The Philosophical Library, 1949).

5 Elizabeth Mary Wright, *Rustic Speech and Folk-Lore* (London: Oxford University Press, 1913), p. 252.

6 Ibid.

7 E. Wright, 'Scraps of English Folklore, II', *Folklore*, Vol. 20, No. 2 (1909), pp. 218–19.

GOOD FRIDAY, GOOD BREAD

1 *Lichfield Mercury*, 26 August 1921.

2 L. Salmon, 'Folklore in the Kennet Valley', *Folklore*, Vol. 13, No. 4 (1902), pp. 418–29.

3 'Rustic Superstition', *Notes and Queries*, 4 April 1868.

4 J. Glyde, *The Norfolk Garland* (Jarrold and Sons, 1872).

5 Rosamond Bayne-Powell, *Housekeeping in the Eighteenth Century*, Vol. I (London: John Murray, 1956), p. 190.

6 Enid M. Porter, 'Folk Life and Traditions of the Fens', *Folklore*, Vol. 72, No. 4 (1961), pp. 584–98.

BANNOCKS

1 Kristina Killgrove, 'Inside The Last Meals Of Ancient Victims Of Sacrifice And Murder', *Forbes*. www.forbes.com/sites/kristinakillgrove/2019/01/30/inside-the-last-meals-of-ancient-victims-of-sacrifice-and-murder/

2 Sam O'Brien, 'Why 18th-Century Scots Performed Mock Human Sacrifices Over Cake', *Atlas Obscura*. www.atlasobscura.com/articles/how-to-make-beltane-bannock-oatcake

3 John Gregorson Campbell, *Superstitions of the Highlands & Islands of Scotland* (Glasgow: James MacLehose and Sons, 1900), p. 232.

4 Ibid.

5 'St Columba's Bannock', CooksInfo. www.cooksinfo.com/st-columbas-bannock

6 Florence Marrian McNeill, *The Silver Bough: A calendar of Scottish national festivals* (Glasgow: Maclellan, 1959).

7 Walter Gregor, Janet Davidson, Mrs Robertson, Mrs Munro, G. Maclean, J. Farquharson and H. Macintosh, 'Notes on Beltane Cakes', *Folklore*, Vol. 6, No. 1 (1895), pp. 2–5.

Pie Lore

1 James Hamley Tregenna, *The Autobiography of a Cornish Rector*, Vol. I (London: Tinsley Brothers, 1872), pp. 234–6.

2 J. B. Partridge, 'Cotswold Place-Lore and Customs (Continued)', *Folklore*, Vol. 23, No. 4, pp. 443–57.

3 P. H. Ditchfield, *Old English Customs Extant at the Present Time* (London: George Redway, 1896), p. 131.

4 John Harland and T. T. Wilkinson (eds), *Lancashire Folk-lore: Illustrative of the Superstitious Beliefs and Practices, Local Customs of the People of the County Palatine* (London: Frederick Warne and Co., 1867), p. 226.

5 Lisa Dawson, 'Fig Pie Rolling at Wybunbury', BBC News. www.bbc.co.uk/stoke/content/articles/2006/06/12/wybunbury_fig_pie_rolling_2006_feature.shtml

6 'A History of Denby Dale Pies.' www.denbydalepiehall.co.uk/pie-history/

7 L. Winstanley and H. J. Rose, 'Welsh Folklore Items, III', *Folklore*, Vol. 39, No. 2 (1928), pp. 171–8.

Cake Lore

1 G. F. Northall, *English Folk Rhymes* (London: Kegan Paul, Trench, Trubner & Co., 1892), p. 148.

2 Quoted on 'Custom Demised: Thomasing on St. Thomas' Day', Traditional Customs and Ceremonies. traditionalcustomsandceremonies.wordpress.com/2013/12/31/custom-demised-thomasing-on-st-thomas-day/

3 Ibid.

4 *Star*, 31 July 1883.

5 J. D. Rolleston, 'The Folklore of Children's Diseases', *Folklore*, Vol. 54, No. 2 (1943), pp. 287–307.

KING ALFRED'S BAKING MISHAP

1 Martin Wainwright, 'King Alfred's cakes reduced to crumbs', *Guardian*, 2007. www.theguardian.com/uk/2007/mar/13/britishidentity.research
2 The Venerable Bede, *De Temporum Rationale*.
3 Rowena Hill, 'Meet the Firestarting Fungus', Kew Gardens. www.kew. org/read-and-watch/king-alfreds-cakes-fungus
4 Walter Gregor, 'Bread', *The Folk-Lore Journal*, Vol. 7, No. 3 (1889), pp. 195–8.

WITCH CAKES

1 *Caledonian Mercury*, 6 July 1778.
2 Peter Charles Hoffer, *The Salem Witch Trials: A Legal History* (Lawrence: University Press of Kansas, 1997), pp. 37–8.
3 Rosemary Guiley, *The Encyclopedia of Witches, Witchcraft and Wicca* (Facts on File, 2010), p. 351.
4 *Liverpool Echo*, 18 April 1913.
5 Pitt Rivers Museum, Object number 1985.51.1060 is a witch cake collected from Flamborough some time before 1933.

PANCAKES

1 Henry Bourne, *Observations on Popular Antiquities; Including the Whole of Mr. Bourne's Antiquitates Vulgares*, Vol. XI (New Castle: J. White, 1810), p. 369.
2 Available from the University of Michigan website. quod.lib.umich. edu/e/eebo/A13439.0001.001
3 Edward Dunnicliff, 'Correspondence', *Folklore*, Vol. 44, No. 4 (1933), p. 420.
4 H. B. Wheatley, 'Catalogue of Brand Material', *Folklore*, Vol. 26, No. 4 (1915), pp. 358–88.
5 Ibid.
6 'Blood sports at School: The Eton Hare-Hunt.' www.henrysalt.co.uk/ library/essay/blood-sports-at-school/
7 E. F. Coote Lake, 'Folk Life and Traditions', *Folklore*, Vol. 60, No. 2 (1949), pp. 300–302.
8 Anna-Eliza Bray, *Legends, Superstitions, and Sketches of Devonshire on the Borders of the Tamar and the Tavy, Illustrative of Its Manners, Customs,*

History Antiquities, Scenery, and Natural History, Vol. II (London: John Murray, 1844), p. 286.

9 T. W. Bagshawe, 'Pancake Bell, Toddington, Bedfordshire', *Folklore*, Vol. 61, No. 3 (1950), p. 167.

EASTER CAKES

1 'The Folk Lore of a Cornish Village', *Notes and Queries*, 20 October 1855.

2 'Good Friday's Bread', *The Athenaeum*, No. 1004 (1847).

3 *Eastbourne Gazette*, 5 April 1939.

4 'Pax Cakes – A Rare Custom', Church of England. www.achurchnear you.com/church/10705/page/51199/view/

5 A. W. Moore, *Folklore of the Isle of Man* (London: D. Nutt, 1891).

6 L. Salmon, 'Folklore in the Kennet Valley', *Folklore*, Vol. 13, No. 4 (1902), pp. 418–29.

7 Ibid.

8 'Whirlin Cakes', Foods of England. www.foodsofengland.co.uk/whirl incakes.htm

9 Richard Pearse, 'Devonshire Calendar Customs I, Moveable Feasts', The Devonshire Association, 1936. Available online. devonassoc.org. uk/devoninfo/devonshire-calendar-customs-i-movable-festivals-1936/

10 John Timbs, *Something for Everybody: A Garland for the Year* (London: Lockwood and Co., 1861), p. 30.

11 H. C. Ellis, 'Monmouthshire Notes', *Folklore*, Vol. 15, No. 2 (1904), p. 221.

12 Alexander Lee, 'Have your Simnel Cake and Eat it', *History Today*, Vol. 69, No. 4, 2019.

13 E. Gutch, *County Folklore, Vol. II, Examples of Printed Folk-lore Concerning the North Riding of Yorkshire, York & the Ainsty* (London: D. Nutt, 1901), pp. 243–4.

WEDDING CAKES

1 W. Warde Fowler, 'Confarreatio: A Study of Patrician Usage', *Journal of Roman Studies*, Vol. 6 (1916), pp. 185–95.

2 Thomas Dawson, *The Good Huswife's Jewell*, 1596. Available online. www.medievalcookery.com/notes/ghj1596.txt

3 Robert May, *The Accomplisht Cook* (London: Obadiah Blagrave, 1685), pp. 234–6.

4 John Aubrey, *Remaines of Gentilisms and Judaisme* (London: W. Satchell, Peyton, and Co., 1881), pp. 22–3.

5 Laura Reynolds, 'How The Tiered Wedding Cake Was Inspired By St Bride's', *The Londonist*. londonist.com/london/history/was-the-tiered-wedding-cake-really-inspired-by-st-bride-s

6 Simon Charsley, *Wedding Cakes and Cultural History* (Taylor & Francis, 2022).

7 *Manchester Courier and Lancashire General Advertiser*, 2 July 1853.

8 Simon Charsley, *Wedding Cakes and Cultural History* (Taylor and & Francis, 2022).

GROANING CAKES

1 John Brand, *Observations on Popular Antiquities: Chiefly Illustrating the Origin of our Vulgar Customs, Ceremonies, and Superstitions*, Vol. 2, edited by Henry Ellis (London: 1849), pp. 70–77.

2 *Barnet Press*, 17 June 1899.

3 William Henderson, *Notes on the folk-lore of the northern counties and the borders* (London: W. Satchell, Peyton and Co., 1879).

4 Ibid., p. 12.

5 A. Moutray Read, 'Country Tales From Cornwall', *Folklore*, Vol. 28, No. 3 (1917), pp. 317–18.

6 *Hartlepool Northern Daily Mail*, 24 June 1893.

7 M. A. Courtney, *Cornish Feasts and Folk-lore* (Penzance: Beare and Son, 1890), pp. 157–8.

FARM CAKES

1 Lavender M. Jones, 'Some Worcestershire Calendar Customs', *Folklore*, Vol. 72, No. 1 (1961), pp. 320–22.

2 Elizabeth Mary Wright, *Rustic Speech and Folk-Lore* (Oxford: Oxford University Press, 1913), p. 301.

3 A. Nutt, 'Sympathetic Bees', *Folklore*, Vol. 3, No. 1 (1892), p. 138.

CHRISTMAS CAKES

1 Ellen Castelow, 'Stir-Up Sunday', *Historic UK*. www.historic-uk.com/CultureUK/Stir-Up-Sunday/

2 Andreea Szasz, 'Harwich mayor-making traditions continue after 4 centuries', *Daily Gazette*. www.gazette-news.co.uk/news/18443844.harwich-mayor-making-traditions-continue-4-centuries/

3 Elizabeth Mary Wright, *Rustic Speech and Folk-Lore* (Oxford: Oxford University Press, 1913), pp. 303–4.
4 M. A. Courtney, *Cornish Feasts and Folk-lore* (Penzance: Beare and Son, 1890), pp. 6–7.

SOUL CAKES

1 Thomas Blount, *Glossographia*, available online. quod.lib.umich.edu/cgi/t/text/text-idx?c=eebo;idno=A28464.0001.001
2 Charlotte S. Burne, 'Souling, Clementing, and Catterning. Three November Customs of the Western Midlands', *Folklore*, Vol. 25, No. 3 (1914), pp. 285–99.

FUNERAL CAKES

1 John Harland and T. T. Wilkinson (eds), *Lancashire Folk-lore: Illustrative of the Superstitious Beliefs and Practices, Local Customs of the People of the County Palatine* (London: Frederick Warne and Co., 1867), p. 270.
2 E. Sidney Hartland, 'Avril-Bread', *Folklore*, Vol. 28, No. 3 (1917), pp. 305–10.
3 *The Englishwoman's Domestic Magazine 1872–1877*, Vol. 22, p. 115.

HOT CROSS BUNS

1 Quoted on St Albans Cathedral Website. www.stalbanscathedral.org/the-alban-bun
2 John Strype, *Survey of London*, 1598.
3 Chris Hastings and Elizabeth Day, 'Hot cross banned: councils decree buns could be "offensive" to non-Christians', *Daily Telegraph*, 16 March 2003.
4 P. H. Ditchfield, *Old English Customs Extant at the Present Time* (London: George Redway, 1896), p. 75.

MAGIC BUNS

1 *The Epicure,* Issues 109–130, Vol. 10 (1903), p. 150.
2 R. Chambers (ed.), *The Book of Days* (London: W. & R. Chambers, 1863), p. 418.
3 R. C. Nichols, 'Notes and Queries', *The Folk-Lore Journal*, Vol. 3, No. 1 (1885), pp. 90–92.

4 Rachel Nuwer, '5 Great Historical Myths And Traditions About Hot Cross Buns, a Pre-Easter Pastry', *Smithsonian Magazine*. www.smithsonianmag. com/smart-news/five-great-myths-about-hot-cross-buns-traditional-pre-easter-pastry-180951130

5 Oliver Thring, 'Consider the Hot Cross Bun', *Guardian*, 2011. www. theguardian.com/lifeandstyle/wordofmouth/2011/apr/19/consider-the-hot-cross-bun

6 Leopold Wagner, *A new book about London: a quaint and curious volume of forgotten lore* (London: Allen & Unwin, 1921).

7 'Hot Cross Bun Ceremony, The Bell Inn, Horndon on the Hill, 2016', *Essex Sounds*. www.essexsounds.org.uk/content/catalogue_item/hot-cross-bun-ceremony-2016

Love Magic

THE DUMB CAKE

1 Angelina Parker, 'Oxfordshire Village Folklore (1840–1900)', *Folklore*, Vol. 24, No. 1 (1913), pp. 74–91.

2 Wirt Sikes, *British Goblins: Welsh Folk-lore, Fairy Mythology, Legends and Traditions* (London: William Clowes and Sons, 1879), pp. 304–5.

3 M. C. F. Morris, *Yorkshire Folk-Talk* (Oxford: Horace Hart, 1892), pp. 230–31.

4 William Henderson, *Notes on the folk-lore of the northern counties and the borders* (London: W. Satchell, Peyton and Co., 1879), p. 71.

5 Thomas Firminger Thiselton-Dyer, *British Popular Customs, Present and Past Illustrating the Social and Domestic Manners of the People. Arranged According to the Calendar of the Year* (London: G. Bell, 1900), pp. 284–5.

6 A. W. Moore, *Folklore of the Isle of Man* (London: D. Nutt, 1891).

7 William Hone, *The Every-Day Book and Table Book*, Vol. I (London: Thomas Tegg, 1830), pp. 260–61.

FINDING LOVE

1 Elizabeth Mary Wright, *Rustic Speech and Folk-Lore* (London: Oxford University Press, 1913), p. 260.

2 Henry Graves Bull (ed.), *The Herefordshire pomona, containing coloured figures and descriptions of the most esteemed kinds of apples and pears* (London: Journal of Horticulture Office, 1878), p. 52.

3 Elizabeth Mary Wright, *Rustic Speech and Folk-Lore* (London: Oxford University Press, 1913), p. 259.

4 G. F. Northall, *English folk-rhymes: a collection of traditional verses relating to places and persons, customs, superstitions, etc.* (London: Kegan, Paul, Trench, Trubner & Co, 1892), p. 116.

5 Angelina Parker, 'Oxfordshire Village Folklore, II', *Folklore*, Vol. 34, No. 4 (1923), pp. 322–3.

6 Jonathan Ceredig Davies, *Folk-lore of West and Mid-Wales* (Aberystwyth: Welsh Gazette, 1911), p. 37.

Fairy Food Lore

1 Robert Herrick, *Hesperides*, 1684.

2 John Gregorson Campbell, *Superstitions of the Highlands & Islands of Scotland* (Glasgow: James MacLehose and Sons, 1900), pp. 21–3.

3 J. Maxwell Wood, *Witchcraft and Superstitious Record in the South-Western District of Scotland* (Dumfries: J. Maxwell and Son, 1911), p. 180.

4 Robert Kirk, *The Secret Commonwealth of Elves, Fauns & Fairies* (London: D. Nutt, 1893).

5 'Notes on Irish Folklore', *Folklore*, Vol. 27, No. 4 (1916), pp. 419–26.

6 John Ewart Simpkins, *County Folk-Lore* – Volume VII – *Examples of Printed Folk-Lore Concerning Fife with Some Notes on Clackmannan and Kinross-Shires* (London: Sidgwick, 1914), pp. 311–13.

7 Jonathan Ceredig Davies, *Folk-lore of West and Mid-Wales* (Aberystwyth: Welsh Gazette, 1911), p. 135.

8 *Folklore and Legends: Scotland* (London: W. W. Gibbings, 1889), p. 100.

9 John Gregorson Campbell, *Superstitions of the Highlands & Islands of Scotland* (Glasgow: James MacLehose and Sons, 1900), pp. 150–52.

10 *Folklore and Legends: Scotland* (London: W. W. Gibbings, 1889), p. 187.

11 Ronald M. James, 'Knockers, Knackers, and Ghosts: Immigrant Folklore in the Western Mines', *Western Folklore*, Vol. 51, No. 2, (1992), pp. 153–77.

12 Katharine Mary Briggs, *The Fairies in Tradition and Literature* (London: Routledge, 1967).

Drink Lore

1 H. Hodson Rugg, *Observations on London Milk*, 1850.
2 Edwin Radford and Mona Radford, *Encyclopedia of Superstitions* (New York: The Philosophical Library, 1949).
3 Ibid.

WATER

1 Linda-May Ballard, 'An Approach to Traditional Cures in Ulster', *Ulster Medical Journal*, Vol. 78, No. 1 (2009), pp. 26–33.
2 Mabel Peacock, Katherine Carson and Charlotte S. Burne, 'Customs Relating to Iron', *Folklore*, Vol. 12, No. 4 (1901), pp. 472–5.
3 'Notices and News', *The Folk-Lore Journal*, Vol. 1, No. 5 (1883), pp. 167–8.
4 Thomas Firminger Thiselton-Dyer, *Domestic Folklore* (London: Cassell, Petter, Galpin & Co., 1881), p. 20.
5 Wirt Sikes, *British Goblins: Welsh Folk-lore, Fairy Mythology, Legends and Traditions* (London: William Clowes and Sons, 1879), pp. 255–6.
6 W. Grant Stewart, *Popular Superstitions of the Highlands* (1823).
7 Walter Gregor, 'New Year Customs', *The Antiquary*, January 1882, pp. 1–6.
8 John Aubrey, *Miscellanies on Various Subjects*. Accessed via The Gutenberg Project. www.gutenberg.org/ebooks/4254

BEER

1 'Alewives In Oxford: A History Of Female Brewing', Museum of Oxford. museumofoxford.org/alewives-in-oxford-a-history-of-female-brewing
2 J. Harvey Bloom, *Folk Lore, Old Customs and Superstitions in Shakespeare Land* (Read Books Limited, 2017).
3 Walter Gregor, *Notes on the Folk-Lore of the North-East of Scotland* (London: Elliot Stock, 1881), p. 89.
4 John Aubrey, *Miscellanies upon Various Subjects* (London: Reeves and Turner, 1890), pp. 83–4.
5 M. A. Courtney, *Cornish Feasts and Folk-lore* (Penzance: Beare and Son, 1890), p. 19.

WINE

1 Edwin Radford and Mona Radford, *Encyclopedia of Superstition* (New York: The Philosophical Library, 1949).
2 Ibid.

TEA

1 James A. Benn, *Tea in China: A Religious and Cultural History* (Hong Kong University Press, 2015).
2 Shane McCausland, 'Telling images of China', *Irish Arts Review*, Vol. 27, No. 1 (2010), pp. 78–81.
3 James Mew and John Ashton, *Drinks of the World* (London: The Leadenhall Press, 1892).
4 Mary Julia MacCulloch, 'Folklore of the Isle of Skye. III', *Folklore*, Vol. 33, No. 4 (1922), pp. 382–9.
5 Edwin Radford and Mona Radford, *Encyclopedia of Superstitions* (1949).
6 E. J. Ladbury, Charlotte S. Burne and S. O. Addy, 'Scraps of English Folklore, III', *Folklore*, Vol. 20, No. 3 (1909), pp. 342–9.
7 Jonathan Ceredig Davies, *Folk-lore of West and Mid-Wales* (Aberystwyth: Welsh Gazette, 1911), p. 217.
8 Ibid., pp. 14–16.

Free Food and Doles

1 'St Briavels Bread & Cheese Scramble', *Calendar Customs*. calendar customs.com/articles/st-briavels-bread-cheese-scramble/
2 Steven Roud, *The English Year* (London: Penguin Books, 2008).
3 Thomas Firminger Thiselton-Dyer, *British Popular Customs, Present and Past Illustrating the Social and Domestic Manners of the People. Arranged According to the Calendar of the Year* (London: G. Bell, 1900), p. 166.
4 Ibid., pp. 49–50.
5 'Wayfarer's Dole', *Atlas Obscura*. www.atlasobscura.com/places/way farers-dole
6 Christina Hole, *English Traditional Customs* (London: Batsford, 1975), p. 149.
7 Lord Nugent, *Ye Dole of Tichborne* (London: Bemrose and Sons, 1871).

8 Ben Johnson, 'The Tichborne Dole', *Historic UK*. www.historic-uk. com/CultureUK/The-Tichborne-Dole/

9 *Anecdotes and Traditions: Illustrative of Early English History and Literature, Derived from Ms. Sources* (London: Camden Society, 1839), p. 113.

10 Philip Morant, *The history and antiquities of the County of Essex*, Vol. I (London: T. Osborne, 1786).

11 J. Shirley, 'Some Quaint Bequests', *Charity Organisation Review*, New Series, Vol. 8, No. 45 (1900), pp. 218–20.

12 Sisters of Mercy: The Biddenden Maids', *History Extra*. www.history extra.com/period/medieval/sisters-of-mercy-the-biddenden-maids/

Conclusion

1 Beth Richardson, 'An Emblem of the Immortal Spirit? "Salt Plates" for St James's and Park Street Burial Grounds', *Museum of London Archaeology*. molaheadland.com/salt-plates-from-st-james-and-park-street-burial-grounds/

2 William Henderson, *Notes on the folk-lore of the northern counties of England and the borders* (London: Publications of the Folk-lore Society, 1879), p. 36.

Unbound is the world's first crowdfunding publisher, established in 2011.

We believe that wonderful things can happen when you clear a path for people who share a passion. That's why we've built a platform that brings together readers and authors to crowdfund books they believe in – and give fresh ideas that don't fit the traditional mould the chance they deserve.

This book is in your hands because readers made it possible. Everyone who pledged their support is listed below. Join them by visiting unbound.com and supporting a book today.

Chance A-R
Ace
Charlotte Addams
James Afford
Melissa Agsaulio
Buket Akgün
Adam Alexander
Syeda Ali
Ashley Allen
Daniel Fenton Anderson
Bernard Angell
Pip Askew
Tom Atkinson

Nic Attwood
James Aylett
Amber B
Liam Babington
Shannon Bailey Grace
Tamsyn Ball
Holly Bamford
Lynne Barnsley
Amelia Bayliss
Emma Bayliss
Elizabeth Beall
Bob Beaupré
Mike Beck

Peter Beecham
Katherine Beesley
Charlotte Bence
Becky and Dean Benkert
Steve Bennett
Phillip Bennett-Richards
Margo Benson
Bee Benton
Terry Bergin
Steve Besley
Sam Bilton
Adam Binnington
Steven R. Bitgood
Charlie Blackie-Kelly
Ronia Blake
Shannon Blanch
Tharin Blumenschein
Bobby and Lillie
Aaron Bobick
Aurora Bonati
Andy Brereton
Stacia Briggs
Bethan Briggs-Miller
Beverley Bright
Alice Broadribb
Isabella Brown
Brian Browne
Mike Bull
Gillian, Hann & Tony Bunn
David Burgess
Sarah Burgess
Nick Burton
Chris Bush
Anna Calvert

Jacq Calvert
Stacey Calvert
HL Campbell
Kenith and Kathy Capen
Sharon Carr-Wu
Beth Carter
Nicola Carter
Iris Abril Castañeda C
Sam Castriotta
Susan Chadwick
Dee Dee Chainey
Anna Chamberlain
Caroline Champion
Paul Charlton
Diana Chiu
Katarzyna Churchill
Indigo Clardmond
Helen Clark
Roger Clarke
Ross Clarke
Mathew Clayton
Matt Clifton
Freyalyn Close-Hainsworth
Candice Cloud
Claire Cock-Starkey
Andrew Cogburn
Kate Coldrick
Lucy Coleman Talbot
Gina Collia
Hattie Collins
Maria Connor
Matthew Cope
Jo Cosgriff
Hanna Cowan

Yvonne Cresswell
River Cronin
Katherine Crouch
Rita Csernátony
Jennifer Culver
Daddy, Sammi and Mr Wolf
Kae Dale
Laura Davis
Lynwen Davison
Kat Day
Noah de Koning
Lynne Deakin
Megan Delahunty-Light
Clare Dempsey
Megan Derr
Patric ffrench Devitt
Sara 'Willie' Didier
Diane Dodd
Martin Dostál
Alex Doyle
Vikki Drummond
Sarah Duce
Sarah Dudley
Kiara Duncan
Dan Early
Eli the Bearded
Felicity Ellacombe
Laura Elliff
Marie Ellis
Holly Elsdon
Nik Elvy
Reinhard Eschbach
Sarah Evans
Charlotte Everitt

M.J. Fahy
Paul Fairie
Louise Farquharson
Charlie Farquharson-Roberts
Lucille Farrell
Neil Fazakerley
Hannah Filipski
Beth Filmore
Victoria Finney
Em Fleming
Edwina Fletcher
Fran Foot
Jean Forbes
Jacqueline Ford
Elizabeth Fraser
Charlotte Freeman
Karla Freeman
Zoë Froggatt
Daisy Fry
Lisa Fryer
Alex Gallacher
Majda Gama
Heather Gardner
Matthew Gilbert
Laura Jayne Gill
Rina Gill
Anna Gillespie
Barbara Gittes
Fiona & David Goggin
Stephanie Goldberg
Felicity Goodall
Boyd Goode
Annie Gray
Sharon Gray

Karen Green
Hannah Grego
Mike Griffiths
Kate Grinnell
Victoria Grundle
Raul Guerrero
Natalie Guest
Diana Guibord
Sarah Gurney
Cynthia Gyure
Pauline Haak
Mathew Haigh
Denise Hair
Elizabeth Hall
Kay Hall
Laura E. Hall
Matt Hall
Lilly Hanrahan
Brian Ch. Hanson
Elizabeth Hanson
Max Harding
Jonathan Hargreaves
Emily Harris
Ruth Harris
Karen Hart
Stuart Hawkes
Scían Hayes
John Hayward
Sanjay Hazarika
Heather & Rose
Pamela Henderson
Charity Hendrix
Lucy Henzell-Thomas
Karen Herbert

Stuart Herkes
Max Higgins
Nigel Higgins
Tina Hoggatt
Bethan Holdridge
Lisa Holdsworth
Cheryl Holland
Sophie Hollinshead
Elizabeth Hopkinson
Eric Horstman
Jamie Houston
Deborah Louise Hudson
Cory Hughart (Crock of Time)
Martin Hughes
Tom Hughes
Karrie Hyatt
April Jackson
Bill & Terra Jackson
Ellen Jackson
Jan Jackson
Susan Janson
Jane Jeans
Beth Jenkins
Simon Jerrome
Julie Jones
Mary Jones
Nye Jones
Jeana Jorgensen
Yuki Kameda
Katie
Emma Kay
Sarah Keeyes
Tricia Kelly
Tobias Kenning

Zoe Kenyon

Alim Kheraj

Tim Kinsey

Amy Koester

Allison Koster

Diane Kovacs

Helene Kreysa

Janice Kuechler

Lisa Labovitch

Aylwin Lambert

Alice Langley

Lee Lantry

Rachael Lawrence

Lucy Lawson

Ric & Anton Le Poidevin

Melanie Leach

John R R Leavitt

Caroline Lee

Kelsey Lee

Ian & Tina Leonardi

Paul Levy

Joshua Lilly

Taryn Lindhorst

Mark Lorch

Jane Loveday

Brigitte Colleen Luckett

Murray Lynes

Jamie M

Jessie M

Gillian Macdonald

Kristin Selinder MacDonald

Matt Macfarlane

Edward MacGregor

Alexander H. MacLeod IV

April Madden

Rebecca Magnis

Laura Mahony Mahony

Carol Malaab

Victoria Maloy

Scott Malthouse

Ava Mandeville

Valentina Marenco

Sarah Markham

Sara Marsden

Matilda & Max

Jamie McAllister

Katie McCarroll

Duncan McClau

Ian McDonald

Robert McDowell

Cat McGill

Lucy McGough

Neil McKenna

Kasey McKeral

Mark Mclaughlan

Lesley McLellan

Emily McMichael

Brunhilde Merk-Adam

Kristina Meschi

Danielle Milbank

Helen Miller

Max Miller

Phillip Mitchell

Ayesha Mohammed

Ken Monaghan

I Moon

Bonnie Kay Morgan

Dan Morgan

Rosemary Morgan

Ann Morris

Carl Moss

Stacy Murtagh

Owen Myers

Georgia Nakos

Carlo Navato

David Neill

Dawn Nelson

Natalie Nelson

Kay Nettle

Joachim New

Bridget Newbery

Ian Nield

Carly North

Louise O'Mahony

Cassandra Oliver

Gregory Olver

Emily Oram

Angela Osborne

Angela Oster

Chris Otto

Sand Owen

Leann Pace

Paula Page

Susan Page

Jessica Pankhurst

Steph Parker

Tom Parker Bowles

Julie Parkinson

Graham Partridge

Michelle Patel

Richard Patey

Sue Patrick

Denise Peacock

Oliver Pearcey

Chris Pennell

Dan Peters

Sara Peterson

Shelley W. Peterson

Brian Petro

Neil Philip

Robert Phillips

Karen F. Pierce

Jennifer Piercy

Alessandra Pino

Kristin Plant

Steve Pont

Dion Potter

Tracy Powell

Kerrie Power

Rhianna Pratchett

David Pratt

Louise Pratt

Janet Pretty

Felicity Pritchett

Sophie Proctor

Lorelai Prosser

Caroline Pulver

Rachel

Rebecca Rajendra

Colette Reap

Val Reid

Rowena Relf

Electra Rhodes

Elaine Richardson

Leslie Rieth

Suzy Rillie

Gatsby Robertson

Louis Robertson

Andrew Robeson

Mark Robinson

Peter Robinson

Cat Rocketship

Natalie Roe

Jeri Rolfe

Tom Roper

Eva Rose

Rebecca Rose

Lynn Rosskamp

Ann Rottersman

Stephen Rötzsch Thomas

Janette Rowland

Karen Rowland

Liberty Rowley

Elle Rudd

Bonnie Russell

Teraza Salmon

Bernie Sammon

Thea Sandall

John Sanders

Adam Sargant

Deborah Schauffler

Inka Schönfeld

Lydia Schubert

Amberly Woods Schulz

Heidi Schulz

Fabienne Schwizer

Christine M. Scott

Gemma Scott

Jonathan Seaman

Mary Seaton

Icy Sedgwick

Karl E. H. Seigfried

Dick Selwood

Seven Fables Dulverton

Victoria Sharratt
  McConnell

Heather Shattuck

Alison Shaw

C.R. Shelidon

Martin Shewen

Mary Nicole Silva

Kathleen Simonton

Jill Singer

Betty Skelton

Debbie Slater

Barendina Smedley

Emma Smith

Jeffrey Smith

Margaret Smith

Michael Smith

Steph Smith

Simon Smith & Schwirl Smith

Helen Somers

Paul Sparrow-Clarke

Liam Spinage

Judith Stafford

Patrycja Stańczyk

Charlotte Stark

Louise Starkowsky Dancause

Emily Starling

Mary Steele

Rick Steele

Amanda Steinke

Jane Stemp

Alex Stevens

Brice Stratford

Trevor Stuart

Dan & Gill Sumption

Tim Suter

Toby Swallow

Barry Syder

Kirsty Syder

Deb Taylor

Kay Taylor

Michael Taylor

The Witching Museum

Chris Theophilus-Bevis

Emma Thimbleby

Holly Thomas

Edward Thompson

Nicholas Thompson

Andrea Thomson

Gypsy Thornton

Harley-Anna Tillotson

To Eve, love from Adam.
   March 2023.

Michael Townley

Jess & Olly Tracy

Lindsay Trevarthen

Mary Elizabeth Trujillo

Emma Tucker

Anna Tuckett

Simon Tudor

William Tyler

Laura Underhill

Lindy Usher

McKinley Valentine

Grace Varley

Charlotte Vassell

Bart Vervoort

Eric Vondran

John Wainwright

Chee Lup Wan

Lucinda Ward

Glen Warren

Stephanie Wasek

Ken Washburn

Elaine Waters

Wendy Watson

Sophia Waugh

Rachel Webb

Ange Weeks

Ivy Noelle Weir

Nigel Welham

Alexandra Welsby

Lesley West

Sarah West Alin

Lizzie Westbrook

Jo Westman

Katie Weston

James Whelan

Vicki Whitehead

Helen Whitham

Simon Wilcox

Annie Wiles

Annette Wilkinson

John Wilkinson

Monica Willett

Andrew David Williams

Shaun Williams

Susan Williams

Wendy R. Williams

Samantha Willis-Hall
Janice Winkler
Willow Winsham
Nastassja Wiseman
Theresa Witziers
Dee Wolstenholme

Lucy Wood
Techla Wood
Joanna Wootten
Christina Wray
Gayle Yeomans
Donna Zillmann